Study Guide
for use with
Adolescence
Tenth Edition

John W. Santrock
University of Texas at Dallas

Prepared by

Daniel D. Houlihan
Minnesota State University

Boston   Burr Ridge, IL   Dubuque, IA   Madison, WI   New York   San Francisco   St. Louis
Bangkok   Bogotá   Caracas   Kuala Lumpur   Lisbon   London   Madrid   Mexico City
Milan   Montreal   New Delhi   Santiago   Seoul   Singapore   Sydney   Taipei   Toronto

The **McGraw·Hill** Companies

McGraw-Hill Higher Education

Study Guide for use with
ADOLESCENCE, TENTH EDITON
JOHN W. SANTROCK

This book is printed on acid-free paper

1 2 3 4 5 6 7 8 9 0 BKM/BKM 0 9 8 7 6 5 4

ISBN 0-07-299363-4

http://www.mhhe.com

CONTENTS

PREFACE

HOW TO USE THE STUDY GUIDE

You are about to undertake the challenging and exciting task of learning about biological, cognitive, and sociocultural influences on adolescents. This *Study Guide* will assist you as you read *Adolescence* by John W. Santrock. It will help you learn and test your understanding of key terms and key persons as well as facts and theories covered in the text. Do remember, however, that its use should **supplement** rather than **substitute for** a careful and thorough reading of the text. Each chapter of this *Study Guide* contains several features designed to help you master the content of the chapter in *Adolescence:*

- ■ Learning Goals with Key Terms in Boldface
- ■ Key Terms
- ■ Key People
- ■ "Dr. Detail's" Mastery Exercises
- ■ Section Reviews
- ■ Cognitive Challenge
- ■ Adolescence in Research
- ■ Comprehensive Review
- ■ Adolescence in Books
- ■ Adolescence in Movies and Videos
- ■ Answer Key

Each chapter of the *Study Guide* presents a detailed set of learning goals in which key terms designated by the author appear in boldface. These objectives have been organized by major chapter headings and subheadings, and numbered accordingly. For example, the first section after the Preview and Images of Adolescents in each chapter is numbered 1.0, and the associated goals are numbered 1.1, 1.2, and so forth. These goals cover the bulk of the material in the chapter. The learning goals indicate as specifically as possible what you should be able to do after you have read and mastered the material in a chapter.

It is recommended that you make extensive use of the learning goals. For example, it is a good idea to review the key terms before and after you read each section, or subsection, of a chapter. In addition, you should review the learning goals as you do the section reviews, in that there is substantial overlap. Consistent and extensive review of the learning goals will help you better learn and remember the chapter content, and that, in turn, will help you do your best on the examinations.

Key Terms

Devise your own definitions for these key terms based on your understanding of the text's definitions or on how you use the key terms in completing a sentence. This is important because you will not know whether you really understand a term until you can define it and use it in your own way.

Key People

This feature asks you to match the key person involved in adolescent research (related to the chapter's content) to the idea or concept with which they are associated. Some of these people will be featured in the margins of the main text with quotations about their theories and research. In all cases, the individual's research will have been discussed in the chapter.

Dr. Detail's Mastery Exercises

Most chapters will have a section titled "Dr. Detail's." These mastery exercises can cover almost anything relevant to the chapter. Some might cover percentages, whereas others might present "not so key" people in the chapter. Still others may be crossword puzzles or theory mastery exercises. The intent of this section is to give you a review of material that might not be the "primary focus" of the chapter, but might still appear on a test.

Section Review

All sections have their own Section Review consisting of a variety of exercises that help you review and study particularly important concepts and material in the chapter. The activities include matching, classifying, completing tables, defining terms, and providing short-answers to many questions.

Cognitive Challenge

Each chapter has one or more exercises that asks you to think about specific concepts and principles and apply them to your own life and respond from your personal experience and opinion. For these activities there are generally no answers provided, because they will be unique to each student. Nonetheless, these responses are an important guide as to how well you can work with the information you are learning in class and from your text.

Adolescence in Research

Some research articles discussed in the chapter have been chosen; and you are asked to analyze the research hypothesis, methods, and conclusions and suggest the relevance of the findings for adolescent development.

Comprehensive Review

Each chapter contains a selection of multiple-choice questions that covers the main content of the chapter. These questions can be either factual or conceptual in nature. They help prepare you to take a multiple-choice exam as well as reviewing the entire chapters' content one last time.

Adolescence in Books and Movies

After the comprehensive review, you will find suggestions for books and movies that explore or depict some facet of the chapter material.

Answer Key

At the end of each Study Guide chapter is the Answer Key. Keep in mind that the answers given for short-answer questions are merely a guide, as individual responses will vary. If you have any questions about whether your answer is accurate after referring to the answer given, always refer to the text for confirmation and clarification.

Some Final Thoughts ...

This *Study Guide* contains activities that will enhance your ability to learn, retrieve, and remember knowledge about *Adolescence*. However, effective studying involves more than the specific things you do to learn the material; it includes developing good general study habits, time management, and strategies that can help to lead to active learning. The learning activities in the *Study Guide* are designed to encourage you to be an active learner. Research has shown that study activities do not really help you unless you use them in a very active way (e.g., working through the section review, studying on your own, and checking the material you could not remember). Likewise, practice makes perfect. You will, therefore, note that many issues are addressed more than once in the guide. This should allow for easier mastery of difficult materials. If you agree with this, I hope that all of the activities in this *Study Guide* will be useful both as ready-made suggestions for study and as models for activities that you invent on your own to help you achieve your own course goals.

To also help you in developing effective study strategies, the publishers have included in this guide a brief section on "Being an Excellent Student." Read this section, written by Anita Rosenfield of DeVry Institute of Technology, Southern California, for more in-depth tips and suggestions on how to succeed in this and other courses.

Enjoy the class!

Dan Houlihan

Being an Excellent Student

by Anita Rosenfield

DeVry Institute of Technology, Southern California

Most students who are in college want to be good students, and most students have some particular goal in mind, which is probably why they chose the particular college or university they are attending. As you chose your college or university, and perhaps even an area of major interest or concentration, you had certain goals in mind, which likely included doing well in school, earning good grades, and graduating.

Unfortunately, many students do not do as well in college as they had hoped and expected. Let's examine some of the reasons for this disappointing outcome to see how to avoid them and to learn, instead, how to be a good student and guide your behavior to improve your chances of achieving your goals.

A common definition of education is that it is "how people learn stuff." For most of our history, educators have focused on the "stuff." Teachers were required to be masters of their respective academic fields. Even today, some states have requirements that speak only to the need to be qualified in the subject matter one teaches, not in the teaching methods themselves.

In the 1960s, we became more interested in the "people" part of the definition, which was evidenced by moving to strategies like open classrooms and free universities. The idea was that, given the opportunity to do so, people will naturally learn. Although these experiments were dismal failures, they taught us something.

The key to the definition of education is the word *how*. Today, thanks to a wealth of research on the principles that guide the phenomenon of learning, and on the nature of learning and memory, we know much more about how learning occurs, and how we can make it better. By using these principles, we can become better students.

Formulating the Plan

Anything worth having is worth planning for. Whether you hope to learn to teach, to fly, to write for profit, or to change diapers correctly, you have in mind a goal. An everyday question from the first days in elementary school is, "What do you want to be when you grow up?" The answer to this question is one way of formulating a goal. Now that you are a college student, many people will expect you to know what you want to do for a profession or career. Yet you may not have the foggiest notion, or you might have an idea that is still slightly foggy. That is OK. What is clear, however, is that you want to succeed in your college courses. This is a relatively long-range goal, and as such can serve a purpose in keeping you on track.

But our day-to-day behavior is often hard to connect to our long-range goals. We need short-term goals to keep us organized and to be sure that the flow of our activities is in the direction we want to be going. To accomplish our long-range goals, we need to focus on three types of short-term goals. First, we need goals for the day; second, we need goals for the week; and third, we need goals for the semester or term. Let's look at each of these separately.

Goals for Today

It is helpful to keep a daily checklist, diary, or schedule as a reminder of what must be done each day. Check off the things as you accomplish them. A pocket calendar is particularly helpful for this task.

Goals for the Week

Students who are successful in college also schedule their time weekly. Sometime during the course of registration, you made up a schedule showing your classes for the whole week. If you have a job, you must allow time for that, too. Also, many college or university students have family obligations that need to be considered as well. Finally, everyone needs some time for relaxing, eating, sleeping, and playing (even in graduate school we were advised that we needed to find some time to have fun in order to keep our balance). With all these things in mind, it is no wonder many students find little time to study.

But good students do all these things, too, yet they study. Do they have more time? No, we all have the same amount of time. But successful students schedule their time carefully. So, make up a weekly schedule and block off time for all these necessary events: classes, work, relaxation, eating, sleeping, playing, family, and studying. Students who actually schedule their time and keep to their schedules are amazed at how much time they find they have!

As you make up your weekly schedule, you may find your study time in a large block. If this is true, please remember to take a short break every twenty to thirty minutes. This is called distributed practice and is far more efficient than studying for hours on end. After the first twenty or thirty minutes, most of us become much less efficient anyway. When you take that break, reward yourself somehow; then get back to your studying. Something I always tell my students is never to try to read a whole chapter in one sitting. In fact, when I am preparing for a new class or have changed texts in a class I have been teaching, I take that advice myself!

Goals for the Semester

At the beginning of each semester, we find ourselves immersed in many new courses. Often, you will be confronted by several new professors with whom you have never worked before. It is difficult to sort out the expectations and demands of these several courses. However, it is important to organize the information that will be needed for completing all of the course requirements in order to be successful in the courses.

If you can, obtain a large wall calendar and mark on it all the dates of tests, exams, and term paper due dates, being sure to write on the calendar the course for which each date applies. Now, estimate how long it will take you to make final preparations for those exams, and mark those dates as warning or alert dates. Look over the dates on which papers are due, and see if they are bunched together. If your college is typical, they will probably be close. You can help yourself to avoid the last-minute all-nighters if you simply determine a spread of due dates for yourself, and mark those on the calendar too. As you do this step, please be sure to avoid any days that have personal significance for you, such as birthdays, anniversaries, and so on. This calendar gives you an overview of major dates in your semester.

If you have followed this carefully, you now have a large semester calendar plastered on your wall, a weekly schedule of major life events, classes, and study times taped over your desk, and a daily checklist of must-do items in your pocket or purse. **So, your scheduling is on its way. Let's look now at other important strategies.**

Attending Classes

Many students believe that, since they are in college, they can decide whether to go to class at all. This is true. Some students also believe that attendance in class is not important to their grade. This is not true! Some colleges or universities have attendance requirements, so that if students miss a given number of classes it will either lower their grade a full letter grade, or the instructor may drop the student from the course; some instructors have in-class activities that count toward students' grades, so if students are not in class, they do not get credit for participating. Even without such strategies, students who do not attend class sessions almost always do more poorly on the tests and exams. Perhaps they were absent when a crucial item was discussed, or when the instructor lectured over the material this examination requires. Remember, that more often than not, instructors will include information in their lectures that is not in your textbook, and that information (whether from class lecture, videos shown in class, guest lectures, and so on) is fair game for tests. Moreover, if you are not there, the instructor cannot get to know you, and therefore cannot give you the benefit of the doubt on your answers. It should come as no surprise that in study after research study, the data clearly show that those students who attend class regularly receive the highest grades and actually learn more, too! So, the first rule of being an effective student is to attend classes. Besides, how else can you get your money's worth?

But okay, now that you've determined you will go to every class, what will you do?

Benefiting from Lectures

Sometimes students think that if they come to class and "pay attention," they will remember what the instructor talked about; they think that if they take notes, they will miss much of what the instructor says. But sitting and paying attention is difficult. For one thing, most people can think much faster than they can speak. While the instructor lectures at 80 words per minute, the student thinks at about 350 words per minute! If the student is using this extra "thinking capacity" to focus on what the instructor is saying, it is fine. This rarely lasts more than five minutes at a time, however. Most of the time, this extra "thinking capacity" is used in daydreaming!

Daydreaming can be helpful in resolving our emotional problems, planning the course of our lives, and avoiding work. Often, it is motivated by the desire to avoid work. For whatever motive, however, daydreaming is not compatible with attending a lecture. Human beings simply cannot attend to more than one stimulus at one time. And you have to admit, your daydreams can be ever so much more interesting than your professor's lectures.

Benefiting from lecture notes is best achieved by taking notes. Use plenty of paper, and leave blank lines at regular intervals, or leave wide side margins. You will use these spaces later (they are not wasted!). If the instructor permits it, be brave and interrupt with questions if you do not understand what is being said. One thing I try to stress to my students is that I may know what I am talking about, but it may be unclear to them—and if it's unclear to one student, it may well be unclear to other students. So, for the sake of the other students who didn't understand what I was talking about, each student should take on the responsibility of asking me to clarify what I said, or to expand in a way that will help them understand. Remember that lectures have a way of progressing and building on earlier information. It is important to understand each point, or later points will be lost. (But please, DO NOT ask the person sitting next to you what the professor said—it disrupts the class, disturbs your neighbor, and you are likely NOT to get an accurate response!)

When you take notes, write out the major points, and try to just make simple notes on the supporting minor points. If you miss something, and you cannot ask a question about it, approach the instructor immediately afterward, when it is likely to still be fresh in both your minds. DO NOT try to write down every word, and DO try to use abbreviations or symbols, or, you could do what I did—learn shorthand! (Or, make up your own.)

Often my students will ask if they may tape record my lectures. Personally, I have no objection to having students do this. In fact, I did this my first term back in college but found it was terribly tedious trying to transcribe the lecture. The students for whom this may be particularly helpful are those who have visual, auditory, or motor impairments. However, do not ever tape record a lecture without first asking for and obtaining the professor's permission.

Within one or two hours after the lecture, on the same day, go back over your notes, and do two things. First, fill in the rest of the minor points. This often amounts to completing the sentence or other element. Second, write brief summaries and any questions that you now have in the blank spaces (lines or margins) you left earlier (clever of you to leave those spaces!). These few minutes spent reviewing and organizing your notes will pay off in greatly improved memory. The questions you have, you can ask in class or during the instructor's office hours, and reap two benefits. First, you will get the answers. Second, you will demonstrate that you are a serious student, and that will impress your instructor.

One other thing about going to class, while this is not always true, I have found that typically my best students sit in front. And most students seem to have a need to have "their seat," while a few students have a need to move around, sitting in one seat one day and a different seat the next. It wasn't until my graduate school days that I realized why I needed "my seat"—as a student, we are being overwhelmed with new information, a stressful experience; we need some structure we can count on to reduce that stress. So, if you are one of those who likes to wander, be considerate of your classmates' needs for stress reduction.

By the way, to get the most out of the lectures, do complete the assigned reading BEFORE the class begins so you are familiar with the material. This will help you keep up with what the instructor is talking about, will reduce the amount of information you do not understand, but may also bring up important questions for you to ask in class if the instructor does not talk about them.

Reading for Learning

We all know how to read. You are proving it by reading these words. Hopefully, you are also realizing some ideas as a result of reading. If you are only reading words, please WAKE UP! STOP DAYDREAMING!

We can read a variety of things: newspapers, movie reviews, novels, magazines, and textbooks. Textbooks are unlike all the others and must be read with a strategy all their own.

There are many reading and studying strategies, and all of them work to an extent. Perhaps you learned one or more in the course of going to high school. Perhaps you even took a how-to-study course when you entered college. If so, you probably learned one or two of these systems. If you have one you like that works for you, keep it. If you are interested in learning a new one, read on.

The PQ4R Method

One of the most successful and most widely used methods of studying written material was the SQ3R method, first developed at The Ohio State University. Researchers had noted that students who were more successful were more active readers. More recently, this method has been updated to the PQ4R Method, which adds an additional step. This method teaches you the same skills that have made many thousands of students successful. If you use this method when you read and study, you will be more successful, too. I have outlined the steps below, and the text describes this method in Chapter 13.

The P stands for PREVIEW. After you have read the overview or chapter outline and the list of learning objectives, you should survey the chapter in the text. This is also called skimming. Look at the headings and subheadings, and get the gist of the major points in this chapter. Check off each point in the outline of this Study Guide as you pass it in the pages of the text.

The Q stands for QUESTION. Reading is greatly enhanced if you are searching for the answers to questions. For this text, the Student Study Guide provides learning objectives that can serve as questions. For other texts, make up questions for yourself, based on the chapter overview or on your own survey of the chapter. Be sure that you have at least one question for each major unit in the chapter; you will be less efficient at studying those units for which you do not have questions.

The first of the four Rs is for READ. As you read, look for the answers to the questions you posed, or to the study or learning objectives furnished for you. When you find material that answers these questions, put a mark (X) or a "post-it" note in the margin next to that material. This will help now, since you are actively involved, and later, when you review. It is a good idea to wait to underline or highlight lines of text until after you have read the entire chapter at least once, so you will know what is and what is not most important. (In fact, although some "authorities" suggest you underline or highlight no more than 10% of what you are reading, I find that when most of us begin to underline or highlight, we wind up doing it to most of the chapter. (I suggest not doing it at all because it becomes too passive, which counteracts your attempts to read "actively.")

The second R stands for REFLECT. As you are reading, stop every so often and reflect on the material to increase its meaningfulness. This includes analyzing the material, thinking about how to apply it to your own life, interpreting the information, and connecting it with information you already have in your long-term memory.

The third R is for RECITE. One of the oldest classroom techniques in the world (Aristotle used it) is recitation. In the classroom version, the teacher asks the questions and the students answer them. Unless you can get your teacher to study with you regularly, you'll have to play both roles. Periodically stop in your reading and say aloud (if possible) what the author is telling you. Try to put it in your own words, but be sure to use technical terms as you learn them. If you are not in a situation where you can recite out loud, do it in writing. Just thinking it is not enough. When should you pause to recite? A good rule of thumb is that each time you come to the end of a major subheading, you should recite. One professor encourages his students to recite at least one sentence at the end of each paragraph, and two or three or more sentences at the end of each subunit (when you come to a new heading).

People who do not use recitation usually forget half of what they read in one hour and another half of the half they remembered by the end of the day. People who use recitation often remember from 75 to 90 percent of what they studied. This technique pays off. By the way, if anyone questions why you are talking to yourself, tell them that a psychologist recommended it.

The fourth R is for REVIEW. You should review a chapter soon after you have studied it (using the PQ and first 3Rs). You should review it again the day or evening before a test. It is not usually helpful to cram the night before a test, and particularly not the day of the test! That type of studying does not produce good memory and is likely to make you more anxious during the test itself.

Taking Tests

One of the things students fear most is failure. Failure signifies that things are not going well, and alerts us to the possibility that we may not achieve our goals. Unfortunately, many students see tests and exams as opportunities to fail. They prepare by becoming anxious and fearful, and trying to cram as much as possible right before the exam. These students rarely do well on the exam. They often fail, thus accomplishing just what they feared.

Taking tests requires strategy and planning. First, it is helpful to know what type of tests you will have. Your instructor probably told you during the first class meeting, or it may be in the class syllabus or course outline. If you do not know, ask.

If you are going to be taking essay exams, the best way to prepare is by writing essays. Before you do this, it is a good idea to find out what types of questions the instructor asks, and what is expected in a response. Again, it is helpful to ask the instructor for this material. Perhaps you can even see some examples of essay questions from previous years—some instructors at some colleges have copies of their exams on file in the department office or in the library. By finding out what is expected, you can formulate a model against which you can evaluate your answers.

Now, using the learning objectives or some essay questions you wrote, actually sit down and write out the answers. I have prepared at least two essay questions for each chapter in this text. HINT: If you usually feel more anxious during a test, it may help you to practice writing your essays in the room in which the test will be given. Simply find a time when the room is vacant, and make yourself at home.

If your instructor gives multiple-choice tests, then you should practice taking multiple-choice tests. For each chapter, either use questions provided in the Student Study Guide or make up your own. You may find it helpful to work out an arrangement to pool questions with other students, thereby reducing the amount of work you have to do, and developing a network of friends. Or, you may ask your professor if he or she would entertain the idea of having students write some of the exam questions—some of my professors did that in my undergraduate classes, and it is something I sometimes have my students do.

Whichever way you do it, the important thing is to prepare for tests and exams. Preparation is about 95 percent of the secret to getting a good grade. (Yes, there is some actual luck or chance involved in test scores, as even your instructor will admit!) Preparation is not only a good study and review technique, but also helps to reduce anxiety.

Dealing with Test Anxiety

Anxiety can be a helpful response when it occurs at low levels. In 1908, Yerkes and Dodson showed that the amount of anxiety that could benefit performance was a function of the difficulty and complexity of the task. As the difficulty of the task rose, anxiety became less helpful and more likely to interfere with performance.

If you have ever been so anxious in a test situation that you were unable to do well, even though you knew the information, you have test anxiety. If you get your exams back, and are surprised that you marked wrong answers when you knew the correct answers, or if you can only remember the correct answers after you leave the examination room, you too may have test anxiety.

Strategy Number One: Effective Study

Use study habits that promote learning and make the best use of time. Strategies, such as scheduling your time and using the PQ4R system, reduce anxiety by increasing confidence. As you come to realize that you know the material, your confidence rises and anxiety retreats.

Strategy Number Two: Relaxation

Each of us develops a unique pattern of relaxation. Some people relax by going to a specific place, either in person or mentally. Others relax by playing music, by being with friends, by using autogenic relaxation phrases, or by meditating. Whatever you do, be aware of it, and try to practice relaxation techniques. If you are good at relaxing, try thinking about those situations that make you anxious, and relax while you think of them. To do this, allow yourself to think only briefly (fifteen to thirty seconds at a time) of the situation that makes you anxious, and then relax again. After a number of such pairings, you will find that thinking about that situation no longer makes you anxious. At this point, you may be surprised to find that the situation itself also no longer produces anxiety. You may find that it is helpful to think about these anxiety-provoking situations in a sequence from those that produce very little anxiety to those that are more anxiety-evoking. Such a list, from low to high anxiety, might look something like this:

1. Your instructor announces that there will be a test in four weeks.
2. Your instructor reminds you of the test next week.
3. As you study, you see on the course outline the word *test*, and remember next week's test.
4. One of your friends asks you if you want to study together for the test, which is the day after tomorrow.
5. You choose not to go out with your friends because of the test tomorrow.
6. As you get up in the morning, you remember that today is the day of the test.

7.   You are walking down the hall toward the classroom; thinking about what questions might be on the test.

8.   The instructor enters the classroom, carrying a sheaf of papers in hand.

9.   The instructor distributes the papers, and you see the word *test* or *exam* at the top.

10. After reading the first five questions, you have not been able to think of the answer to any of them.

If you work at it gradually and consistently, pairing these types of thoughts (briefly) with relaxation and remembering to let go and relax after each one, this will dispel test anxiety and make test taking a more productive and successful experience.

Strategy Number Three: Thinking Clearly

Most students who have test anxiety think in unclear and unproductive ways. They say to themselves things like: "I can't get these answers correct . . . I don't know this stuff . . . I don't know anything at all . . . . I'm going to fail this test . . . I'm probably going to flunk out of school . . . I'm just a dumb nerd." These thoughts share two unfortunate characteristics: they are negative and they are absolute. They should be replaced.

When we tell ourselves negative and absolute thoughts, we find it impossible to focus on the test material. The result is that we miss questions even when we know the answers. Our thinking prevents us from doing well.

A good strategy for replacing these negative and absolute thoughts is to practice thinking positive and honest thoughts, such as: "I may not know all the answers, but I know some of them . . . I don't know the answer to that right now, so I will go on to the next one and come back to that . . . I don't have to get them all right . . . I studied hard and carefully, and I can get some of them correct . . . I am a serious student, and have some abilities . . . I am prepared for this test, and know many of the answers . . . This test is important, but it is not going to determine the course of my entire life and if I don't do well, it doesn't mean I'm a horrible person or a dummy."

By thinking clearly, honestly, and positively, we quiet the flood of anxiety and focus on the task at hand. Students who use this technique invariably do better on the tests. It takes practice to think clearly, but it is worth the effort. After a while, you will find that it becomes natural and does not take any noticeable effort. And as anxiety is reduced, more energy is available for studying and for doing well on examinations. The eventual outcome is more enjoyment with learning, better learning, more success in college, and the achievement of your goals.

Strategy Number Four: Guided Imagery

Something I often do with my students before a test is to have them relax (see Strategy Two), close their eyes, and visualize themselves walking into a tall building. They go into the elevator in the building and take it to the top floor, which is fifty-six stories up. They walk out of the elevator, and go to the stairwell, then climb to the top of the building. There is no railing on the top of the building. I direct them to walk over to the very edge of the building and put their toes at the very edge, then look down. I ask them to think about how they are feeling as they are looking down onto the street from the top of this building. I then tell them to back up, have the realization that they can fly—just spread out their arms and they can fly. Then they are directed back to the edge of the building, knowing that they can fly. They put their toes on the edge, look down, and then spread their arms and fly, eventually flying down to land safely on the ground below. Next I have them visualize themselves in the classroom; on the desk before them is their test. They look at the test and see themselves reading the questions saying, "I know that answer. Yes, I remember learning that." They visualize themselves being successful, answering all the questions correctly, and feeling good about themselves. Then I have them visualize getting their tests back, with a big "A" on the test.

Some students are much better able to visualize than others. You can try combining Strategy Two with this strategy to help you improve your visualization, since it can be an effective success strategy.

Strategy Number Five: Do the Easy Ones First

One technique I learned while studying for the GRE (Graduate Record Exam) was to read each question and answer the ones I knew, then go back to the harder ones. Two things to watch out for on this: first, be sure you get the answers in the right place—sometimes when we skip a question or two, we wind up marking the wrong space, so check that your answer to question 10 is in space 10; second, you may find you're stumped by the first several questions—don't let that throw you, just keep going because there is bound to be one you jump on and say, "Yes! I know that one." Answer the easy ones first, then go back to the others after you've built up your confidence seeing you DO know "stuff." Then, always go back over the whole test to be sure you answered every question (the exception here is if you have a professor who takes more than one point off for wrong answers—in that case, it's better not to answer than to answer wrong, but I don't know anyone who does that).

Strategy Number Six: State Dependent Learning

Research has found that we remember information best when we are in the same "state" we were in when we first learned the information. So, for example, you might remember a certain song when prompted by a specific stimulus (seeing someone who reminds you of your "first true love"); or, we will remember things we learned when we were particularly happy if we are again in that mood. This goes for physical contexts as well—so that we have an advantage if we take an exam in the same room where we learned the information in the first place. But it also goes to physical context in terms of our bodies—if you drink coffee or caffeine-laden sodas when you study, try to do the same before your exam. On the other hand, if you don't consume caffeine when you study, by all means, DO NOT suddenly have a cup of coffee before your exam. Because of the power of this phenomenon, you may want to create a particular mental context for yourself when you study so that you can put yourself into the same mental context when you take your exams.

Strategy Number Seven: Take a Break

If you find yourself getting stressed out during the test, take a break. Put your pencil down, breath deeply, you may even want to put your head down on the desk (please, do not fall asleep!). Use the relaxation techniques or the guided imagery strategy; visualize yourself looking at the test and suddenly realizing that you DO know the answers to at least most of the questions. Then go back to taking the test.

Remember, that with all of these test-taking strategies, if you don't do the first one, none of the others will help! Passing the course requires that you actively study the material.

Memory Techniques

No matter how much you read, it won't help you if you don't remember *what* you read. The most critical factor in remembering is being able to apply what you have learned. Of course, some things such as people's names, or certain dates, or statistical information are not easily applied to your life, so you'll have to use other techniques. But first, let's talk about the "easy way."

Apply It to Your Life

If you can take the material you are learning and use it in your everyday life, you will remember it without any problem. Connect it with what you already know, either from life experience or other courses you have taken. Sometimes what you are learning fits nicely with what you already knew; sometimes it will contradict what you learned before. This is an opportunity to look at how the new information fits in with the old—were there new research findings? Or, is it merely a difference of opinion? Make these associations—don't keep the information for any class neatly compartmentalized—if you do, you'll have a hard time trying to find it when you need it.

Teach It to Someone Else!

When we start teaching something to someone else, we find we HAVE TO learn it, and by trying to explain the material to another person, we examine it and think about it differently. So, take the material you are learning in this class (or any class) and teach it to someone else. When they ask you questions, you can look them up and find the answers, or think them out together, or ask someone else. As you explain these concepts to someone else (your children, your friends, or even your dog), you will suddenly see them in a totally different light.

Mnemonic Techniques

Some things are just really difficult to apply to your own life. Dates, names, places, statistics, and such may not have a great deal of meaning for you. In that event, use the tricks that memory specialists use—mnemonics. There are many different types. For example, one famous mnemonic is an acronym for remembering the Great Lakes: HOMES = Huron, Ontario, Michigan, Erie, and Superior; or the colors of the rainbow is a man's name: ROY G. BIV = Red, Orange, Yellow, Green, Blue, Indigo, and Violet (if not for this "man," I'd never remember indigo!) You can make up your own acronyms by taking the first initial of any term, person, etc. It's easiest, though, if it's something that makes sense to you.

Another mnemonic technique is called the ***method of loci,*** and I've been told it's one that medical students use to remember body parts. You list the things you need to remember, and then visualize yourself walking around a familiar place (like your living room), putting one item on a particular piece of furniture. Then, when you need to remember that item, you go through your "living room" to see where it is.

One other mnemonic technique is the story method. Take the information you need to remember and put it into a story.

Be an "Information Dropper"

This is similar to the suggestion to teach, but less formal. Ask your friends to "indulge" you by listening to what you learned in your Life Span Development class (or any other class). Then *tell* them what you are learning. You may, in fact, find that you have managed to help one of your friends by sharing this information!

Rote Memory

If you can remember back to grade school when you learned to multiply, somehow the only way that seemed to happen was by repeating the multiplication tables over and over and over again. Personally, I think this is about the worst way to learn most anything, but for some things (like multiplication tables) it works. The Flashcards that are included in each chapter of this Study Guide are a way to help you learn through repeating the material you don't know until you are able to answer the questions posed without looking at the reverse side of the cards. Hopefully you will then go further and apply the information to other areas of your life.

Most Important

Remember this: Professors don't actually "teach" their students, rather, they facilitate learning so students end up teaching themselves. Although we try really hard to motivate our students, keep them interested, and present information in a way that helps students to understand, the ultimate responsibility for learning rests with the students. Some students have learned *despite* their professors, others don't learn even with the very best of professors. So keep your goals in mind, study hard, ask questions, and aim for success!

Further Resources

Online Learning Center

http://www.mhhe.com/santrocka10

An expansive resource for students, this site includes:

- Self-assessment quizzes for each chapter
- Study tools, including crossword puzzles
- Links to relevant websites
- Adolescent Development Image Gallery
- Interactive scenarios

McGraw-Hill Developmental Psychology Supersite

http://www.mhhe.com/developmental

This website provides valuable resources to help you, such as Interactive exercises, simulations, and links to some of the best developmental psychology sites on the Web.

For those of you with "Print Disabilities" including blindness, visual impairment, learning disabilities or other physical disabilities, please check out the **Recording for the Blind and Dyslexic website** at

www.rfbd.org/ or call customer service at **(800) 221-4792.** This educational library has 77,000 taped titles including textbooks and reference and professional materials for people who cannot read standard print because of a disability.

APA Style

For information on APA writing style and guidelines, please refer your students to the American Psychological Association's website at http://www.apa.org, or link to this site by visiting Santrock's *Adolescence* Online Learning Center at http://www.mhhe.com/santrocka10.

Using the Internet

There are numerous possibilities or ways to use the Internet with Adolescence courses. In fact, the sheer vastness of available information is often overwhelming for both instructors and students alike. Most of you have some idea about how to search for information available on the Internet, but you need to have the critical thinking skills necessary to discern whether the information you are locating is valid and useful. The following five criteria may be helpful in assisting you with analyzing the appropriateness of information available on the Internet.

1.   **Accuracy**

2.   **Authority**

3.   **Objectivity**

4.   **Currency**

5.   **Coverage**

You can often struggle with search strategies or become easily frustrated if you cannot locate the type of information you want. There are several excellent tutorials available online which can assist in this process, and most libraries have resources designed to help students create more sophisticated searching methodologies. The following sites may provide some assistance.

Tutorial for Beginning Users:

http://www.lib.berkeley.edu/TeachingLib/Guides/Internet/FindInfo.html

Created by the library staff of the University of California at Berkeley, this is an excellent place for both instructors and students to learn more about using the Internet. The tutorial is divided into two sections with the first providing information about how to access the Internet and use Netscape. The second part of the tutorial discusses how to search for information and includes a comparative chart of the best five search engines, explanations of meta-search tools, and convenient handouts, which can be used for class exercises. Also available in the handouts section are PowerPoint slides and instructor's notes.

Guide to Meta-search Engines:

http://www.indiana.edu/~librcsd/search/meta.html

This is a useful description of 13 meta-search engines with links to each and can aid both instructors and students in searching for Internet resources.

⌘

Chapter 1   Introduction

Learning Goals with Key Terms and Key People in Boldface

1.0   DESCRIBE THE HISTORICAL PERSPECTIVE ON ADOLESCENCE
    A.   Early History
        1.1   Compare and contrast Plato's and Aristotle's views of adolescence.
        1.2   In which ways are the views regarding adolescence expressed by Plato and Jean-Jacques Rousseau similar?
    B.   The Twentieth Century
        1.3   What was the driving force behind the changing views of adolescence that emerged between 1890 and 1920?
        1.4   What factors led historians to label **G. Stanley Hall** the "father of the scientific study of adolescence"?
        1.5   What was Hall's **storm-and-stress view** concept of adolescence?
        1.6   In what ways were Hall's views similar to those of Charles Darwin?
        1.7   Why was **Margaret Mead**'s sociocultural view of adolescence considered pathbreaking in the early 1900s?
        1.8   What factors have led to a debate over the accuracy of Mead's findings?
        1.9   What is the **inventionist view** of adolescence?
        1.10   Why do historians call the period of 1890 to 1920 the "age of adolescence"?
        1.11   How are schools, work, and economics important dimensions of the inventionist view?
        1.12   Why do some historians suggest that changing laws, in effect, created adolescence?
        1.13   What challenges were presented to adolescents during the Great Depression and World War II?
        1.14   What factors combined in the 1960s and 1970s to challenge the position of prominence achieved by adolescents in the 1950s?
        1.15   How was life different for an adolescent in 1920 as opposed to 1970?
        1.16   Which females and individuals from ethnic minorities have contributed to the study of adolescents?
    C.   Stereotyping Adolescents
        1.17   What is a **stereotype**, and what are the contemporary stereotypes of adolescence?
        1.18   What is the purpose served by a **stereotype?**
        1.19   What did Joseph Adelson mean by the **adolescent generalization gap?**
    D.   A Positive View of Adolescence
        1.20   In what way did research by **Daniel Offer** and his colleagues challenge existing stereotypes of adolescence?

1.21   Do adolescents deserve the negative portrayal they get from adults today? Support your answer with information from the book and your own experience.

2.0   DISCUSS TODAY'S U.S. ADOLESCENTS AND SOCIAL POLICY ISSUES INVOLVING ADOLESCENTS

A.   Current Status of U.S. Adolescents

2.1   Why is today both the best of times and the worst of times for adolescents?

2.2   How would you compare the current status of adolescents and public attitudes toward them with that of adolescents of several decades ago?

2.3   What differences in development among adolescents render them a heterogeneous group?

B.   Social Contexts

2.4   How do **contexts** of development influence adolescent development?

2.5   Why is the cultural context for U.S. adolescents changing today?

C.   Social Policy and Adolescents' Development

2.6   What is **social policy,** and why do we need one that is concerned with adolescent development?

2.7   According to **Marian Wright Edelman,** how are today's politicians falling short in practicing what they preach, i.e., "family values?"

2.8   In the U.S., how have older generations been disproportionately benefiting from social policy?

2.9   What is **generational inequity** and how does it relate to social policy issues?

2.10   In what ways are future generations more likely to be challenged by generational inequality?

2.11   Why should the well-being of adolescents be one of America's foremost concerns?

2.12   Why is it important to not diminish the role of youth in future generations?

2.13   Why does **Reed Larson** believe that more adolescents need opportunities to extend their capacity for initiative?

3.0   CHARACTERIZE THE CURRENT GLOBAL PERSPECTIVE ON ADOLESCENCE

A.   Youth Around the World

3.1   What traditions remain for adolescents around the globe?

3.2   What are some ways in which adolescents around the globe vary in the ways they develop?

3.3   Why are youth in the United States marrying later, while youth in some other countries are marrying earlier?

B.   Global Traditions and Changes in Adolescence

3.4   How has adolescent health and well-being changed in recent years?

3.5   Around the world, are there becoming more opportunities for females?

3.6   What are some trends occurring in families around the world?

3.7   Are schools around the world improving?

3.8   What is the role of peers in Western cultures?

4.0   SUMMARIZE THE DEVELOPMENTAL PROCESSES, PERIODS, TRANSITIONS, AND ISSUES RELATED TO ADOLESCENCE

A.   What Is Development?

4.1   What do we mean when we speak of an individual's **development?**

B.   Processes and Periods

4.2   What are the three major processes that shape adolescent development?

4.3   Differentiate between **cognitive processes** and **socioemotional processes** and their roles in adolescent development.

4.4   What are the three major developmental periods and their subperiods from conception to death?

4.5   What are the four (4) periods of childhood development?

4.6   What factors reflect the role of **biological processes** in the adolescent's development?

4.7   Why would it be inappropriate to suggest that a child enter **adolescence** as a blank slate?

4.8   What is **adolescence** and what are its two periods?

4.9   Why do developmentalists no longer believe that change ends with adolescence?

4.10   How do cultural and gender differences impact when children enter adolescence?

4.11   Do adolescents enter **adulthood** at the same time?

4.12   What are the three periods of adult development?

C.   Developmental Transitions

4.13   What is meant by the saying, "Adolescence begins in biology and ends in culture?"

4.14   What are some biological changes associated with adolescence?

4.15   What transitional period was **Kenniston** referring to when he proposed the term **youth?**

4.16   Contrast **youth** and emerging adulthood.

4.17   Which personal and social assets are linked to well-being in adolescents?

D.   Developmental Issues

4.18   What are the three major issues of adolescent development?

4.19   What is the **nature-nurture issue** and how is it relevant to the concept of **maturation** and experience?

4.20   Differentiate between **continuity of development** and **discontinuity of development.**

4.21   Contrast the views of **nature** proponents with those of **nurture** proponents.

4.22   What are the main issues in **early-later experience issue** debate?

4.23   What recent changes in the choices being made by young women are reflective of the role **nurture** plays?

4.24   How do beliefs about significant developmental experiences differ in various cultures?

4.25   How do nature differences influence differences between adolescent boys and girls?

4.26   Why do developmentalists usually refrain from taking extreme positions on developmental issues?

5.0   EXPLAIN WHAT MATTERS IN UNDERSTANDING ADOLESCENCE

A.   Understanding Adolescence: What Matters?

5.1   What seven things matter in understanding adolescence?

B.   History Matters

5.2   How can historical events and factors significantly alter the lives of adolescents?

C.   Biological Processes Matter

5.3   What are **biological processes** and why do they matter?

5.4   Why does science matter in understanding adolescent development?

D.   Cognitive Processes Matter

5.5   What are **cognitive processes** and why do they matter?

E. **Social and Personality Development Matter**
    5.6   Which important aspects of adolescents' lives involve social and personality development?

F. **Contexts Matter**
    5.7   Which **contexts** are significant in adolescent development?

G. **Problems Matter**
    5.8   What problems and disorders can restrict optimal adolescent development?

H. **Reflective and Critical Thinking Matter**
    5.9   What does it mean to be a critical thinker?
    5.10   Why is the ability to think critically an important milestone in adolescence?

Exercises

KEY TERMS COMPLETION EXERCISE

Each key term is presented in the form of an incomplete sentence. Complete each sentence by either defining the term or giving an example of it. Compare your definitions with those given at the end of the study guide chapter.

1.   The **storm-and-stress view** of adolescence suggests that

    _____

    _____.

2.   According to the **inventionist view,** adolescence began

    _____

    _____.

3.   If I were to invoke a common **stereotype,** I would view adolescents

    _____

    _____.

4.   Evidence that an **adolescent generalization gap** exists is

    _____

    _____.

5.   Examples of **contexts** are

    _____

    _____.

6.   In the United States, **social policy** has resulted in

_____

_____.

7.   In the United States, the biggest threat of **generational inequity** stems from

_____

_____.

8.   Development is the

_____

_____.

9.   **Biological processes** affect a person by

_____

_____.

10.   The best evidence of changing **cognitive processes** in adolescence is

_____

_____.

11.   Confirmation of **socioemotional processes** in adolescence is

_____

_____.

12.   The **prenatal period** is from

_____

_____.

13.   A child in its **infancy** is often seen

_____

_____.

14.   **Early childhood** is marked by

_____

_____.

15. During **middle and late childhood,** children

_____

_____ .

16. The change from childhood to **adolescence** involves

_____

_____ .

17. **Early adolescence** is characterized by

_____

_____ .

18. The activities that make up **late adolescence** are

_____

_____ .

19. You can tell that Susan is in **early adulthood** because

_____

_____ .

20. **Middle adulthood** is marked by

_____

_____ .

21. A person in **late adulthood** might

_____

_____ .

22. According to Kenniston, **youth** is

_____

_____ .

23. **Emerging adulthood** is represented by

_____

_____ .

24.   The **nature-nurture issue** refers to

_____

_____.

25.   The **continuity–discontinuity issue** suggests

_____

_____.

26.   Theorists debating the **early-later experience issue** suggest

_____

_____.

KEY PEOPLE IN THE STUDY OF ADOLESCENCE

Match the name with the concept, issue, or topic related to adolescence with which they are associated.

___ 1. G. Stanley Hall   A. Studied teenagers in Samoa
___ 2. Margaret Mead   B. Coined the term "youth"
___ 3. Leta Hollingsworth   C. The father of the scientific study of adolescence
___ 4. Daniel Offer   D. His work challenged the negative stereotypes of adolescents
___ 5. Marian Wright   E. First used the term "gifted" and challenged the theory of male
         Edelman   superiority
___ 6. Bernice Neugarten   F. Argued that adolescents need more opportunities to develop the
                                        capacity for initiative
___ 7. Kenneth & Mamie   G. A child's rights advocate, who champions improvements in social
         Clark   policies affecting young people and their families
___ 8. Kenneth Kenniston   H. Believes that many segments of society, not just adolescents, are
                                        affected by inequities in our social and economic policies
___ 9. George Sanchez   I. Conducted research on the self-esteem of African-American
                                        children
___ Reed Larson   J. Documented cultural bias in intelligence tests
   10.

"DR. DETAIL'S" MATCHING EXERCISE

Match the correct percentage with the appropriate statement or question.

___ 1. From 1910 to 1930, the number of 10- to 15-year olds gainfully   A. More than 70%
         employed dropped by this:
___ 2. Between 1900 and 1930 the number of high school graduates increased B. More than 20%
         by this:
___ 3. Daniel Offer and his colleagues studied the self-images of adolescents C. 75%
         around the world and found that ____% had a healthy self-image.
___ 4. What percentage of adolescents today are giving birth?   D. 600%
___ 5. College students who said being an adult means accepting responsibility E. 73%
         for the consequences of one's actions:

___ 6. This is the percentage of local TV coverage devoted to crime   F.   Two-thirds
        victimization, accidents, and violent crime involving adolescents.

___ 7. The number of Asian Indian adolescents accepting their parents' choice   G.   46%
        of a marital partner for them.

HISTORICAL PERSPECTIVE
SECTION REVIEW

1.   Why were the views proposed by Jean-Jacques Rousseau regarding adolescence considered more
     enlightened than those proposed by Plato and Aristotle?

     _____

     _____

2.   Compare and contrast Hall's storm-and-stress perspective of adolescence with Margaret Mead's
     sociocultural view.

     _____

     _____

3.   Why were Hall's views regarding adolescence strongly influenced by Darwin?

     _____

     _____

4.   Why were Margaret Mead's Samoan findings met with criticism?

     _____

     _____

5.   Describe the factors that led to the period between 1890 and 1920 being known as the "age of
     adolescence."

     _____

     _____

6.   What accounted for the prominence adolescents gained in society from 1920 to 1950, and what
     factors would challenge this distinction?

     _____

     _____

7.   How did Daniel Offer and his colleagues challenge the negative views of adolescents, and what
     empirical support did they find?

     _____

     _____

KEY PEOPLE IN SECTION (describe the contributions of this individual to the study and understanding of adolescence).

Plato —

_____

_____.

Aristotle —

_____

_____.

Jean-Jacques Rousseau —

_____

_____.

G. Stanley Hall —

_____

_____.

Charles Darwin —

_____

_____.

Margaret Mead —

_____

_____.

Leta Hollingworth —

_____

_____.

Kenneth and Mamie Clark —

_____

_____.

George Sanchez —

_____

_____.

Joseph Adelson —

_____

_____.

Daniel Offer —

_____

_____.

TODAY'S ADOLESCENTS
SECTION REVIEW

1. List three facts of contemporary life that makes today "the best of times" for adolescents.

    _____

    _____

2. List three facts of contemporary life that makes today "the worst of times" for adolescents.

    _____

    _____

3. What are four examples that suggest that today's adolescents are growing up in a less stable environment than that of adolescents several decades ago?

    _____

    _____

4. Why are contexts important in understanding adolescent development?

    _____

    _____

5. Why should the well-being of adolescents be one of the major concerns for makers of social policy?

    _____

    _____

6.   Why does Marian Wright Edelman believe that we must reexamine our nation's policies for families?

_____

_____

7.   What would be the risk associated with ignoring a problem like generation inequity?

_____

_____

8.   How are advances in transportation and telecommunication impacting youth around the globe?

_____

_____.

KEY PEOPLE IN SECTION (describe the contributions of this individual to the study and understanding of adolescence).

Peter Benson —

_____

_____.

Marian Wright Edelman —

_____

_____.

Bernice Neugarten —

_____

_____.

Reed Larson —

_____

_____.

THE NATURE OF DEVELOPMENT
SECTION REVIEW

1.   Complete the table by giving the name and a brief description of the eight periods of development corresponding to the given ages.

Age	Name	Description
Prenatal		
Birth to 18–24 months		
2 to 5–6 years		
6 to 10–11 years		
10–13 to 18–22 years		
Late teens to early 20s and 30s		
35–45 to 55–65 years		
60–70 years until death		

2. Explain why biological, cognitive, and socioemotional processes are unavoidably interwoven.

   _____

   _____

3. Is there a specific age at which an adolescent becomes an adult?

   _____

   _____

4. Which personal and social assets are linked to well-being in adolescence and emerging adulthood?

   _____

   _____

5. Explain the nature/nurture issue in your own words, using any facet of adolescent physical, cognitive, or emotional development as an example.

   _____

   _____

6. How does the continuity-discontinuity issue apply to today's youth?

   _____

   _____

7. Why is the early-later experience issue still such a hotly debated topic?

_____

_____

KEY PEOPLE IN SECTION (describe the contributions of this individual to the study and understanding of adolescence).

Kenneth Kenniston —

_____

_____.

Jerome Kagan —

_____

_____.

Jacqueline Eccles —

_____

_____.

UNDERSTANDING ADOLESCENCE: WHAT MATTERS?
SECTION REVIEW

1. How do historical events and times affect the lives and development of adolescents?

_____

_____

2. In what ways do changes in adolescent thinking and cognitive skill affect their lives?

_____

_____

3. What is a central aspect of biological processes in adolescence?

_____

_____

4.   What does it mean to be a critical thinker?

_____

_____

5.   List nine characteristics and cognitive processes of critical thinkers.

_____

_____

KEY PEOPLE IN THE SECTION (describe the contributions of this individual to the study and understanding of adolescence).

Luis Vargas —

_____

_____.

EXPLORATIONS IN ADOLESCENCE

1.   Have you ever been the target of a stereotype (race, gender, ethnicity, religion, social class, etc.)? Consider what type of stereotype it may have been, and then consider how it may have changed your thinking. How have you been affected by this: positively, or negatively?

2.   In recent years, adolescents have appeared featured on the covers of prominent magazines and featured in many documentaries? The tone of these discussions is becoming increasingly negative. How might this impact today's children who are just starting to enter adolescence?

3.   Is the modern emphasis on education and career training adversely affecting the formation of the family?

COGNITIVE CHALLENGE

1.   Imagine you could time-travel. How would your life, as an adolescent, have been different in each of these different time periods?
      a.   1890 – 1920

_____

_____

      b.   1920 – 1950

_____

_____

c.   1960 – 1980

_____

_____

2.   Choose any ethnic group other than your own. Imagine how your experiences would have been different in the following domains. Write the ethic group or culture that you have chosen here:

a.   relationship with your parents

_____

b.   relationship with your peers

_____

c.   high school experience

_____

d.   your physical health and development

_____

e.   your moral and spiritual development

_____

f.   your intellectual development

_____

g.   your dating behavior and romantic relationships

_____

h.   the neighborhood in which you lived

_____

i.   your family's socioeconomic status

_____

j.   how you would be different today as a result of these variations in experience

_____

3.   Referring to the list of areas in number 2, pick the five areas that you think were the most influential in making you who you are today. Discuss the impact of your experiences in these areas on your adult development.

_____

_____

ADOLESCENCE IN RESEARCH

Concerning Daniel Offer's 1988 study of the negative stereotyping of adolescents, state the hypothesis, the research methods (if known), the research conclusions, and the implications and applications for adolescent development.

_____

_____

 ## COMPREHENSIVE REVIEW

1. That these times are the best of times for today's adolescents is indicated by the observation that
    a. crack cocaine is more addictive and deadly than marijuana.
    b. individuals have longer life expectancies than ever before.
    c. most families include a father who is the breadwinner, a mother, and children.
    d. television transmits powerful messages about sex and violence.

2. According to Plato, the distinguishing feature of the adolescent period was the development of
    a. reason.
    b. self-determination.
    c. virtues and morals.
    d. conformity to societal standards.

3. According to Aristotle, this is the most important aspect of adolescence.
    a. emotional stability
    b. virtues and morals
    c. the ability to choose
    d. reasoning

4. Stanley Hall described adolescence as a period of
    a. emotional stability.
    b. passivity and conformity.
    c. considerable upheaval.
    d. gradual socioemotional development.

5. This century marked the beginning of the scientific exploration of adolescence.
    a. the 19th century
    b. the 15th century
    c. the 4th century
    d. the 20th century

6. G. Stanley Hall was strongly influenced by the views of
    a. Rousseau.
    b. Mead.
    c. Darwin.
    d. Freud.

7.   Margaret Mead proposed that adolescents develop easily into adulthood if their environments are appropriately designed, after observing adolescents in
    a.   Samoa.
    b.   the Philippines.
    c.   the Trobriand Islands.
    d.   Mangia.

8.   The current view of Margaret Mead's research on Samoan adolescents is that
    a.   it was unbiased and error-free.
    b.   it supports the inventionist view rather than G. Stanley Hall's view of adolescence.
    c.   it exemplifies the adolescent generalization gap.
    d.   their lives are more stressful than Mead observed.

9.   Because they believe it was during this time frame that the concept of adolescence was formed, historians now call this period the "age of adolescence."
    a.   1910 to 1940
    b.   1890 to 1920
    c.   1920 to 1950
    d.   1960 to 1980

10.   Which of the following factors did *not* contribute to the invention of the concept of adolescence?
    a.   child-saving legislation
    b.   increased adolescent employment during the Great Depression
    c.   the separation of work and the home
    d.   the creation of a system of compulsory education

11.   As compulsory laws regarding youth were enacted in the early twentieth century, employment of adolescents _____ and school attendance _____ .
    a.   decreased; increased
    b.   decreased; decreased
    c.   increased; decreased
    d.   increased; increased

12.   You are reading a book about how children and adolescents have historically been treated by their parents. The book describes how a mother tries to imitate her daughter's dance steps. The historical passage probably referred to the
    a.   1890s.
    b.   1920s.
    c.   1940s.
    d.   1960s.

13.   What event led to the increase in adolescent rebellion and protest?
    a.   the discovery of marijuana
    b.   the bombing of Pearl Harbor
    c.   the Vietnam War
    d.   the Great Depression

14.   Which of the following is most likely to be true concerning perceptions of adolescents of the mid 1970s to the 1980s?
    a.   They are less interested in physical fitness.

b.   They are more achievement-oriented.

c.   They engage in more radical protests than in the 1970s.

d.   They are less sexually permissive.

15.   If you categorized all adolescents as rebellious, lazy, smart alecks, you would be using a(n)

a.   context.

b.   inventionist view.

c.   stereotype.

d.   generation gap view.

16.   When you were an adolescent, your parents accused your generation of being lazy and having no respect for authority. Based on the research concerning parents' and adolescents' attitudes, you might have told your parents:

a.   "I guess we just have an insurmountable generation gap."

b.   "What you call a generation gap, I would call a generalization gap."

c.   "Although the majority of adolescents have a generation gap, I don't."

d.   "Only the parents of deviant adolescents have a generalization gap."

17.   The research by Daniel Offer and his colleagues in 1988, which examined the self-images of adolescents around the world, had what effect on the belief that adolescents are highly stressed?

a.   It supported that belief.

b.   It challenged its accuracy.

c.   It showed depression to be a larger problem than stress.

d.   It was inconclusive and therefore had no impact.

18.   Sociocultural context refers to

a.   the setting in which development occurs.

b.   studies that allow comparisons between different cultures.

c.   the most important influences on development according to G. Stanley Hall.

d.   a term associated with inferiority and deficits in the cultural group in questions.

19.   _____conducted important research on adolescent development, mental retardation, and gifted children.

a.   Leta Hollingworth

b.   George Sanchez

c.   Kenneth Clark

d.   Daniel Offer

20.   _____ was the first to document cultural bias in intelligence tests for children and adolescents.

a.   Leta Hollingworth

b.   George Sanchez

c.   Kenneth Clark

d.   Daniel Offer

21.   A national government's actions that influence the welfare of its citizens defines the concept of

a.   family values.

b.   generational inequity.

c.   the inventionist viewpoint.

d.   social policy.

22.   According to Marian Wright Edelman, president of the Children's Defense Fund, the most important function of our society should be
    a.   eliminating violence.
    b.   restructuring our educational system.
    c.   parenting and nurturing the next generation.
    d.   developing a healthy knowledge of the body and sexuality.

23.   The concern that older members of the society benefit disproportionately more than younger members of the society in terms of national allocations of resources is the concept of
    a.   generational inequity.
    b.   social policy.
    c.   the adolescent generalization gap.
    d.   the storm and stress view.

24.   Which of the following is *not* a major process contributing to the scientific study of development?
    a.   cognitive
    b.   biological
    c.   socioemotional
    d.   personal

25.   This represents the pattern of change that begins at conception and continues throughout one's life span
    a.   context
    b.   adolescence
    c.   development
    d.   continuity

26.   According to G. Stanley Hall, the dominant process of adolescent development would be
    a.   biological.
    b.   cognitive.
    c.   sexual.
    d.   socioemotional.

27.   Alterations in an individual's thinking and intelligence suggest a change in
    a.   cognitive processes.
    b.   biological processes.
    c.   Context.
    d.   socioemotional processes.

28.   First grade typically marks the end of this period.
    a.   prenatal period
    b.   infancy
    c.   toddlerhood
    d.   early childhood

29.   Developmentalists subdivide the period of development before adolescence into _____ periods.
    a.   two
    b.   six

c.   four
d.   eight

30.   If Kenneth Kenniston is correct, a youth would be expected to
    a.   live in several different places.
    b.   be confused about sexual orientation.
    c.   avoid dating.
    d.   be unable to secure full-time employment.

31.   The most widely recognized marker of entry into adulthood is
    a.   the first sexual experience.
    b.   the decision to get married.
    c.   taking a job that is more or less permanent and fulltime.
    d.   learning to drive a car.

32.   On the issue of maturation and experience, most developmentalists
    a.   agree with the position of G. Stanley Hall.
    b.   agree with the position of Margaret Mead.
    c.   agree with the inventionist viewpoint.
    d.   recognize the importance of their interaction.

33.   Many developmentalists believe that humans progress through a number of defined stages in the
course of their lives. John Santrock, the author of *Adolescence,* would say that these
developmentalists see human development
    a.   as discontinuous.
    b.   as unstable.
    c.   as dominated by environment.
    d.   much as G. Stanley Hall did.

34.   Which of the following examples is the best example of discontinuity in development?
    a.   a seedling growing into an oak.
    b.   a worm growing into a night crawler.
    c.   a caterpillar becoming a butterfly.
    d.   a leaf falling from a tree.

35.   Most developmentalists avoid taking extreme positions on major developmental issues because
    a.   differences between male and female adolescents are growing larger.
    b.   heredity is nearly always a stronger force than environment
    c.   adolescents are beginning their sexual encounters at earlier ages.
    d.   simplistic explanations deny the complexity of human development.

36.   The fact that many previously well-established differences between adolescent males and
females are diminishing as females pursue careers in male-dominated areas and seek greater
autonomy supports this perspective.
    a.   social policy
    b.   nature
    c.   nurture
    d.   context

37.   Which of the following is not an important context in the lives of adolescents?
    a.   music
    b.   family
    c.   school
    d.   peers

ADOLESCENCE ON THE SCREEN

■   *Cider House Rules* is about an orphaned boy whose identity search leads him back to what his foster father wanted for him.

■   *The Talented Mr. Ripley* depicts a highly educated and charming sociopath.

■   *Girl, Interrupted* concerns an adolescent's 1960s hospitalization in a private psychiatric facility.

■   *October Sky* tells the story of budding rocket scientists in the 1950s in rural West Virginia.

■   *Good Will Hunting* portrays the life and friends of a boy who grew up in foster homes and has learned to be self-sufficient, working as a janitor and living in a lower socioeconomic class neighborhood.

■   *Tumbleweeds* follows a displaced single mother and her teenage daughter as they move from place to place and live on a shoestring while the mother looks for a man who will give them a better life.

■   *Liberty House* depicts the changing sociopolitical climate of the 1950s, including integration, interracial dating, and changing family structure and influence.

■   *Of Hopscotch and Little Girls* is a powerful documentary film that explores the plight of girls growing up to be women in different cultures.

■   *Daughters of the Dust* explores life and development on a barrier island off the coast of South Carolina. The Gullah subculture, an isolated African-American group, is the focus.

■   *The Heart is a Lonely Hunter* shows the plight of adolescence in pre-WWII America.

■   *A Walk to Remember* addresses the issues of peer pressure and youth views on mortality and achievement.

ADOLESCENCE IN BOOKS

■   *You and Your Adolescent (Second Edition),* by Laurence Steinberg (Harper Perennial, 1997), provides a broad, developmental overview of adolescence, with parental advice mixed in.

■   *The Rise and Fall of the American Teenager*, by Thomas Hine (Avon, 1999), traces the evolution of American adolescence as a social invention shaped by the needs of the 20th century.

- *Preparing for Adolescence*, by James C. Dobson (Gospel Light/Regal Books, 1999), examines the preparation of children to handle the stresses of growing up today. Issues such as self-confidence, handling group pressure, and feelings of inferiority are discussed.

- *AdolescenceIisn't Terminal*, by Kevin Leman (Tyndale House Publishing, 2002), examines contemporary topics such as peer pressure, dating and risky adolescent behaviors.

Answer Key

KEY TERMS

1. **storm-and-stress view** G. Stanley Hall's concept that adolescence is a turbulent time charge with conflict and mood swings

2. **inventionist view** The view that adolescence is a sociohistorical creation. Especially important in this view are the sociohistorical circumstances at the beginning of the 20th century, a time when legislation was enacted that ensured the dependency of youth and made their move into the economic sphere more manageable.

3. **stereotype** A broad category that reflects our impressions and beliefs about people. All stereotypes refer to an image of what the typical member of a particular group is like.

4. **adolescent generalization gap** Adelson's concept of widespread generalizations about adolescents based on information about a limited, highly visible group of adolescents.

5. **contexts** Settings in which development occurs. These settings are influenced by historical, economic, social, and cultural factors.

6. **social policy** A national government's course of action designed to influence the welfare of its citizens.

7. **generational inequity** The unfair treatment of younger members of an aging society in which older adults pile up advantage by receiving inequitably large allocations of resources, such as Social Security and Medicare.

8. **development** The pattern of change that begins at conception and continues through the life cycle. Most development involves growth, although it also includes decay (as in death and dying).

9. **biological processes** Changes in an individual's physical nature and appearance.

10. **cognitive processes** Changes in an individual's thinking and intelligence.

11. **socioemotional processes** Changes in an individual's relationships with other people, emotions, personality, and social contexts.

12. **prenatal period** The time from conception to birth.

13.　　**infancy** The developmental period that extends from birth to 18 or 24 months.

14.　　**early childhood** The developmental period extending from the end of infancy to about 5 or 6 years of age; sometimes called the preschool years.

15.　　**middle and late childhood** The developmental period extending from about 6 to about 11 years of age; sometimes called the elementary school years.

16.　　**adolescence** The developmental period of transition from childhood to early adulthood; it involves biological, cognitive, and socioemotional changes.

17.　　**early adolescence** The developmental period that corresponds roughly to the middle school or junior high school years and includes most pubertal change.

18.　　**late adolescence** Approximately the latter half of the second decade of life. Career interests, dating, and identity exploration are often more pronounced in late adolescence than in early adolescence.

19.　　**early adulthood** The developmental period beginning in the late teens or early twenties and lasting into the thirties.

20.　　**middle adulthood** The developmental period that is entered at about 35 to 45 years and exited at about 55 to 65 years of age.

21.　　**late adulthood** The developmental period that lasts from about 60 to 70 years of age until death.

22.　　**youth** Kenniston's term for the transitional period between adolescence and adulthood that is a time of economic and personal temporariness.

23.　　**emerging adulthood** Occurs from approximately 18 to 25 years of age and is characterized by experimentation and exploration.

24.　　**nature-nurture issue** *Nature* refers to an organism's biological inheritance, *nurture* to environmental experiences. "Nature" proponents claim that biological inheritance is the most important influence on development; "nurture" proponents claim that environmental experiences are the most important.

25.　　**continuity-discontinuity issue** Continuity is the gradual, cumulative change from conception to death. Discontinuity is development progressing through distinct stages in the life span.

26.　　**early-later experience issue** This issue focuses on the degree to which early experiences (especially early in childhood) or later experiences are the key determinants of development.

KEY PEOPLE IN THE STUDY OF ADOLESCENCE

1. C	**4.** D	**7.** I	**10.** F
2. A	**5.** G	**8.** A	
3. E	**6.** H	**9.** J	

"DR. DETAIL'S" MATCHING EXERCISE

1. C	**3.** E	**5.** A	**7.** F
2. D	**4.** B	**6.** G	

HISTORICAL PERSPECTIVE
SECTION REVIEW

1. Rousseau restored the belief that being a child or an adolescent is not the same as being an adult.

2. Hall believed that adolescence is a turbulent time charged with conflict and mood swings. Mead believed that when a culture proves a smooth, gradual transition from childhood to adulthood, little storm and stress occurs.

3. Hall believed that all development is controlled by genetically determined physiological factors and that environment plays a minimal role in development. This view was based on the scientific and biological dimensions of Darwin's views.

4. Theorists currently state that Somoan adolescence is more stressful than Mead had suggested, and that delinquency does occur. Her work has been criticized as biased and error-prone.

5. It is believed that during this time period the concept of adolescence was invented. Adolescence was the end result of changes in the law that changed the way adolescents lived.

6. During the roaring '20s, adolescence took a turn for the better. The depression and war would soon challenge this new status; however, those who survived the war years received new distinction and responsibilities in its aftermath. This would again change in the 1960s as a result of unsettledness associated with the Vietnam War.

7. In measuring the self-images of adolescents around the world, Offer and his colleagues found a healthy self-image in 73 percent of the adolescents studied.

8. Advances in transportation and telecommunication are spawning a global youth culture in which adolescents everywhere wear the same type of clothing and have similar hairstyles, interests, and expressions.

KEY PEOPLE IN SECTION

Plato — suggested that reasoning is not a characteristic of children, but rather makes its first appearance in adolescence.

Aristotle — argued that the most important aspect of adolescence is the ability to choose and that this self-determination becomes the hallmark of maturity.

Jean-Jacques Rousseau — credited with restoring the belief that being a child or an adolescent is not the same as being an adult.

G. Stanley Hall — credited as being the father of the scientific study of adolescence. Proposed the storm-and-stress view regarding adolescent mood swings.

Charles Darwin — famous evolutionary theorist. His scientific and biological views were applied by Hall to the study of adolescence.

Margaret Mead — studied adolescents on the South Sea island of Samoa. She concluded that the basic nature of adolescence is not biological, but rather sociocultural.

Leta Hollingworth — conducted important research on adolescent development, mental retardation, and gifted children. Was the first individual to use the term 'gifted' to describe youth who scored exceptionally high on intelligence tests.

Kenneth and Mamie Clark — conducted research on the self-esteem of African-American children.

George Sanchez — documented cultural bias in intelligence tests for children and adolescents.

Joseph Adelson — called the widespread stereotyping of adolescents so widespread as to represent an "adolescent generation gap."

Daniel Offer — found evidence contradicting the negative view of adolescence. Offer found 73 percent of adolescents around the world had healthy self-images.

TODAY'S ADOLESCENTS
SECTION REVIEW

1.   computers; longer life expectancies; television, satellites, and air travel

2.   crack cocaine; television images of violence and sex; contradictory messages about sex

3.   high divorce rates; high adolescent pregnancy rates; increased geographic mobility of families; adolescent drug use.

4.   Without a reference to historic, economic, social, and cultural factors, there would be no basis by which to judge the behavior of adolescents today.

5.   The future of youth is the future of society. If adolescents don't reach their full potential they will be able to contribute less to society.

6.   Edelman doesn't believe that policies currently don't reflect the words of politicians. She believes that we need better health care, safer schools and neighborhoods, better parent education, and improved family support programs.

7.   Not addressing generation inequity could result in alienation, distrust, and ill-will between the generations.

KEY PEOPLE IN SECTION

Peter Benson — his Search Institute has determined through research that a number of assets (e.g., family support) serve as a buffer to prevent adolescents from developing problems while making the transition to adulthood.

Marian Wright Edelman — president of the Children's Defense Fund and a tireless advocate of children's rights.

Bernice Neugarten — believed in developing a spirit of support for improving the range of options of all people in society.

Reed Larson — argued that adolescents need more opportunities (e.g., sports & art) to develop the capacity for initiative.

THE NATURE OF DEVELOPMENT
SECTION REVIEW

Age	Name	Description
Conception to birth	Prenatal	Growth from a single cell to a complete organism
Birth to 18–25 months	Infancy	Dependency on adults; early psychological development
2 to 5 – 6 years	Early childhood	Children lean to care for self, develop school readiness, and play with peers
6 to 10–11 years	Middle and late childhood	Master reading, writing, and arithmetic, exposure to culture; self-control increases; achievement becomes a theme
10–13 to 18–22 years	Adolescence	Biological, cognitive, and emotional changes; career interests, dating, and identity options explored in late adolescence
Late teens to early 20s and 30s	Early adulthood	Establishing personal and economic independence; career development; starting a family
35–45 to 55–65 years	Middle adulthood	Transmitting values to the next generation; enhanced concerns about one's body; reflection on meaning of life
60–70 years to death	Late adulthood	Adjusting to decreasing strength and health, retirement and reduced income; adapting to changing social roles; increased freedom; parenthood

2. Socioemotional processes shape cognitive processes, cognitive processes advance or restrict socioemotional processes, and biological processes influence cognitive processes.

3. Is there a specific age at which an adolescent becomes an adult? Early adulthood usually begins in the late teens or early twenties and lasts through the thirties.

4. Jacqueline Eccles recently examined research and concluded that three types of assets are especially important: intellectual, psychological, and social.

5. For instance, nature influences physical differences between boys and girls, but nurture accounts for changing gender roles.

6. It helps to refine the process of maturation and growth and makes it a more understandable process.

7.   Some believe that unless infants experience warm, nurturant caregiving in the first year of life, their development will never be optimal. Others argue that children and adolescents are malleable throughout development and that later sensitive caregiving is just as important as earlier sensitive caregiving.

KEY PEOPLE IN SECTION

Kenneth Kenniston—proposed that a transition occurs between adolescence and adulthood that can last two to eight years or longer.

Jerome Kagan—pointed out that even children who show the qualities of an inhibited temperament, which is linked to heredity, have the capacity to change their behavior.

Jacqueline Eccles—concluded that three types of assets are linked to well-being in adolescence and emerging adulthood: intellectual, psychological, and social.

UNDERSTANDING ADOLESCENCE: WHAT MATTERS?
SECTION REVIEW

1.   Wars, legislation, economic upheavals, and advances in technology have modified how many adolescents experience their lives.

2.   Helps them to solve social as well as academic problems encountered in life.

3.   Puberty and the changes associated with it.

4.   What does it mean to be a critical thinker? It means that you can ask yourself how you know something. Critical thinkers are open-minded and intellectually curious.

5.   Critical thinkers think reflectively and productively and evaluate evidence. They are open-minded, intellectually curious, and look for multiple determinants of behavior. They analyze, infer, connect, synthesize, criticize, create, evaluate, think, and rethink.

KEY PEOPLE IN SECTION

Luis Vargas—one of his special interests is the treatment of Latino youth for delinquency and substance abuse.

EXPLORATION IN ADOLESCENCE

No answers given—personal reflection

COGNITIVE CHALLENGE

No answers given—personal reflection

ADOLESCENCE IN RESEARCH

Offer and his colleagues tested the hypothesis that adolescents were deserving of many of the negative stereotypes bestowed on them (e.g., the storm-and-stress portrayal of adolescence). Their cross-cultural study showed no support for this negative view of adolescence. They sampled the self-images of adolescents around the world and found that at least 73 percent of the adolescents studied reported a healthy self-image.

⊠ COMPREHENSIVE REVIEW

1. b	10. b	19. a	28. d
2. a	11. a	20. b	29. c
3. c	12. b	21. d	30. a
4. c	13. c	22. c	31. c
5. d	14. b	23. a	32. d
6. c	15. c	24. d	33. a
7. c	16. b	25. c	34. c
8. d	17. b	26. a	35. d
9. b	18. a	27. a	36. c
			37. a

⌘

Chapter 2   The Science of Adolescent Development

Learning Goals with Key Terms and Key People in Boldface

1.0   DESCRIBE THE MAJOR THEORIES OF DEVELOPMENT

A.   Theories of Development

1.1   What are the four steps of the scientific method?

1.2   Describe a theory.

1.3   What is a hypothesis?

B.   Psychoanalytic Theories

1.4   What does **psychoanalytic theory** describe?

1.5   How did **Sigmund Freud** develop his ideas about **psychoanalytic theory?**

1.6   What are the id, ego, and superego?

1.7   What are defense mechanisms?

1.8   What is repression?

1.9   What did **Sigmund Freud** mean by his iceberg analogy?

1.10   How did **Peter Blos** and **Anna Freud** help to shape the understanding of adolescence?

1.11   What are the characteristics of Freud's oral, anal, phallic, genital, and latency stages of psychosexual development?

1.12   What did Freud mean by the Oedipus complex?

1.13   What was the feminine-based criticism of Freud's theory?

1.14   How does **Erik Erikson's theory** differ from that of Freud?

1.15   How do psychosocial stages differ from psychsexual stages?

1.16   What are the characteristics of Erikson's eight life span stages—trust versus mistrust, autonomy versus shame and doubt, initiative versus guilt, industry versus inferiority, identity versus identity confusion, intimacy versus isolation, generativity versus stagnation, and integrity versus despair?

1.17   What are the primary contributions of **psychoanalytic theories** of adolescent development?

1.18   What are the main criticisms of **psychoanalystic theories?**

C.   Cognitive Theories

1.19   What are the three major theories of cognitive development?

1.20   What are the characteristics of **Piaget's** stages of cognitive development—the sensorimotor, preoperational, concrete operational, and formal stages?

1.21   How does the cognitive theory of **Lev Vygotsky** differ from that of **Piaget?**

1.22   How has **Vygotsky's** view stimulated interest in the view that knowledge is situated and collaborative?

1.23   What is the main emphasis of the **information processing approach?**

1.24   What are the primary contributions of the cognitive theories of adolescent development?

1.25   What are the main criticisms of the cognitive theories?

D.   **Behavioral and Social Cognitive Theories**

1.26   What do **behavioral** and **social cognitive** theories emphasize?

1.27   What is the main emphasis of **behaviorism?**

1.28   What role does the mind play in development according to **Skinner?**

1.29   Who are the architects of the contemporary version of **social cognitive theory?**

1.30   What is the essence of Bandura's **social cognitive theory?**

1.31   What are the primary contributions of the **behavioral and social cognitive theories** of adolescent development?

1.32   What are the main criticisms of the **behavioral and social cognitive theories?**

E.   **Ecological, Contextual Theories of Development**

1.33   How does Urie Brofenbrenner's **ecological, contextual theory** explain adolescent development?

1.34   What are the characteristics of the five systems that make up Brofenbrenner's ecological theory—the **microsystem, mesosystem, exosystem, macrosystem, and chronosystem?**

1.35   What are the primary contributions of the **ecological, contextual theory** of adolescent development?

1.36   What are the main criticisms of the **ecological, contextual theory?**

F.   **An Eclectic Theoretical Orientation**

1.37   What is meant by an **eclectic theoretical orientation?**

2.0   **EXPLAIN HOW RESEARCH ON ADOLESCENT DEVELOPMENT IS CONDUCTED**

A.   **Types of Research**

2.1   Explain the role of **descriptive research** in studying adolescent behavior.

2.2   What skills does scientific observation require?

2.3   What role does a **laboratory** play in research?

2.4   What are some drawbacks of **laboratory** research?

2.5   How does **naturalistic observation** differ from scientific observation in general?

2.6   What is the role of interviews and surveys in adolescent research?

2.7   What are some problems with using surveys and interviews?

2.8   What is a **standardized test?**

2.9   What are some advantages and criticisms of **standardized tests?**

2.10   Describe the **experience sampling method (ESM).**

2.11   How are physiological measures used in assessing adolescent development?

2.12   What are **case studies?**

2.13   What is the goal of **correlational research?**

2.14   Why does correlation not equal causation?

2.15   What does **experimental research** allow us to conclude about behavior?

2.16   What is the difference between the **independent variable** and the **dependent variable?**

2.17   What are the functions of the experimental group and the control group?

2.18   Why is it important to have both experimental and control groups when conducting research?

2.19   What is the value of random assignment?

B.   Time Span of Research

2.20   What is the difference between **cross-sectional research** and **longitudinal research?**

2.21   What is the value of **longitudinal research?**

C.   The Field of Adolescent Development Research

2.22   Why were researchers so neglectful of adolescence until recently?

2.23   What is the role played by journals and professional meetings in the distribution of scientific information about adolescence?

3.0   DISCUSS THREE RESEARCH CHALLENGES IN ADOLESCENT DEVELOPMENT

A.   Research Challenges

3.1   What are three challenges faced by researchers in adolescent development?

B.   Ethics

3.2   What ethical considerations guide researchers?

3.3   Why did the American Psychological Association (APA) adopt a code of ethics?

3.4   What are the four main issues in ethical guidelines designed to protect subjects from harm?

C.   Minimizing Bias

3.5   What gender considerations do researchers need to take into account?

3.6   What do ethnicity and culture have to do with research into adolescent development?

3.7   What is **ethnic gloss?**

3.8   What research errors can ethnic gloss result in?

D.   Being a Wise Consumer of Information About Adolescent Development

3.9   What six rules should you follow in order to be a wise consumer of information about adolescent development?

3.10   What is nomothetic research?

3.11   What is meant by idiographic needs?

Exercises

KEY TERMS COMPLETION EXERCISE

Each key term is presented in the form of an incomplete sentence. Complete each sentence by either defining the term or giving an example of it. Compare your definitions with those given at the end of the study guide chapter.

1.   A **theory** can be helpful to

_____

_____

2.   **Hypotheses** are used to

_____

_____

3. According to **psychoanalytic theory** the personality is

    _____

    _____

4. **Erikson's theory** addresses development from

    _____

    _____

5. The four stages in **Piaget's theory** are

    _____

    _____

6. **Vygotsy's theory** is a sociocultural cognitive theory that emphasizes

    _____

    _____

7. According to the **information-processing theory,**

    _____

    _____

8. **Social cognitive theories** emphasize

    _____

    _____

9. **Ecological, contextual theory** consists of

    _____

    _____

10. A therapist applying an **eclectic theoretical orientation** might try

    _____

    _____

11.   **Descriptive research** is a

_____

_____

12.   A **laboratory** is often used in conducting

_____

_____

13.   A **naturalistic observation** is done

_____

_____

14.   **Standardized tests** are useful in

_____

_____

15.   The **experience sampling method (ESM)** can be used to

_____

_____

16.   You might use a **case study** when you are

_____

_____

17.   In **correlational research,** the goal is to

_____

_____

18.   The goal of **experimental research** is to

_____

_____

19.   In research, the **independent variable** is

_____

_____

20.   In research, the **dependent variable** is

_____

_____

21.   **Cross-sectional research** involves

_____

_____

22.   **Longitudinal research** involves

_____

_____

23.   **Ethnic gloss** can result in

_____

_____

KEY PEOPLE IN THE STUDY OF ADOLESCENCE

Match the name with the concept, issue, or topic related to adolescence with which they are associated.

____	1. Sigmund Freud	A.	Associated with social cognitive theory
____	2. Peter Blos	B.	Eight psychosocial stages
____	3. Anna Freud	C.	Four cognitive stages
____	4. Karen Horney	D.	Five systems in which adolescents develop
____	5. Nancy Chodorow	E.	Associated with behaviorism
____	6. Erik Erikson	F.	Proposed a sociocultural cognitive theory that emphasized developmental analysis, the role of language, and social relations.
____	7. Jean Piaget	G.	Five psychosexual stages
____	8. B. F. Skinner	H.	Believed that regression is a normal aspect of puberty
____	9. Albert Bandura	I.	Believed that women define themselves in terms of relationships
____	10. Lev Vygotsky	J.	Believed that defense mechanisms are the key to understanding adolescent adjustment
____	11. Urie Bronfenbrenner	K.	Believes that thinking is information processing
____	12. Robert Siegler	L.	Associated with the first feminist-based criticism of Freud's theory
____	13. Walter Mischel	M.	Used ESM and found that adolescents experienced emotions that were more extreme and more fleeting than those of their parents

____ 14. Reed Larson &   N.   Initially labeled cognitive social learning theory
          Maryse Richards

"DR. DETAIL'S" MATCHING EXERCISE

Match the stage with the correct developmental information associated with that stage across each of the following theories.

Freud's Psychosexual Stages

____ 1. Genital stage   A. Between 1 and 3 yrs. Pleasure involves the anus and the process of eliminating.

____ 2. Oral stage   B. Occurs between age 6 and puberty. The child focuses on intellectual development while repressing sexual interest.

____ 3. Phallic stage   C. Goes from puberty onward. The source of sexual pleasure now becomes someone outside of the family.

____ 4. Latency stage   D. First 18 months of life. Pleasure centers around the mouth.

____ 5. Anal stage   E. Occurs between ages 3 and 6. Pleasure focuses on the genitals.

Erikson's Eight Life-Span Stages

____ 1. Autonomy vs. Shame and Doubt   A. Experienced during late adulthood, when people look back and evaluate what they have done with their lives.

____ 2. Identity vs. Identity Confusion   B. Experienced during middle adulthood. This stage marks what a person has done to help the next generation.

____ 3. Trust vs. Mistrust   C. Experienced during early adulthood. Individuals face the developmental task of forming intimate relationships with others.

____ 4. Integrity vs. Despair   D. Experienced during the adolescent years. A time when the individual needs to find out who they are.

____ 5. Intimacy vs. Isolation   E. Experienced in the elementary school years. Success in school brings a sense of pride; failure brings about a sense of not being good enough.

____ 6. Initiative vs. Guilt   F. Experienced in the first year of life. A sense of well-being depends upon whether or not one's needs are being met.

____ 7. Generativity vs. Stagnation   G. Experienced between ages 1 and 3. Is a stage in which infants begin to discover that their behavior is their own.

____ 8. Industry vs. Inferiority   H. Experienced during the preschool years. Children are asked to accept responsibility for their bodies, their behavior, their toys, and their pets.

Piaget's Stages of Cognitive Development

____ 1. Concrete Operational stage   A. Infants construct an understanding of the world by coordinating sensory experiences with physical actions.

____ 2. Preoperational stage   B. Children begin to represent the world with words, images, and drawings.

____ 3. Formal Operational stage   C. A child in this stage is likely not to be able to imagine the steps needed to complete an algebraic equation.

____ 4. Sensorimotor stage   D. The child begins to think in more abstract and logical terms.

Bronfenbrenner's Ecological, Contextual Theory

___	1.	Chronosystem	A. Includes the person's family, peers, school, and neighborhood.
___	2.	Microsystem	B. The relation of family experiences to school experiences, school experiences to work experiences, and family experiences to peer experiences.
___	3.	Macrosystem	C. Experiences in another social setting influence what the individual experiences in an immediate context.
___	4.	Mesosystem	D. Involves the culture in which a person lives.
___	5.	Exosystem	E. Involves the patterning of environmental events and transactions over the life course and sociohistorical circumstances.

THEORIES OF ADOLESCENT DEVELOPMENT
SECTION REVIEW

1.   Label each stage of the scientific method and describe what would be done in each stage of a scientific study of mentoring.

Number	Name	Description
One		
Two		
Three		
Four		

PSYCHOANALYTIC THEORIES

1.   According to Freud, the personality has three structures. Explain the role of each of these structures.

_____

_____

2.   How did Freud come to conceptualize the personality to be like an iceberg?

_____

_____

3.   Explain the role that ego defense mechanisms have in protecting the personality.

_____

_____

4.   Compare the views of Anna Freud with those of Peter Blos.

_____

_____

5.   Discuss some of the criticisms of Freud's views.

_____

_____

6.   For each of the Freudian stages, state the age and focus of development and pleasure.

Stage	Age	Focus of Development/Pleasure
Oral		
Anal		
Phallic		
Latency		
Genital		

7.   For each of the Erikson stages, provide the age range and focus of psychosocial development.

Stage	Age	Focus of Development
Trust vs. mistrust		
Autonomy vs. shame and doubt		
Initiative vs. guilt		
Industry vs. inferiority		
Identity vs. identity confusion		
Intimacy vs. isolation		
Generativity vs. stagnation		

Integrity vs. despair		

8. In what ways did Erikson's theory extend the theory presented by Freud?

_____

_____

COGNITIVE THEORIES

1. Compare and contrast cognitive theories with psychoanalytic theories.

_____

_____

2. What two processes underlie Piaget's cognitive construction of the world, and what purpose did they serve?

_____

_____

3. What occurs in the Formal Operations Stage that differentiates it from Piaget's other stages?

_____

_____

4. For each of Piaget's cognitive stages, state age and manner in which the child/adolescent thinks and understands the world.

Stage	Age	Way of Thinking and Understanding
Sensorimotor		
Preoperational		
Concrete operational		
Formal operational		

5.   Why has Vygotsky's views on adolescence become an important addition to the understanding of adolescent cognitive development?

_____

_____

6.   What are the primary contributions of cognitive theories to the understanding of adolescent development?

_____

_____

7.   What are the main criticisms of the cognitive theories?

_____

_____

BEHAVIORAL AND SOCIAL COGNITIVE THEORIES

1.   In Skinner's view, what is development?

_____

_____

2.   Contrast Skinner's view with that of Albert Bandura?

_____

_____

3.   What role does empirical research play in studying development from both the social cognitive and behavioral perspectives?

_____

_____

4.   What are some of the contributions of the behavioral and social cognitive theories of development?

_____

_____

5.   What are some of the criticisms of the behavioral and social cognitive theories of development?

_____

_____

ECOLOGICAL, CONTEXTUAL THEORY

1.   What are some of the contributions of ecological, contextual theory to the overall understanding of adolescent development?

_____

_____

2.   What does it mean to say someone follows an eclectic theoretical orientation?

_____

_____

3.   Describe the five systems in Bronfenbrenner's ecological theory.

System	Description
Microsystem	
Mesosystem	
Exosystem	
Macrosystem	
Chronosystem	

KEY PEOPLE IN SECTION (describe the contributions of this individual to the study and understanding of adolescence).

Sigmund Freud —

_____

_____.

Peter Blos —

_____

_____.

Anna Freud —

_____

_____.

Karen Horney —

_____

_____.

Nancy Chodorow —

_____

_____.

Erik Erikson —

_____

_____.

Jean Piaget —

_____

_____.

Lev Vygotsky —

_____

_____.

Robert Siegler —

_____

_____.

B.F. Skinner —

_____

_____.

Albert Bandura —

_____

_____.

Walter Mischel —

_____

_____.

Urie Bronfenbrenner —

_____

_____.

RESEARCH ON ADOLESCENT DEVELOPMENT
SECTION REVIEW

1. What are some common types of descriptive research methods?

    _____

    _____

2. What skills are required for scientific observation?

    _____

    _____

3. What is a laboratory?

    _____

    _____

4. What are some drawbacks to laboratory research?

    _____

    _____

5. What is a benefit of naturalistic observation?

    _____

    _____

6.   What is a problem encountered with surveys and interviews?

_____

_____

7.   What are advantages and disadvantages of standardized tests?

_____

_____

8.   What has led to a flurry of research studies on the brain activities of adolescents?

_____

_____

9.   When is it appropriate to use case studies in conducting research?

_____

_____

10.   What is the goal of correlational research?

_____

_____

11.   Compare and contrast independent and dependant variables used in research studies.

_____

_____

12.   Why is it important to randomly assign participants to experimental or control groups when conducting a study?

_____

_____

TIME SPAN OF RESEARCH

1.   What are some strengths and limitations of cross-sectional research studies?

_____

_____

2.   What are some positives and drawbacks of longitudinal research studies?

_____

_____

THE FIELD OF ADOLESCENT DEVELOPMENT RESEARCH

1.   Explain the role played by journals in the advancement of scientific theory.

_____

_____

2.   Explain which information goes in respective sections of a journal article.

Section	Description
Abstract	
Introduction	
Method	
Results	
Discussion	
References	

FACING UP TO RESEARCH CHALLENGES
SECTION REVIEW

CONDUCTING ETHICAL RESEARCH

1.   Explain the importance of informed consent, confidentiality, debriefing and deception in conducting ethical research?

_____

_____

MINIMIZING BIAS

1.   How might gender be a bias that influences the choice of theory, questions, hypotheses, participants, and research design?

_____

_____

2.   What is ethnic gloss, and what are its implications regarding adolescent research?

_____

_____

BEING A WISE CONSUMER OF INFORMATION ABOUT ADOLESCENCE

1.   Why must we always be cautious when reading about adolescent research in the popular media?

_____

_____

2.   Contrast nomothetic and idiopathic research and needs.

_____

_____

EXPLORATIONS IN ADOLESCENCE

Find an article in a research journal (such as Developmental Psychology, Child Development, Journal of Research on Adolescence, Journal of Early Adolescence, or Journal of Youth and Adolescence) about any topic in the text. Then look for an article on the same subject in either a newspaper or are a magazine. Compare how the research article on the topic differs from the newspaper or magazine article. What are the differences between the nature, type, and quality of information presented?

COGNITIVE CHALLENGE

In the chapter, we were given a brief look at the lives of Jean Piaget and Erik Erikson. From that look at their lives, we are given a glimpse at what factors might have led them to formulate the theories they did. In looking back at your life (childhood, adolescence, college experience), what kind of theory could you formulate and what factors would contribute to this.

ADOLESCENCE IN RESEARCH

Concerning Albert Bandura's and Walter Mischel's research on social cognitive theory, state the hypothesis, the research methods (if known), the research conclusions, and the implications for adolescent development.

 COMPREHENSIVE REVIEW

1.   Which of the following is NOT one of the steps in the scientific method?
    a.   draw conclusions
    b.   replication
    c.   collect research information
    d.   analyze the data

2.   Sigmund Freud developed his ideas about psychoanalytic theory
    a.   while being held in a Nazi detention camp
    b.   while reviewing the published theories of Erik Erikson
    c.   from work he did with mental patients
    d.   while studying to become a medical doctor

3.   Which of the following is NOT one of Freud's three structures of the personality?
    a.   ego
    b.   repression
    c.   superego
    d.   id

4.   Developing a study schedule is a function of the
    a.   id.
    b.   ego.
    c.   superego.
    d.   ego-ideal.

5.   Feeling guilty over adolescent sexual exploration is a result of
    a.   ego.
    b.   libido.
    c.   superego.
    d.   id.

6.   Which of the following is an example of an ego defense mechanism?
    a.   autonomy
    b.   latency
    c.   Oedipus complex
    d.   repression

7.   Unconsciously hating your younger brother might be an example of
    a.   ego-centrism.
    b.   repression.
    c.   the Oedipus complex.
    d.   id-ideals.

8.   According to Peter Blos and Anna Freud,
    a.   it is permissible to make generalizations about the role of defense mechanisms in adolescent development on the basis of small or clinical samples of subjects.
    b.   research on adolescent defense mechanisms should be nonsexist.
    c.   defense mechanisms are a normal aspect of adolescent development.
    d.   Sigmund Freud's original analysis of the role of defense mechanisms in adolescent development has been confirmed many times.

9.   Louella believes all boys have "cooties." She devotes herself to athletics and caring for various pets. A psychoanalyst would say Louella is
    a.   behaving normally for someone in the latency stage.
    b.   being overly controlled by her superego.
    c.   experiencing unconscious conflicts between her ego and id.
    d.   fixated at the phallic stage of development.

10. Max tells his mom, "When I grow up I'm going to marry you." Freud might consider this an example of
    a. repression.
    b. the Oedipus complex.
    c. latency.
    d. the id.

11. Horney and Chodorow criticized Freud for
    a. his conceptualization of the Oedipus complex.
    b. male-bias reflected in his theories.
    c. discussing children's sexuality too extensively in his theories.
    d. ignoring sexuality in the elderly.

12. The decision to get married might indicate that Johnny is in which of Freud's psychosexual stages?
    a. latency
    b. oral
    c. genital
    d. phallic

13. An infant left to cry in her crib for long periods of time might, according to Erikson, develop
    a. autonomy.
    b. guilt.
    c. initiative.
    d. mistrust.

14. Sheree changed her major three times in college, and now that she has graduated she still cannot decide what type of job she wants. Erik Erikson would describe Sheree as going through a period of
    a. shame and doubt.
    b. identity confusion.
    c. despair.
    d. generativity and stagnation.

15. According to Mavis Hetherington, life in a family following a divorce returns to a stable state after what period of time has elapsed?
    a. 5 years
    b. It never becomes stable.
    c. 1 year
    d. 2 years

16. Diana often finds herself daydreaming about boys and wondering what her life will be like when she gets married. According to Piaget, Diana is likely in which stage?
    a. sensorimotor stage
    b. preoperational stage
    c. concrete operational stage
    d. formal operational stage

17. The information processing approach emphasizes
    a. the quality of thinking among adolescent of different ages.
    b. overcoming age related problems or "crises."
    c. age appropriate expressions of sexual energy.
    d. perception, memory, reasoning ability, and problem solving.

18. Which of the following is NOT a limitation of laboratory research?
    a. It is almost impossible to conduct research without the subject knowing they are being studied.
    b. It is a controlled setting that removes many of the complex factors of the "real world."
    c. It is an unnatural setting.
    d. People willing to participate may not reflect the general population.

19. Sam is shy when around his friends, teachers, and family. Skinner would suggest that this behavior is
    a. modeled after his father's behavior.
    b. learned.
    c. repressed.
    d. ecological.

20. One of the strong points of behavior theory is its
    a. belief that cognitive processes are irrelevant for understanding development.
    b. emphasis on the relationship between environmental stimuli and adolescent behavior.
    c. emphasis on reducing adolescent behavior to fine-grained elements.
    d. emphasis on the role of information processing as a mediator between behavior and environment.

21. Cara receives a job promotion that requires her to travel often. Because of this, she has less time to spend with her adolescent son and it hurts their relationship. According to Bronfenbrenner, this is an example of a(n)
    a. microsystem.
    b. mesosystem.
    c. chronosystem.
    d. exosystem.

22. From B. F. Skinner's point of view, the best way to explain adolescent behavior is to
    a. pay attention to the external consequences of that behavior.
    b. pay attention to the self-produced consequences of that behavior.
    c. focus on adolescent cognitive interpretation of environmental experiences.
    d. identify the biological processes that determine adolescent maturation.

23. The frequent finding that adults who abuse their children and adolescents typically comes from families in which they themselves were abused, supports which theory of development?
    a. Freudian psychoanalytic theory
    b. information processing theory
    c. ecological theory
    d. social cognitive theory

24. A researcher who takes the best aspect from many theories in constructing a research model could be said to be applying
    a. ecological theory.
    b. information processing theory.
    c. eclectic theory.
    d. social cognitive theory.

25. A major strength of ecological theory is its framework for explaining
    a. environmental influences on development.
    b. biological influences on development.
    c. cognitive development.
    d. affective processes in development.

26. Many developmentalists have chosen to subscribe to an eclectic viewpoint because
    a. they cannot afford to subscribe to all the other viewpoints; the annual dues are too high.
    b. none of the current theories is at all correct.
    c. they believe that not enough data have been collected so far to even begin proposing a definitive theory.
    d. each of the major theories has both valid points and flaws.

27. Which of the following is true about theories that endeavor to explain adolescent development?
    a. If theorists keep working at it they will eventually come up with one theory that explains development.
    b. Cognitive, psychoanalytic, and humanistic theories have nothing in common and can never be reconciled.
    c. The theories proposed should be thought of as complementary rather than competitive.
    d. One theory from biology, one theory from cognitive psychology, and one theory from social psychology are all that is needed to explain development.

28. One difficulty of doing research on adolescents in a laboratory setting is that
    a. an unnatural behavior may occur.
    b. random assignment is impossible.
    c. extraneous factors are difficult to control.
    d. the experimenter's judgments are of unknown reliability.

29. An investigator interested in gender differences in helping behavior spends three hours a day in the mall watching who opens doors for shoppers burdened with packages. Which of the following methods of data collection is being used?
    a. naturalistic observation
    b. experimental
    c. correlational
    d. case studies

30. Which of the following is TRUE about correlation research?
    a. Correlation means causation.
    b. Correlation ranges from 0 to +1.00.
    c. Correlation does not mean causation.
    d. A correlation of −.40 is less than a correlation of +.20.

31. Which of the following is NOT a section typically found in a research article published in a journal?
    a. discussion
    b. statistical design
    c. results
    d. method

32. A psychologist treats Brent's irrational fear of balloons. The assessment of Brent's problem and his treatment is an example of a(n)
    a. hypothesis.
    b. correlational research.
    c. case study
    d. context

33. The experimental factor that is manipulated in an experiment is
    a. independent variable.
    b. dependent variable.
    c. control group.
    d. method

34. The factor that is measured as the result of an experiment is
    a. independent variable.
    b. dependent variable.
    c. control group.
    d. method.

35. The assignment of participants to experimental and control groups by chance is
    a. naturalistic observation.
    b. longitudinal research.
    c. random assignment.
    d. experimental research.

36. In conducting her research on adolescent self-esteem, Professor Radcliff gathered information from 14-year-old students in 20 different states. This is an example of
    a. case study research.
    b. longitudinal research.
    c. cross-sectional research.
    d. correlational research.

37. When Clint was in pre-school, he was part of a large study on temperament. The same researchers would again observe Clint's behavior in the 5th grade, the 10th grade, and when he turned 30 years old. Clint was likely a subject in which type of study?
    a. case study research.
    b. longitudinal research.
    c. cross-sectional research.
    d. correlational research.

38. Which of the following is NOT an important topic in research ethics?
    a. informed consent.
    b. naturalistic observation

    c.   confidentiality

    d.   debriefing

39.   Stating that your research study contained 10 "Latino" subjects is an example of

    a.   informed consent

    b.   random assignment

    c.   debriefing

    d.   ethnic gloss

ADOLESCENCE ON THE SCREEN

- *Good Will Hunting* concerns an adolescent named Will (played by Matt Damon) in treatment for attachment problems brought on by his being abandoned by his biological parents and abused by his foster parents. Will's therapist Sean (played by Robin Williams) uses a psychodynamic treatment model.

- *Ordinary People* portrays a surviving son's guilt and suicidal depression over what he feels was his role in his brother's death. He pulls through with the help of hospitalization and a psychodynamic therapist whom he trusts.

- *American Flyers* portrays a youngest son's difficulty in following in the steps of a highly successful older brother who is dying.

ADOLESCENCE IN BOOKS

Two recent biographies about Erikson and Freud demonstrate how individual life events—as well as historical events, time, and place—influenced their theories:

- *Freud: A Life for Our Time*, by Peter Gay (W.W. Norton, 1998), is a balanced and comprehensive biography of Sigmund Freud that places his theories in the context of the times.

- *Identity's Architect: A Biography of Erik H. Erikson*, by Lawrence J. Friedman (Simon & Schuster, 1999), traces the origins of Erikson's concern with identity and identity crises to his early life experiences.

- *Self-efficacy in Changing Societies*, by Albert Bandura (Cambridge University Press, 1997), takes a look at changing views of self in adolescents across time.

Answer Key

KEY TERMS

1.   **theory** An interrelated, coherent set of ideas that helps to explain and make predictions.

2.   **hypotheses** Specific assumptions and predictions that can be tested to determine their accuracy.

3. **psychoanalytic theory** Describes development as primarily unconscious—that is, beyond awareness —and is heavily colored by emotion.

4. **Erikson's theory** Eight stages of development that unfold as we go through the life span. Each stage consists of a unique developmental task that confronts individuals with a crisis that must be faced.

5. **Piaget's theory** States that individuals actively construct their understanding of the world and go through four stages of cognitive development.

6. **Vygotsky's theory** A sociocultural cognitive theory that emphasizes developmental analysis, the role of language, and social relations.

7. **information-processing theory** Emphasizes that individuals manipulate information, monitor it, and strategize about it. Central to this approach are the processes of memory and thinking.

8. **social cognitive theories** Emphasis is placed on the importance of studying environmental experiences and observable behavior. Social cognitive theorists emphasize person/cognitive factors in development.

9. **ecological, contextual theory** Bronfenbrenner's view of development, involving five environmental systems—microsystem, exosystem, ecosystem, macrosystem, and chronosystem. These emphasize the role of social contexts in development.

10. **eclectic theoretical orientation** Not following any one theoretical approach, but rather selecting from each theory whatever is considered the best in it.

11. **descriptive research** Has the purpose of observing and recording behavior.

12. **laboratory** A controlled setting from which many of the complex factors of the real world have been removed.

13. **naturalistic observation** Observation made in the "real world" outside of the laboratory.

14. **standardized tests** Commercially prepared tests that assess performance in different domains. A standardized test often allows an adolescent's performance to be compared to that of other adolescents of the same age.

15. **experience sampling method (ESM)** Involves providing participants with electronic pagers and then beeping them at random times, at which time they are asked to report on various aspects of their lives.

16. **case study** An in-depth look at an individual.

17. **correlation research** Describes the strength of the relationship between two or more events or characteristics.

18. **experimental research** Allows researchers to appropriately determine the causes of behavior.

19. **independent variable** The manipulated, influential, experimental factor.

20. **dependent variable** The factor that is measured in an experiment.

21. **cross-sectional research** Research that studies all people at one time.

22. **longitudinal research** Involves studying the same individuals over a period of time, usually several years or more.

23. **ethnic gloss** Using an ethnic label such as African American or Latino in a superficial way that portrays an ethnic group as being more homogeneous than it really is.

KEY PEOPLE IN THE STUDY OF ADOLESCENCE

1. G	4. L	7. C	10. F
2. H	5. I	8. E	11. D
3. J	6. B	9. A	12. K
			13. N
			14. M

"DR. DETAIL'S" MATCHING EXECISE

Freud's Psychosexual Stages
1. C   4. B
2. D   5. A
3. E

Erikson's Eight Life-Span Stages

1. G	3. F	5. C	7. B
2. D	4. A	6. H	8. E

Piaget's Stages of Cognitive Development
1. C   3. D
2. B   4. A

Bronfenbrenner's Ecological, Contextual Theory
1. E   3. D   5. C
2. A   4. B

THEORIES OF ADOLESCENT DEVELOPMENT
SECTION REVIEW

Number	Name	Description
One	Conceptualize the problem	Identify the problem; develop hypothesis that mentoring will improve achievement of adolescents from impoverished backgrounds.
Two	Collect information (data)	Conduct the mentoring program for six months and collect data before and after program begins.

| Three | Draw conclusions | Analyze the data that show improvement over period of program; conclude that mentoring helped increase achievement. |
| Four | Revise research conclusions and theory | Research will increase likelihood that mentoring will be considered an important component to help improve achievement of low-income adolescents. |

PSYCHOANALYTIC THEORIES

1. *Id* — consists of instincts, which are an individual's reservoir of psychic energy. *Ego*—the structure of the personality that deals with the demands of reality. *Superego*—the moral branch of the personality.

2. Freud felt that most of our personality exists below our level of awareness. Just as an iceberg has its greatest mass below the surface of the water and out of sight.

3. Ego defense mechanisms are unconscious methods the ego uses to distort reality and protect itself from anxiety.

4. Blos stated that regression during adolescence is actually not defensive at all, but rather an integral, normal, inevitable, and universal part of puberty. Anna Freud developed the idea that defense mechanisms are the key to understanding adolescent adjustment.

5. Most contemporary psychoanalytic theorists place less emphasis on sexual instincts and more emphasis on cultural experiences as determinants of an individual's development. Most theorists today also feel that conscious thought makes up more of the iceberg than Freud envisioned. Lastly, Freud's theories have been viewed as too focused on males.

6.

Stage	Age	Focus of Development/pleasure
Oral	0–1 1/2 years	Pleasure focused on the mouth; sucking reduces tension.
Anal	1 1/2–3 years	Pleasure involves the anus; eliminative functions reduce tension.
Phallic	3–6 years	Pleasure focuses on the genitals; child discovers self-manipulation is enjoyable.
Latency	6 years–puberty	Child represses interest in sexuality and develops social and intellectual skills
Genital	Adolescence–adulthood	Sexual pleasure is focused on those outside of the family.

7.

Stage	Age	Focus of Development
Trust vs. mistrust	Infancy	Feeling of physical comfort and minimal amount of fear and apprehension.
Autonomy vs. shame and doubt	1–3 years	Begin to assert independence or autonomy in behavior.
Initiative vs. guilt	3–5 years	Engage in active, purposeful behavior to cope with challenges of the world.

Industry vs. inferiority	6 years–puberty	Direct energy toward mastering knowledge and intellectual skills.
Identity vs. identity confusion	10–20 years	Finding out who they are, what they are about, and where they are going in life.
Intimacy vs. isolation	20s and 30s	Forming intimate relationships.
Generativity vs. stagnation	40s and 50s	Assist younger generation in developing and leading useful lives.
Integrity vs. despair	60s to death	Look back and evaluate life's accomplishments.

8.   For Freud, the primary motivation for human behavior was sexual in nature; for Erikson it was social and reflected a desire to affiliate with other people.

COGNITIVE THEORIES

1.   Whereas psychoanalytic theories stress the importance of adolescents' unconscious thoughts, cognitive theories emphasize their conscious thoughts.

2.   Organization and adaptation. We organize our experiences and adapt our thinking to include new ideas.

3.   In formal operations, hypothetical or abstract thinking is possible. This greatly increases the thinking capacity of the child in this stage.

4.

Stage	Age	Way of Thinking and Understanding.
Sensorimotor	Birth–2	Coordinates sensory experiences with physical actions.
Preoperational	2–7	Uses words and images to represent the world.
Concrete operational	7–11	Reason logically about concrete events and classify objects.
Formal operational	11–adulthood	Reasons in abstract, idealistic, and logical ways.

5.   Vygotsky's theory has stimulated considerable interest in the view that knowledge is situated and collaborative. That is to say, that within our communities we are immersed in an environment rich with knowledge.

6.   They present a positive view of development. They emphasize the individual's active construction of understanding. They underscore the importance of examining developmental changes in children's thinking. The information-processing approach offers detailed descriptions of cognitive processes.

7.   There is skepticism about the pureness of Piaget's stages. The cognitive theories do not give adequate attention to individual variations in cognitive development. The information processing does not give an adequate description of developmental changes in cognition. Psychoanalytic theorists argue that the cognitive theories do not give enough credit to unconscious thought.

BEHAVIORAL AND SOCIAL COGNITIVE THEORIES

1.   For Skinner, development is behavior.

2.   Bandura believes observational learning is a key aspect of how we learn. This adds a cognitive component that differs from Skinner's views.

3.   Like Skinner's behavioral approach, the social cognitive approach emphasizes the importance of empirical research in studying development.

4.   An emphasis on the importance of scientific research. A focus on the environmental determinants of behavior. An underscoring of the importance of observational learning. An emphasis on person and cognitive factors.

5.   Too little emphasis on cognition. Too much emphasis on environmental determinants. Inadequate attention to developmental changes. Too mechanical and inadequate consideration of the spontaneity and creativity of humans.

ECOLOGICAL, CONTEXTUAL THEORY

1.   A systematic examination of macro and micro dimensions of environmental systems. Attention to connections between environmental settings. Consideration of sociohistorical influences on development.

2.   An eclectic theoretical orientation does not follow any one theoretical approach, but rather selects and uses whatever is considered the best in each theory.

3.

System	Description
Microsystem	family, peers, school, neighborhood
Mesosystem	school and parents; parents and friends
Exosystem	lack of facilities for a handicapped person
Macrosystem	ethnic or racial group
Chronosystem	wider range of gender roles for men and women

KEY PEOPLE IN SECTION

Sigmund Freud—a medical doctor who specialized in neurology; he developed his ideas about psychoanalytic theory from work with mental patients.

Peter Blos—a British psychoanalyst who felt that regression during adolescence is actually not defensive at all, but rather a normal part of puberty.

Anna Freud—Sigmund's daughter Anna developed the idea that defense mechanisms are the key to understanding adolescent adjustment.

Karen Horney—developed a model of women with positive feminine qualities and self-evaluation; she was a critic of Sigmund Freud's male oriented theories.

Nancy Chodorow—another Freud critic; she noted that many more women than men define themselves in terms of their relationships with others.

Erik Erikson—developed the theory that people develop in psychosocial stages; Erikson emphasized developmental changes throughout the human life span.

Jean Piaget—he proposed that individuals actively construct their understanding of the world and go through four stages of cognitive development.

Lev Vygotsky—he proposed a sociocultural cognitive theory that emphasizes developmental analysis, the role of language, and social relations.

Robert Siegler—he is a leading expert on children's information processing, and believes that thinking is information processing.

B.F. Skinner—to Skinner, development is behavior; the mind, conscious or unconscious, is not needed to explain behavior and development.

Albert Bandura—believes that observational learning is a key aspect of how we learn.

Walter Mischel—along with Bandura, he is an architect of the contemporary version of social cognitive theory, which Mischel initially labeled *cognitive social learning theory*.

Urie Bronfenbrenner—proposed a strong environmental view of children's development that is receiving increased attention today: Ecological, Contextual Theory.

RESEARCH ON ADOLESCENT DEVELOPMENT SECTION REVIEW

TYPES OF RESEARCH

1.   Observation, surveys, interviews, standardized tests, experience sampling, physiological measures, and case studies.

2.   Must be systematic, know what you are observing, and know where to observe.

3.   A controlled setting that removes many of the complex factors present in the "real world."

4.   It is almost impossible to conduct research without the participants' knowing that they are being studied. The lab setting is unnatural. People willing to come to a lab might not represent the real population of people. Some adolescent behaviors are not able to be studied in a lab setting.

5.   Behavior observed is more likely to reflect real behavior, as opposed to lab setting.

6. Participants tend to answer in a way they think is socially acceptable or desirable rather than saying what they really think.

7. Advantage—they provide information about individual difference among people. Problem — they do not always predict behavior or performance in a non-test situation.

8. The development of neuroimaging techniques.

9. When for practical or ethical reasons, the unique aspects of an individual's life cannot be duplicated and tested in other individuals. A case study is most relevant when the phenomenon being studied is rare and you want an in-depth look at the individual being studied

10. The goal is to describe the strength of the relationship between two or more events or characteristics.

11. The independent variable is the manipulated, influential factor in an experiment. The dependent variable is measured as the result of an experiment.

12. Random assignment reduces the likelihood that the experiment's results will be due to any preexisting differences between the groups.

TIME SPAN OF RESEARCH

1. The cross-sectional study's main advantage is that the researcher does not have to wait for the children to grow older. However, a disadvantage is that this approach provides no information about the stability of the children's and adolescent's feelings or attitudes over time.

2. A positive is that you can evaluate how the individual children and adolescents change as they get older. However, a drawback is that this approach is costly and time consuming.

THE FIELD OF ADOLESCENT DEVELOPMENT RESEARCH

1. Journals are the main outlets for the vast amount of research being conducted on adolescence.

2. Explain which information goes in respective sections of a journal article?

Section	Description
Abstract	A brief summary that appears at the beginning of the article.
Introduction	Introduces the problem or issue that is being studied.
Method	Consists of a clear description of the participants evaluated in the study, the measures used, and the procedures that were followed.
Results	Reports the analysis of the data collected. Might be difficult for nonprofessionals to understand.
Discussion	Presents the author's conclusions, inferences, and interpretation of what was found. Statements are usually made about whether the hypotheses presented in the introduction were supported, limitations of the study, and suggestions for future research.

References	Gives a bibliographic listing for every source cited in the article.

FACING UP TO RESEARCH CHALLENGES
SECTION REVIEW

CONDUCTING ETHICAL RESEARCH

1.   Informed consent means that the participants' legal guardians have been told what participation will entail and any risks that might be involved. Confidentiality means that researchers are responsible for keeping all of the data they gather completely confidential, and, when possible, completely anonymous. Debriefing consists of informing participants of the purpose and methods used in a study after the study has been completed.

MINIMIZING BIAS

1.   Because most of the early research opportunities in developmental psychology went to men, they tended to study what they were most familiar with, which was males. This means that many hypotheses have not been adequately tested with female participants even to this day.

2.   Ethnic gloss means using an ethnic label in a superficial way that makes an ethnic group look more homogeneous than it really is.

BEING A WISE CONSUMER OF INFORMATION ABOUT ADOLESCENCE

1.   Because the media tend to focus on sensational or dramatic findings. This leads to the potential for inaccuracy.

2.   Nomothetic focuses on the group, whereas idiographic focuses on the individual.

EXPLORATIONS IN ADOLESCENCE

Individual assignment—various articles and responses could be appropriate.

COGNITIVE CHALLENGE

Individual reflection—no answers provided.

RESEARCH IN ADOLESCENCE

The hypothesis was that observational learning is a key aspect of how we learn. The methods varied, but often appeared to be individual case histories. Emphasized a focus on the environmental determinants of behavior, and did show observational learning to play a big role in who we become.

COMPREHENSIVE REVIEW

1. b	11. b	21. d	31. b
2. a	12. c	22. a	32. c
3. b	13. d	23. d	33. a
4. b	14. b	24. c	34. b
5. c	15. d	25. a	35. c
6. d	16. d	26. d	36. c
7. b	17. d	27. c	37. b
8. c	18. b	28. a	38. b
9. a	19. b	29. a	39. d
10. b	20. b	30. c	

⌘

Chapter 3   Puberty, Health, and Biological Foundations

Learning Goals with Key Terms and Key People in Boldface

1.0   DISCUSS THE DETERMINANTS, CHARACTERISTICS, AND TIMING OF PUBERTY
  A.   Determinants of Puberty
    1.1   What is **puberty?**
    1.2   What role does heredity play in puberty?
    1.3   What are **hormones**, and what is their role in **puberty?**
    1.4   What are the two classes of **hormones**, and how do they affect males and females differently?
    1.5   What is testosterone, and what role does it play in male development?
    1.6   What is the role of the endocrine system in puberty?
    1.7   What are the different endocrine glands, and what are their functions?
    1.8   How does the endocrine system work?
    1.9   How does the negative feedback system in the endocrine system work?
    1.10   What are the two phases of **puberty** that are linked with hormonal changes?
    1.11   What role is played **menarche** and **spermarche** with regards to a girl's or boy's entry into gonadarche?
  B.   Growth Spurt
    1.12   What physical changes coincide with the growth spurt?
  C.   Sexual Maturation
    1.13   What is the order of physical changes during sexual maturation?
  D.   Secular Trends in Puberty
    1.14   What does the term secular trends refer to?
    1.15   What is a likely contributor to the earlier maturation of girls today?
    1.16   What are the five pubertal stages of male and female sexual development?
  E.   Psychological Dimensions
    1.17   What accounts for adolescents' preoccupation with their bodies?
    1.18   What are some gender differences in adolescents' perception of their bodies?
    1.19   How do hormones affect behavior in adolescents?
    1.20   What is the typical reaction of young girls to **menarche?**
    1.21   What effect does early or late maturation have on a developing boy or girl?
    1.22   Are the effects of puberty exaggerated?
  F.   Pubertal Timing and Health Care
    1.23   What can be done to help off-time maturers who are at risk for health problems?
2.0   DESCRIBE THE DEVELOPMENTAL CHANGES IN THE BRAIN DURING ADOLESCENCE
  A.   Neurons
    2.1   What are **neurons?**
    2.2   What are the three basic parts of the **neuron?**

4.7   What is a **twin study?**

4.8   How do **twin studies** examine the difference between identical twins and fraternal twins?

4.9   What are some issues that develop as a result of **twin studies?**

4.10   What is an **adoption study?**

4.11   What is the basis of the enthusiasm regarding the study of molecular genetics?

4.12   What is a genome?

4.13   What is the importance of the Human Genome Project?

C.   Heredity-Environment Interaction

4.14   According to behavior geneticist Sandra Scarr, what are three ways heredity and environment are correlated?

4.15   What distinguishes Scarr's concepts of **passive genotype-environment correlations, evocative genotype-environment correlations,** and **active (niche-picking) genotype-environment correlations?**

4.16   What is the difference between **shared environmental influences** and **nonshared environmental influences?**

4.17   What are the most reasonable conclusions we can make about the interaction of heredity and environment?

4.18   Why are the views of Judith Harris both intriguing and controversial?

Exercises

KEY TERMS COMPLETION EXERCISE

Each key term is presented in the form of an incomplete sentence. Complete each sentence by either defining the term or giving an example of it. Compare your definitions with those given at the end of the study guide chapter.

1.   One of the early signs of **puberty** is

_____

_____

2.   **Hormones** play a major role in

_____

_____

3.   Testosterone is an **androgen** that

_____

_____

4.   Estradiol is an **estrogen** that

_____

_____

5.   Suzy is probably entering **menarche** because

_____

_____

6.   John is probably entering **spermarche** because

_____

_____

7.   **Neurons** are made up of

_____

_____

8.   **Basal metabolism rate (BMR)** gradually declines

_____

_____

9.   **Evolutionary psychology** is the study of

_____

_____

10.   **Chromosomes** play a major role in

_____

_____

11.   **DNA** is responsible for

_____

_____

12.   **Genes** determine

_____

_____

13.   A **genotype** is a

_____

_____

14.   A girl's **phenotype** can be observed in her appearance by

_____

_____

15.   The study of **behavior genetics** might involve

_____

_____

16.   In a **twin study,** a comparison is made between

_____

_____

17.   In an **adoption study,** researchers seek

_____

_____

18.   **Passive genotype-environment correlations** lead parents to

_____

_____

19.   **Evocative genotype-environment correlations** might explain Tom's happiness because

_____

_____

20.   **Active (niche-picking) genotype-environment correlations** might explain why athletic boys

seek out

_____

_____

21.   Examples of **shared environmental influences** are

_____

_____

22.   Example of **nonshared environmental influences** are

_____

_____

KEY PEOPLE IN THE STUDY OF ADOLESCENCE

Match the person with the event or concept in adolescent development with which they are associated.

___	1. Sandra Scarr	A.	Studied adolescent sleep patterns. Determined that early school starting times may result in lack of attention and poor performance on tests.
___	2. Mary Carskadon	B.	Described three ways that heredity and environment are correlated.
___	3. Roberta Simmons and Dale Blyth	C.	Studied the effects of being an early or late maturing male or female.
___	4. Robert Plomin	D.	Wrote the book *The Dependent Gene*.
___	5. David Moore	E.	Rejected "one-sided evolution" in which social behavior is seen as the product of evolved biology.
___	6. Albert Bandura	F.	Found that common rearing and environment accounts for little of the variation in adolescents' personality.
___	7. Mihalyi Csikszentimalyi and Jennifer Schmidt	G.	Felt that evolution shapes our physical features, decision making, aggressive behaviors, fears, and mating behaviors.
___	8. David Buss	H.	Argued that evolution has programmed humans to act in predictable ways from puberty into early adulthood.

"DR. DETAIL'S" PUZZLE

Down

1. The main class of female hormones.
2. Powerful chemical substances secreted by the endocrine glands and carried through the body by the bloodstream.
3. The way an individual's genotype is expressed in observed and measurable characteristics.
4. The nervous system's basic units.

Across

1. A girl's first menstrual period.
2. The main class of male sex hormones.
3. A period of rapid physical maturing involving hormonal and bodily changes.
4. A person's genetic heritage.
5. A boy's first ejaculation of semen.

PUBERTY
SECTION REVIEW

1. How can puberty be distinguished from adolescence?

    _____

    _____

2. How is the emergence of puberty timed, and what can have an impact on it?

    _____

    _____

3. Differentiate between the two classes of hormones, and how they specifically impact males and females.

    _____

    _____

4. What physical changes in boys is testosterone associated with?

    _____

    _____

5. What is the endocrine system's role in puberty?

    _____

    _____

6. Contrast the functions of the hypothalamus and pituitary gland.

    _____

    _____

7. How does the endocrine system work?

    _____

    _____

8. Describe the role of the negative feedback system in the endocrine system.

    _____

    _____

9. What are the two phases of puberty linked with hormonal changes?

    _____

    _____

10. What is the order of appearance of physical changes in females?

    _____

    _____

11.   Explain what is meant by secular trends.

_____

_____

12.   Explain the gender differences apparent in how adolescents view their bodies.

_____

_____

13.   Are there links between concentrations of hormones and adolescent behavior?

_____

_____

14.   What are some advantages and disadvantages of being an "early" or "late" maturing adolescent?

_____

_____

15.   If puberty and development are unusually late, what steps can be taken to help the adolescent?

_____

_____

KEY PEOPLE IN SECTION (describe the contributions of this individual to the study and understanding of adolescence).

Roberta Simmons and Dale Blyth —

_____

_____.

THE BRAIN
SECTION REVIEW

1.   What are the three basic parts of the neuron?

_____

_____

2.   How do neurons change in adolescence?

_____

_____

3.   Match the lobe of the brain with its primary function.
   ___ 1. Occipital lobe   A. Involved in bodily sensations
   ___ 2. Parietal lobe   B. Involved in hearing
   ___ 3. Temporal lobe   C. Involved in the control of voluntary muscles,
                                         personality, and intelligence
   ___ 4. Frontal lobe   D. Involved in visual functioning

4.   In what ways, has the development of MRI's (magnetic resonance imaging) enhanced the understanding of how the brain works?

_____

_____

5.   How has the conceptualization of "left-brained" or "right-brained" individuals helped to perpetuate misinformation?

_____

_____

ADOLESCENT HEALTH
SECTION REVIEW

1.   Why is adolescence a critical juncture in the adoption of behaviors related to health?

_____

_____

2.   What is basal metabolism rate, and what role does it play in adolescence?

_____

_____

3.   Are American adolescents getting enough exercise?

_____

_____

4. With regard to eating and exercise, how do U.S. adolescents compare with kids from other countries?

    _____

    _____

5. What are some positive and negative influences sports can have on adolescent development?

    _____

    _____

6. According to Carskadon, what might improve adolescent performance in class and on tests?

    _____

    _____

7. What are the three leading causes of death in adolescence?

    _____

    _____

KEY PEOPLE IN SECTION (describe the contributions of this individual to the study and understanding of adolescence).

Mary Carskadon —

_____

_____.

EVOLUTION, HEREDITY, AND ENVIRONMENT
SECTION REVIEW

1. Explain the difference between genotypes and phenotypes and how each impacts development.

    _____

    _____

2. In the study of adolescence, what has been learned from twin studies and adoption studies?

    _____

    _____

3. Why does behavior geneticist Robert Plomin maintain that shared environment accounts for little of the variation in adolescent's personalities or interests?

    _____

    _____

4. What was the cause of the most recent nature-nurture controversy?

    _____

    _____

5. Explain the epigenetic view.

    _____

    _____

KEY PEOPLE IN SECTION (describe the contributions of this individual to the study and understanding of adolescence).

Sandra Scarr —

_____

_____.

Robert Plomin —

_____

_____.

Charles Darwin —

_____

_____.

Judith Harris —

_____

_____.

David Buss —

_____

_____.

Stephen Jay Gould —

_____

_____.

EXPLORATIONS IN ADOLESCENCE

Which of the following most closely resembles you?

Early maturing male ___
Late maturing male ___
Early maturing female ___
Late maturing female ___

Depending upon which you checked, how might your life (e.g., experiences, opportunities, dating, sports, leadership experiences, etc.) have been affected by how early or late you matured?

_____

_____

_____

_____

_____

COGNITIVE CHALLENGE

Looking at the following characteristics, first circle whether you believe nature or nurture is more responsible for these characteristics in you. Then briefly explain your reasoning.

Height   (nature | nurture)

_____

_____

Weight   (nature | nurture)

_____

_____

Skin color   (nature | nurture)

_____

_____

Temperament   (nature | nurture)

_____

_____

Intelligence   (nature | nurture)

_____

_____

Humor   (nature | nurture)

_____

_____

Hair color   (nature | nurture)

_____

_____

Athleticism   (nature | nurture)

_____

_____

Age at maturation   (nature | nurture)

_____

_____

Academic ability   (nature | nurture)

_____

_____

ADOLESCENCE IN RESEARCH

Concerning the research about early and late maturation by Simmons and Blyth (1987), state the hypothesis, the research methods (if known), the research conclusions, and the implications and applications for adolescent development.

_____

_____

_____

_____

_____

COMPREHENSIVE REVIEW

1. A period of rapid physical maturation involving hormonal and bodily changes that take place primarily in early adolescence.
    a. menarche
    b. heredity
    c. adolescence
    d. puberty

2. These are the main class of male sex hormones.
    a. estrogens
    b. androgens
    c. neurons
    d. spermarche

3. These are the main class of female sex hormones.
    a. estrogens
    b. androgens
    c. menarche
    d. spermarche

4. Powerful chemical substances secreted by the endocrine glands and carried through the body by the bloodstream are
    a. neurons.
    b. hormones.
    c. genotypes.
    d. phenotypes.

5. Which of the following is not monitored by the hypothalamus?
    a. sex
    b. eating
    c. hearing
    d. drinking

6. Which of the following is most similar in function to how the negative feedback system works?
    a. refrigerator
    b. television set
    c. a thermostat-furnace system
    d. a washing machine and dryer unit

7. Sandra Scarr proposed all the following heredity-environment interactions except
    a. passive genotype-environmental interactions.
    b. heritable genotype-environmental interactions.
    c. evocative genotype-environmental interactions.
    d. active genotype-environmental interactions.

8.   This is the only time during development in which growth is faster than during puberty.
   a.   toddlerhood
   b.   middle childhood
   c.   infancy
   d.   young adulthood

9.   On average, females enter puberty at an earlier age than males, and that's why
   a.   women are typically shorter than men.
   b.   fifth- and sixth-grade girls are usually taller than boys.
   c.   girls and boys do not get along well during puberty.
   d.   boys are more muscular, and girls have more fat.

10.   Sue started her menstrual period about two years earlier than Mary, even though both girls are very healthy. A likely explanation for this event is that
   a.   Sue is an athlete.
   b.   Sue has greater body mass than Mary.
   c.   Mary has greater body mass than Sue.
   d.   Sue has better genes than Mary.

11.   Androgens are to males as _____ are to females.
   a.   testosterone
   b.   gonadotropins
   c.   hormones
   d.   estrogens

12.   _____ is important in the pubertal development of females.
   a.   Thyroxin
   b.   Estradiol
   c.   Androgen
   d.   Estrogen

13.   Emily and Ervin are fraternal twins, both in the sixth grade. Ervin gets angry because people tease him about his sister being taller than he. His parents can legitimately tell Ervin that
   a.   although his sister is taller, his sexual maturation is more advanced.
   b.   his sister is probably taller because she doesn't eat as much junk food.
   c.   he needn't worry, because he'll probably catch up with or surpass his sister's height by the end of the eighth grade.
   d.   since his sister was taller than he was during childhood, she'll be taller than he is during adolescence.

14.   The fact that some adolescent males begin puberty as early as 10 years of age and others at 17 (or even later) is an example of
   a.   environmental influences.
   b.   individual differences.
   c.   biologically caused psychological disturbance.
   d.   behavior genetics in action.

15.   In the Berkeley Longitudinal Study, males who matured early
- a.   perceived themselves as more successful in peer relations.
- b.   perceived themselves more negatively because of additional parental pressure.
- c.   were perceived by peers as unattractive due to the accompanying occurrence of acne.
- d.   perceived themselves more negatively because they were "ahead of the others."

16.   In a college course in human sexuality, Jill was asked to describe her initial reactions to menarche. She described the experience very negatively, emphasizing discomfort and messiness. Jill probably was
- a.   well prepared for the event.
- b.   unlikely to tell her mother about the event.
- c.   an early maturer.
- d.   on time in her pubertal development.

17.   Jonathan is just entering puberty. The first of many changes that he is likely to notice is
- a.   minor voice change.
- b.   growth of hair in the armpits.
- c.   appearance of straight pubic hair.
- d.   increase in penis and testicle size.

18.   Jenny is just entering puberty. The first of many changes that she is likely to notice is
- a.   growth of hair in the armpits.
- b.   increase in hip width.
- c.   increase in breast size.
- d.   significant increase in height.

19.   This term refers to patterns over time or across generations.
- a.   menarche
- b.   phenotype
- c.   secular trends
- d.   spermarche

20.   Which of the following has NOT been mentioned as a possible reason for the earlier onset of puberty in the 20th century?
- a.   girlhood obesity
- b.   the deterioration of the ozone
- c.   improvements in health
- d.   improvements in nutrition

21.   Immediately following the onset of menarch, who are girls most likely to discuss the matter with?
- a.   a best friend
- b.   a trusted teacher
- c.   a sibling
- d.   their mothers

22.   Stephanie is a late-maturing female. She has an increased probability of
- a.   being tall and thin.
- b.   being shorter and stockier.

c. having a clear complexion.
d. having to visit a dermatologist for acne treatment.

23. Early-maturing adolescents often date at an earlier age than their later-maturing friends. For females, at least, this early social involvement may be welcomed uneasily by the adolescent, because many adolescent females are
  a. unprepared for puberty.
  b. emotionally secure.
  c. unattractive.
  d. not interested in heterosexual interactions.

24. Which of the following is not one of the three basic parts of a neuron?
  a. cell body
  b. axon
  c. occipital lobe
  d. dendrites

25. What role does the myelin sheath play in the functioning of a neuron?
  a. It carries information away from the cell body to other cells.
  b. It receives information from other cells.
  c. It helps to insulate the axon and speeds transmission.
  d. It provides the neuron with nutrition.

26. Which role does the axon play in the functioning of a neuron?
  a. It carries information away from the cell body to other cells.
  b. It receives information from other cells.
  c. It helps to insulate the axon and speeds transmission.
  d. It provides the neuron with nutrition.

27. Which role does the dendrite play in the functioning of a neuron?
  a. It carries information away from the cell body to other cells.
  b. It receives information from other neurons.
  c. It helps to insulate the axon and speeds transmission.
  d. It provides the neuron with nutrition.

28. Which of the following lobes of the brain is involved in hearing?
  a. temporal
  b. frontal
  c. parietal
  d. occipital

29. Which of the following lobes of the brain is involved in visual functioning?
  a. temporal
  b. frontal
  c. parietal
  d. occipital

30. Which of the following lobes of the brain is involved in bodily sensations?
  a. temporal
  b. frontal

    c.   parietal
    d.   occipital

31.   Which of the following lobes of the brain is most involved in personality?
    a.   temporal
    b.   frontal
    c.   parietal
    d.   occipital

32.   Which of the following structures of the brain is most involved in emotion?
    a.   temporal
    b.   frontal
    c.   amydala
    d.   occipital

33.   Which of the following is not one of the things blamed for the poor physical condition of American adolescents?
    a.   computers
    b.   fast food
    c.   television
    d.   schools

34.   Which of the following hormones is associated with adolescent sleep patterns?
    a.   estrogen
    b.   androgen
    c.   estradiol
    d.   melatonin

35.   Which of the following is not one of the three leading causes of death for adolescents in America?
    a.   homicide
    b.   suicide
    c.   accidents
    d.   HIV/AIDS

36.   The unique arrangement of chromosomes and genes inherited by each adolescent is referred to as the _____ , whereas the adolescent's observed characteristics are called the _____ .
    a.   phenotype; genotype
    b.   phenotype; reaction range
    c.   genotype; reaction range
    d.   genotype; phenotype

37.   _____ is the area concerned with the degree and nature of the hereditary basis of behavior.
    a.   Genetic psychology
    b.   Behavioral psychology
    c.   Behavior genetics
    d.   Developmental genetics

38.   A behavioral geneticist comparing the IQs of monozygotic twins with those of dizygotic twins is applying the
        a.   twin-study method.
        b.   family-of-twins method.
        c.   kinship method.
        d.   habitability method.

ADOLESCENCE ON THE SCREEN

■   *My Left Foot* addresses how a boy deals with physical deformity.

■   *Trainspotting* depicts the decadent lifestyle of Scottish teenagers bent on self-destruction through heroin addiction.

■   *Ordinary People* tells of an adolescent boy's struggle with suicidal tendencies arising out of the guilt he feels for an accident that took his young brother's life.

■   *Antonia's Line* is a longitudinal portrayal of the transformation from early adolescence to womanhood, and life's decisions involved.

■   *The Body Beautiful* is a generative example of how our various bodily and social identities are built and given meaning concurrently.

■   *Daughters of the Dust* portrays life and development on a barrier island among the Gullah subculture, an isolated African-American culture off the coast of South Carolina.

■   *Rain* is the story of a 13-year-old girl who becomes increasingly aware of problems in her parents' marriage, while at the same time beginning to discover her own sexuality.

ADOLESCENCE IN BOOKS

■   *The What's Happening to My Body? Book for Boys,* by Lynda Madaras & D. Ssveddra (Newmarket, 1991), is written for parents and focuses on how to help boys cope with pubertal transitions.

■   *You're in Charge*, by Niels Lauersen & Eileen Stukane (Fawcett, 1993), is written for teenage girls and describes the changing female body.

Answer Key

KEY TERMS

1.   **puberty** A period of rapid physical maturation involving hormonal and bodily changes that occur primarily in early adolescence.

2.   **hormones** Powerful chemical substances secreted by the endocrine glands and carried through the body by the bloodstream.

3.   **androgen** The main class of male sex hormones.

4.   **estrogen** The main class of female sex hormones.

5.   **menarche** A girl's first menstruation.

6.   **spermarche** A boy's first ejaculation of semen.

7.   **neurons** Are the nervous system's basic units.

8.   **basal metabolism rate (BMR)** Is the minimum amount of energy an individual uses in a resting state.

9.   **evolutionary psychology** An approach that emphasizes the importance of adaptation, reproduction, and "survival of the fittest" in explaining behavior.

10.   **chromosomes** Threadlike structures that contain deoxyribonucleic acid, or DNA.

11.   **DNA** A complex molecule that contains genetic information.

12.   **gene** The units of hereditary information, which are short segments composed of DNA.

13.   **genotype** A person's genetic heritage; the actual genetic material.

14.   **phenotype** The way an individual's genotype is expressed in observed and measurable characteristics.

15.   **behavior genetics** The study of the degree and nature of behavior's hereditary basis.

16.   **twin study** A study in which the behavioral similarity of identical twins is compared with the behavioral similarity of fraternal twins.

17.   **adoption study** A study in which investigators seek to discover whether, in behavior and psychological characteristics, adopted children and adolescents are more like their adoptive parents, who provided a home environment, or their biological parents, who contributed to their heredity. Another form of adoption study is to compare adoptive and biological siblings.

18.   **passive genotype-environment correlations** Occur when parents who are genetically related to the child provide a rearing environment for the child.

19.   **evocative genotype-environment correlations** Occur when the adolescent's genotype elicits certain types of physical and social environments.

20.   **active (niche-picking) genotype-environment correlations** Occur when adolescents seek out environments they find compatible and stimulating.

21.   **shared environmental influences** Adolescents common environmental experiences that are shared with their sibling, such as their parents' personalities and intellectual orientation, the family's social class, and the neighborhood in which they live.

22.   **nonshared environmental influences** The adolescent's own unique experiences, both within a family and outside the family that are not shared by another sibling.

KEY PEOPLE IN THE STUDY OF ADOLESCENCE

1. B	**3.** C	**5.** D	**7.** H
2. A	**4.** F	**6.** E	**8.** G

"DR. DETAIL'S" PUZZLE

Down
1. estrogens
2. hormones
3. phenotype
4. neurons

Across
1. menarche
2. androgens
3. puberty
4. genotype
5. spermarche

PUBERTY
SECTION REVIEW

1.   Puberty ends long before adolescence does.

2.   It is programmed into the genes, but can be influenced by the environment.

3.   Androgen plays an important role in male pubertal development. Estrogen plays an important role in female pubertal development.

4.   Testosterone is associated with the development of external genitals, increase in height, and change in voice.

5.   The endocrine system's role in puberty involves the interaction of the hypothalamus, the pituitary gland, and the gonads.

6.   The hypothalamus monitors eating, drinking, and sex. The pituitary gland controls growth and regulates other glands.

7.   The pituitary gland sends a signal via gonadotropins to the appropriate gland to manufacture the hormone. Then the pituitary gland, through interaction with the hypothalamus, detects when the optimal level of hormones is reached and responds by maintaining gonadotropin secretion.

8.   It works in the body like a thermostat-furnace system.

9.   Andrenarche and gonadarche.

10.   First breasts enlarge or pubic hair appears. Later, hair appears in the armpits, height increases, and the hips become wider.

11.   The term refers to patterns over time, especially across generations.

12.   Girls in puberty are less happy with their bodies and have more negative body images compared to boys, who are pleased to see their muscles develop.

13.   Hormonal factors are thought to account for at least part of the increase in negative and variable emotions that characterize adolescents.

14.   Early maturing boys perceived themselves more positively and had more successful peer relations. Early maturing girls had a similar outcome to early boys, but not as pronounced. Some are cognitively not ready for social activities. Late maturing boys faced many challenges, but developed a strong sense of identity; perhaps due to adversity. Late maturing girls develop at a better pace and tend to grow to be tall and slender, which can be socially advantageous.

15.   A physician may recommend hormonal treatment.

KEY PEOPLE IN SECTION

Roberta Simmons and Dale Blyth—longitudinally studied early and late maturing males and females.

THE BRAIN
SECTION REVIEW

1.   The dendrite, cell body, and axon.

2.   Much of the neuron does not change; however, axons develop throughout adolescence.

3.   1. D   2. A   3. B   4. C

4.   MRIs have shown the significant changes that the brain goes through between ages 3 and 15.

5.   The conceptualization of "right" and "left-brained" individuals has oversimplified the acquiring of specific skills in the developing brain.

ADOLESCENT HEALTH
SECTION REVIEW

1.   Because many of the factors linked to poor health habits and early death in the adult years begin during adolescence.

2.   Basal metabolism rate (BMR) is the minimum amount of energy an individual uses in a resting state. BRM declines during adolescence.

3.   Recent studies show they are not getting nearly enough exercise.

4.   U.S. kids exercise less than their counterparts in other countries and eat more junk food that is high in fat.

5.   Positives are they eat healthier, are less likely to use drugs, smoke cigarettes, or drink alcohol. Negatives are that there is more likelihood of a win-at-all-costs attitude to develop among adolescent athletes and their parents.

6.   Carskadon made the suggestion that adolescents might benefit from a later start to the school day.

7.   Accidents, homicide, and suicide are the leading causes of death in adolescence.

KEY PEOPLE IN SECTION

Mary Carskadon—conducted a number of research studies on adolescent sleep patterns.

EVOLUTION, HEREDITY, AND ENVIRONMENT
SECTION REVIEW

1.   A genotype is a person's genetic heritage, the actual genetic material. A phenotype is the way an individual's genotype is expressed and observed.

2.   Twin and adoption studies are often used to study heredity's influence on behavior.

3.   Plomin has noted that even when living under the same roof, experiences are often very different.

4.   Judith Harris's recent book, *The Nurture Assumption*, dramatically downplays the role parents play in the development of their child's personality. This caused much new debate on nature versus nurture.

5.   The epigenetic view emphasizes that development is the result of ongoing, bi-directional interchange between heredity and the environment.

KEY PEOPLE IN SECTION

Sandra Scarr—describes three ways heredity and environment are correlated: passively, evocatively, and actively.

Robert Plomin—believes that common rearing accounts for little of the difference in adolescents' personality or interests.

Charles Darwin—noted that most species reproduce at rates that would cause enormous increases in their population and yet populations remain nearly constant.

Judith Harris her provocative book, *The Nurture Assumption*, ignited the most recent nature-nurture controversy.

David Buss—his ideas on evolutionary psychology have produced a wave of interest in how evolution can explain human behavior.

Stephen Jay Gould—concluded that in most domains, human biology allows for a broad range of cultural possibilities.

EXPLORATIONS IN ADOLESCENCE

No answers provided—individual reflection and response.

COGNITIVE CHALLENGE

No answers provided—individual reflection and response.

ADOLESCENCE IN RESEARCH

This was a longitudinal study, following more than 450 individuals in Milwaukee, Wisconsin, for 5 years, from sixth to tenth grade. The students were individually interviewed, and their achievement test scores and grade point averages were obtained. The researchers found that early-maturing girls had more problems in school, were more independent, and were more popular with boys than late-maturing girls were.

⊠ COMPREHENSIVE REVIEW

1. d	11. d	21. d	31. b
2. a	12. b	22. a	32. c
3. a	13. c	23. a	33. a
4. b	14. b	24. c	34. d
5. c	15. a	25. c	35. d
6. c	16. c	26. a	36. d
7. b	17. d	27. b	37. c
8. c	18. c	28. a	38. a
9. b	19. c	29. d	
10. b	20. b	30. c	

⌘

Chapter 4   Cognitive Development

Learning Goals with Key Terms and Key People in Boldface

1.0   **DISCUSS THE COGNITIVE DEVELOPMENTAL VIEW OF ADOLESCENCE**
   A.   **Piaget's Theory**
       1.1   What is Piaget's theory of cognitive processes?
       1.2   What is a **schema?**
       1.3   What roles do **assimilation** and **accommodation** play in cognitive development?
       1.4   What did Piaget mean by **equilibration?**
       1.5   What are names and defining characteristics of Piaget's four stages of cognitive development?
       1.6   How does an infant learn about the world in the **sensorimotor stage?**
       1.7   What happens in the **preoperational stage?**
       1.8   What are the characteristics of the **concrete operational stage?**
       1.9   What did Piaget mean by **operations?**
       1.10   What are the characteristics of **conservation** and **classification?**
       1.11   What are the indicators of the **formal operational stage?**
       1.12   What is **hypothetical-deductive reasoning?**
       1.13   What were Piaget's main contributions to understanding cognitive development?
       1.14   What are the major criticisms of Piaget's theory?
       1.15   What are the distinctions between **early formal operational thought** and **late** formal operational thought?
       1.16   What principles of Piaget's theory of cognitive development can be applied to education?
       1.17   What were Piaget's main contributions, and has the theory withstood the test of time?
       1.18   Who are the **neo-Piagetians** who expanded and modified Piaget's theory?
       1.19   How strong is the evidence for a fifth, postformal stage of cognitive development?
   B.   **Vygotsky's Theory**
       1.20   What were Vygotsky's main contributions to cognitive developmental theory?
       1.21   What did Lev Vygotsky mean by the **zone of proximal development (ZPD)?**
       1.22   How do the concepts of **scaffolding, cognitive apprenticeship, tutoring, cooperative learning,** and **reciprocal teaching** contribute to cognitive development and learning?
       1.23   Why do we say that Piaget and Vygotsky both were proponents of **constructivism?**
       1.24   What is the difference between a cognitive constructivist approach and a social constructivist approach?

2.0   DESCRIBE THE INFORMATION-PROCESSING VIEW OF ADOLESCENCE?

    A.   Characteristics

        2.1   What, according to Robert Siegler, are the three main characteristics of the information processing approach to cognitive development?

        2.2   What are the components of thinking, change mechanisms, and self-modification?

        2.3   What is encoding?

        2.4   What does automaticity refer to?

    B.   Attention and Memory

        2.5   What are **attention** and **memory** and why are they such important adolescent cognitive processes?

        2.6   What are the functions of short-term memory and long-term memory?

        2.7   Why do many theorists choose to apply the concept of working memory?

        2.8   How is long-term memory different from working memory?

    C.   Decision Making

        2.9   What do we know about adolescent decision-making ability?

        2.10   How is adolescent decision making different from that of children?

    D.   Critical Thinking

        2.11   What does **critical thinking** involve?

        2.12   What are the adolescent cognitive changes that allow improved critical thinking?

        2.13   How does the **Jasper Project** enhance critical thinking skills?

        2.14   What are the two main debates concerning critical thinking and adolescents?

    E.   Creative Thinking

        2.15   What is **creativity?**

        2.16   What is the difference between **convergent thinking** and **divergent thinking?**

        2.17   What are seven strategies that can help adolescents become more creative?

        2.18   What is **brainstorming** and how does it contribute to creative thinking?

    F.   Metacognition and Self-Regulatory Learning

        2.19   What is **metacognition?**

        2.20   How can adolescents develop better learning strategies?

        2.21   What is **self-regulatory learning?**

        2.22   What are five characteristics of self-regulatory learners?

        2.23   How can teachers or parents help students become self-regulatory learners?

3.0   SUMMARIZE THE PSYCHOMETRIC/INTELLIGENCE VIEW OF ADOLESCENCE

    A.   The Psychometric/Intelligence View

        3.1   What does the **psychometric/intelligence view** emphasize?

        3.2   What did Huxley mean when he used the word intelligence?

        3.3   What is the traditional definition of **intelligence?**

    B.   Intelligence Tests

        3.4   What was the first valid intelligence test and why was it developed?

        3.5   What was Binet's concept of **mental age (MA)?**

        3.6   What is an **intelligence quotient (IQ)?**

        3.7   What is a **normal distribution?**

        3.8   What are the Wechsler scales and what kind of IQ scores do they yield?

        3.9   How are the Wechsler and Stanford-Binet scales similar or different?

        3.10   How are intelligence tests misused?

    C.   Theories of Multiple Intelligences

        3.11   What was the concept of general intelligence and what are its origins?

        3.12   Explain Spearman's two-factor theory.

3.13   What were Thurstone's 7 primary mental abilities?

3.14   According to Howard Gardner, what are the eight types of intelligence?

3.15   What are the components of Sternberg's **triarchic theory of intelligence?**

3.16   How are Gardner's and Sternberg's theories different, and how are they the same?

D.   Emotional Intelligence

3.17   What is **emotional intelligence** and who is its major proponent?

3.18   According to Goleman's views, what are the four main areas of **emotional intelligence?**

E.   Controversies and Issues in Intelligence

3.19   Is nature or nurture more important in determining intelligence?

3.20   Why is intelligence increasing around the globe?

3.21   Are there cultural differences in intelligence?

3.22   What are the characteristics of **culture-fair tests?**

3.23   Are intelligence tests culturally biased?

3.24   What controversy was caused with the publication of the book, *The Bell Curve,* by **Herrnstein** and **Murray?**

3.25   What are the appropriate uses of intelligence tests? What uses are inappropriate?

3.26   Does gender influence intelligence?

4.0   EXPLAIN HOW SOCIAL COGNITION IS INVOLVED IN DEVELOPMENT

A.   Adolescent Egocentrism

4.1   What is **adolescent egocentrism** and what types of thinking does it include?

4.2   What does David Elkind believe brings on adolescent egocentrism?

4.3   What is an **imaginary audience?**

4.4   What is the **personal fable?**

B.   Perspective Taking

4.5   What is perspective taking, and how does it influence adolescent egocentrism?

C.   Implicit Personality Theory

4.6   What is **implicit personality theory?**

4.7   Do adolescents conceptualize an individual's personality differently than children do?

D.   Social Cognition in the Rest of the Text

4.8   What areas of adolescent development have been influenced by the concept of social cognition?

Exercises

KEY TERMS

Each key term is presented in the form of an incomplete sentence. Complete each sentence by either defining the term or giving an example of it. Compare your definitions with those given at the end of the study guide chapter.

1.   Piaget's interest in **schemas**

     _____

     _____

2.   **Assimilation** occurs when

     _____

     _____

3.   Suzy demonstrates **accommodation** when she

     _____

     _____

4.   **Equilibration** is a mechanism

     _____

     _____

5.   You can tell that Jeannine is in the **sensorimotor stage** because

     _____

     _____

6.   Jared has now entered the **preoperational stage** in that he

     _____

     _____

7.   In the **concrete operational stage,** children can engage in

     _____

     _____

8.   You can tell that Ramon is in the **formal operational stage** because

     _____

     _____

9.   **Hypothetical-deductive reasoning** is used to

_____

_____

10.   **Neo-Piagetians** argue that

_____

_____

11.   **Post-formal thought** is most likely seen in

_____

_____

12.   The **zone of proximal development (ZPD)** refers to

_____

_____

13.   **The social constructivist approach** is

_____

_____

14.   Alex is good at **critical thinking** because

_____

_____

15.   **Creativity** is the ability to

_____

_____

16.   An example of **convergent thinking** is

_____

_____

17.   An example of **divergent thinking** is

_____

_____

18.   Cognitive psychologists define **metacognition** as

_____

_____

19.   **Self-regulatory learning** consists of

_____

_____

20.   The **psychometric/intelligence view** emphasizes

_____

_____

21.   Some experts describe **intelligence** as

_____

_____

22.   **Mental age (MA)** is an individual's

_____

_____

23.   William Stern created the **intelligence quotient (IQ),** which refers to

_____

_____

24.   A **normal distribution** is

_____

_____

25.   **Emotional intelligence** was proposed as a

_____

_____

26.   **Heritability** is seen as

_____

_____

27.   What are examples of **culture fair tests?**

_____

_____

28.   Chris is going through a stage of **adolescent egocentrism** that is leading him to

_____

_____

29.   **Implicit personality theory** suggests that

_____

_____

KEY PEOPLE IN THE STUDY OF ADOLESCENCE

Match the name with the concept, issue, or topic related to adolescence with which they are associated.

____	1. Jean Piaget	A.	Multiple intelligences
____	2. Lev Vygotsky	B.	Mental age (MA)
____	3. Nathan Brody	C.	Four stages of cognitive development
____	4. Annamarie Palincsar & Ann Brown	D.	General intelligence
____	5. Robert Siegler	E.	Triarchic theory of intelligence
____	6. Robbie Case	F.	Zone of proximal development
____	7. Peter Salovey & John Mayer	G.	Felt that intelligence tests can predict school and job success
____	8. J.P. Guilford	H.	Information processing view
____	9. Mihalyi Csikszentmihalyi	I.	Reciprocal teaching
____	10. Michael Pressley	J.	Automaticity
____	11. Robert Serpell	K.	Creativity
____	12. Alfred Binet	L.	Developed a test that measures emotional intelligence
____	13. William Stern	M.	Strategies
____	14. David Wechsler	N.	Primary abilities related to intelligence

___	15. Charles Spearman	O.	Developed IQ tests with several subscales
___	16. L. L. Thurstone	P.	Emotional intelligence
___	17. Robert Sternberg	Q.	Imaginary audience & personal fable
___	18. Howard Gardner	R.	Perspective taking
___	19. Daniel Goleman	S.	Authors of *The Bell Curve*
___	20. David Elkind	T.	Convergent & divergent thinking
___	21. Robert Selman	U.	Intelligence quotient (IQ)
___	22. Richard Herrnstein & Charles Murray	V.	Studied intelligence in rural African communities

"DR. DETAIL'S" TERM MATCHING EXERCISE

Match the term with the correct definition.

___	1. operations	A.	Refers to changing the level of support over the course of a teaching session
___	2. conservation	B.	An expert stretches and supports the novice's understanding of and use of the culture's skills
___	3. classification	C.	The retention of information over time
___	4. early formal operational thought	D.	Emphasis is on the individual's cognitive construction of knowledge and understanding
___	5. late formal operational thought	E.	May appear during the middle adolescent years
___	6. scaffolding	F.	Involves students taking turns leading a small-group discussion
___	7. cognitive apprenticeship	G.	Mental actions that allow the individual to do mentally what was done before physically
___	8. cooperative learning	H.	Limited capacity memory where information is retained for 30 seconds unless rehearsed
___	9. reciprocal teaching	I.	Emphasizes that individuals actively construct knowledge and understanding
___	10. constructivism	J.	Emphasis is on collaboration with others to produce knowledge and understanding
___	11. cognitive constructivist approach	K.	Piaget's term for an individual's ability to recognize that the length, number, mass, quantity, area, weight, and volume of objects and substances do not change through transformations that alter their appearance
___	12. social constructivist approach	L.	Involves students working in small groups to help each other learn
___	13. memory	M.	Adolescent's have increased ability to think hypothetically
___	14. short-term memory	N.	Piaget's concept of concrete operational thought, in which children systematically organize objects into hierarchies of classes and subclasses
___	15. working memory	O.	Knowing about one's own (and others') knowing
___	16. long-term memory	P.	A sense that adolescents have that they are unique, untouchable, and that no one else can understand them
___	17. meta-knowing skills	Q.	Mental workbench where information is manipulated and assembled to help make decisions

___	18.	imaginary audience	R. A relatively permanent memory system
___	19.	personal fable	S. Adolescents believe they are the main actors in an imagined play, and all others are in the audience
___	20.	encoding	T. The ability to process information with little or no effort
___	21.	automaticity	U. The process by which information gets into memory

PIAGET'S THEORY
SECTION REVIEW

1. Using any event or experience of your choice, describe how an existing schema was changed as a result of disequilibrium, assimilation, and accommodation.

    _____

    _____

2. Compare and contrast assimilation and accommodation.

    _____

    _____

    _____

3. How do children apply the mechanism, equilibration, in everyday life?

    _____

    _____

    _____

4. List and discuss the four stages of cognitive development according to Piaget.

    _____

    _____

    _____

    _____

5. Compare and contrast conservation and classification.

    _____

    _____

6.   What were Piaget's main contributions to developmental theory?

_____

_____

7.   How has Piaget's theory withstood the test of time?

_____

_____

8.   What are some criticisms of Piaget's theory?

_____

_____

9.   What information supports the existence of a fifth, postformal stage in Piaget's theory?

_____

_____

KEY PEOPLE IN SECTION (describe the contributions of this individual to the study and understanding of adolescence).

David Elkind —

_____

_____.

Robbie Case —

_____

_____.

K. Warner Schaie —

_____

_____.

William Perry —

_____

_____.

VYGOTSKY'S THEORY
SECTION REVIEW

1.   Fill in the boxes with the descriptions comparing the views of Piaget and Vygotsky.

Topic	Vygotsky	Piaget
Constructivism		
Stages		
View on Education		
Teaching Implications		

2.   What did Vygotsky mean by the zone of proximal development?

_____

_____

3.   Explain how each of these contemporary cognitive concepts would be utilized in a high school classroom.

a.   scaffolding

_____

_____

b.   cognitive apprenticeship

_____

_____

c.   tutoring

_____

_____

d.   cooperative learning

_____

_____

e.   reciprocal teaching

_____

_____

4.   Contrast the cognitive constructivist approach and social constructiveness approach.

_____

_____

KEY PEOPLE IN SECTION (describe the contributions of this individual to the study and understanding of adolescence)

Barbara Rogoff —

_____

_____.

Ann Brown and Annemarie Palincsar —

_____

_____.

THE INFORMATION-PROCESSING VIEW
SECTION REVIEW

1. Describe the three main characteristics of the information-processing approach.

    _____

    _____

    _____

2. Describe the following types of memory:

    a. short-term memory

    _____

    b. working memory

    _____

    c. long-term memory

    _____

3. How competent are adolescents at making decisions?

    _____

    _____

4. What are some cognitive changes that allow for improved critical thinking in adolescence?

    _____

    _____

5.   Compare and contrast convergent and divergent thinking.

_____

_____

6.   Outline strategies to help adolescents become more creative.

_____

_____

7.   What are critical thinking skills that Sternberg believes adolescents need in everyday living?

_____

_____

8.   What are the characteristics of self-regulatory learners?

_____

_____

KEY PEOPLE IN SECTION (describe the contributions of this individual to the study and understanding of adolescence)

Robert Siegler —

_____

_____.

Robbie Case —

_____

_____.

Robert Sternberg —

_____

_____.

J.P. Guilford —

_____

_____.

Mark Strand —

_____

_____.

Michael Pressley —

_____

_____.

Barry Zimmerman, Sebastian Bonner, and Robert Kovach —

_____

_____.

THE PSYCHOMETRIC/INTELLIGENCE VIEW
SECTION REVIEW

1. Calculate the following I.Q.s using Stern's formula (*IQ=MA/CA x 100*).
    a. MA = 10, CA = 8 _____
    b. MA = 5, CA = 9 _____
    c. MA = 15, CA = 12 _____

2. How do the Wechsler scales differ from the tests developed by Binet?

    _____

    _____

3. What is meant by a normal distribution?

    _____

    _____

4. Match the skills indicative of each of Gardner's eight frames of mind with the profession or vocation they are most likely to be associated with.

    _____ 1. scientists, engineers, accountants   A. verbal skills
    _____ 2. farmers, botanists, landscapers   B. intrapersonal
    _____ 3. teachers and mental health professionals   C. mathematical
    _____ 4. surgeons, dancers, athletes   D. naturalist
    _____ 5. composers and musicians   E. spatial
    _____ 6. theologians and psychologists   F. interpersonal
    _____ 7. authors, journalists, speakers   G. bodily-kinesthetic
    _____ 8. architects, artists, sailors   H. musical

5. Describe how each of components of Sternberg's triarchic theory of intelligence would be utilized in writing a book report.

    _____

    _____

6.   According to the Mayer-Salovey-Caruso Emotional Intelligence Test, emotional intelligence involves four main areas:

_____

_____

_____

7.   Summarize the current status of the following debates about intelligence:

   a.   Nature and nurture

_____

_____

   b.   Ethnicity and culture

_____

_____

   c.   Use and misuse of intelligence tests

_____

_____

KEY PEOPLE IN SECTION (describe the contributions of this individual to the study and understanding of adolescence).

Aldous Huxley —

_____

_____.

Alfred Binet —

_____

_____.

Theophile Simon —

_____

_____.

William Stern —

_____

_____.

Lewis Terman —

_____

_____.

David Wechsler —

_____

_____.

Charles Spearmman —

_____

_____.

L.L. Thurstone —

_____

_____.

Robert Sternberg —

_____

_____.

Howard Gardner —

_____

_____.

Daniel Goleman —

_____

_____.

Nathan Brody —

_____

_____.

John Carroll —

_____

_____.

Robert Serpell —

_____

_____.

Elena Grigorenko —

_____

_____.

Richard Herrnstein and Charles Murray —

_____

_____.

SOCIAL COGNITION
SECTION REVIEW

1.   Do you have a personal fable? What does it consist of? Do you think that it is important to have a personal fable? Why or why not?

_____

_____

2.   Can the imaginary audience lead adolescents to make bad decisions?

_____

_____

3.   How is perspective taking involved in the development of adolescent egocentrism?

_____

_____

4.   Do adolescents conceptualize an individual's personality differently than children do?

_____

_____

5.   In what three ways do adolescents interpret personality differently than other children?

_____

_____

KEY PEOPLE IN SECTION (describe the contributions of this individual to the study and understanding of adolescence).

David Elkind —

_____

_____.

EXPLORATIONS IN ADOLESCENCE

How can the *imaginary audience* and *personal fable* affect you in a positive, or negative way?
    a. imaginary audience

_____

    b. personal fable

_____

COGNITIVE CHALLENGE

If you could go back to high school and restructure the courses and curriculum there, how could you add more critical opportunities?

_____

_____

ADOLESCENCE IN RESEARCH

Concerning Siegler's 1998 research regarding adolescent information-processing, state the hypothesis, the research methods (if known), the research conclusions, and the implications and applications for adolescent development.

_____

_____

⊠ COMPREHENSIVE REVIEW

1.   According to Jean Piaget, the fundamental ways in which adolescents adapt their thinking entails
    a.   conservation and classification.
    b.   social information processing and perspective taking.

    c.   the imaginary audience and the personal fable.

    d.   assimilation and accommodation.

2.   When he learned the value of money, Kenny initially thought that a nickel was worth more than a dime. Recently, as he has begun to buy items, Kenny has come to realize the value of a dime. The process by which Kenny adapted his schema is

    a.   assimilation.

    b.   accommodation.

    c.   equilibration.

    d.   metacognition.

3.   Piaget believed that there is considerable movement between states of cognitive equilibrium and disequalibrium as assimilation and accommodation work in concert to produce cognitive change. He called this

    a.   assimilation.

    b.   accommodation.

    c.   equilibration.

    d.   metacognition.

4.   Which of the following is NOT a stage of cognitive development according to Piaget?

    a.   sensorimotor

    b.   preoperational

    c.   concrete operational

    d.   informal operational

5.   When children begin representing their worlds in images and words, they are in which stage of cognitive development?

    a.   sensorimotor

    b.   preoperational

    c.   concrete operational

    d.   informal operational

6.   Renée begins to pull toys from her toy box; in so doing, she sorts them into piles of cars, trucks, and animals. She also understands that some toys can be switched from one pile to another or can form new piles based on, for example, types having similar colors. Renée's behavior reflects the cognitive ability called

    a.   perspective taking.

    b.   classification.

    c.   organization.

    d.   conservation.

7.   Unlike the concrete operational child, the formal operational adolescent can demonstrate

    a.   assimilation.

    b.   reversible mental operations.

    c.   conservation ability.

    d.   hypothetical-deductive reasoning.

8.   Compared to the early formal operational problem solver, the late formal operational solver

    a.   derives her hypothesis from the problem data.

    b.   looks for a general hypothesis to explain what has happened.

    c.   is satisfied with general statements about cause and effect.

    d.   searches for necessary and sufficient conditions to explain the results.

9.   Which of the following statements does not describe one of Jean Piaget's contributions to the field of cognitive development?

    a.   Jean Piaget contributed a number of important concepts such as conservation and object permanence.

    b.   Jean Piaget demonstrated that culture and education influence cognitive development.

    c.   Jean Piaget demonstrated that we adapt to our environment.

    d.   Jean Piaget made many insightful and systematic observations of children.

10.   Which group of developmentalists believes that cognitive development is more specific in many respects than did Piaget?

    a.   Piagetians

    b.   neo-Piagetians

    c.   competency-based developmentalists

    d.   information processing developmentalists

11.   Perhaps the greatest general criticism is that Piaget's theory tends to underestimate the importance of ____ in cognitive development.

    a.   culture and education

    b.   arts and entertainment

    c.   authority and mystery

    d.   sexuality and role playing

12.   Which of the following is NOT a criticism of Piaget's theory?

    a.   His theory assumes developmental synchrony, but that is often not the case.

    b.   Some cognitive abilities emerge earlier than Piaget thought.

    c.   Some children can be trained to perform at a higher level.

    d.   Piaget's theory focuses too much on childhood sexual development.

13.   Which of the following has been proposed as a probable fifth stage in Piaget's stages of development?

    a.   informal thought

    b.   formal thought

    c.   situational thought

    d.   postformal thought

14.   Tasks too difficult for an individual that can be mastered with the help of more skilled individuals defines what?

    a.   Jean Piaget called it hypothetical-deductive reasoning.

    b.   Lev Vygotsky called it the zone of proximal development.

    c.   Kurt Fisher called them abstract relations.

    d.   Neo-Piagetians called it social information.

15.   This refers to the changing of the level of support over the course of a teaching session.

    a.   intelligence

    b.   metacognition

    c.   scaffolding

    d.   equilibration

16. Adolescent egocentrism is represented by two types of thinking referred to as
    a.   the imaginary audience and the personal fable.
    b.   the abiding self and the transient self.
    c.   narcissism and the imaginary audience.
    d.   the indestructible self and the transient self.

17. Your 20-year-old friend Ellie confesses to you that she has always thought that somehow she was very different from everyone she knew, in her feelings and her understanding of the world. You might suspect that Ellie's sense of herself reflects
    a.   David Elkind's notion of the personal fable.
    b.   an organic pathology, perhaps a temporal lobe tumor.
    c.   a failure to achieve formal operational thought.
    d.   developmental delay of adolescence.

18. The teacher tells Marty to think of how many different sculptures he can make out of snow. This is an exercise in which type of thinking?
    a.   magical
    b.   convergent
    c.   artistic
    d.   divergent

19. Who reported being terrified of taking IQ tests as a child?
    a.   Howard Gardner
    b.   Theophile Simon
    c.   Robert Sternberg
    d.   David Wechsler

20. Who is credited with developing the concept of mental age (MA)?
    a.   William Stern
    b.   Theophile Simon
    c.   Alfred Binet
    d.   David Wechsler

21. Who is credited with developing the formula for calculating I.Q. (IQ = MA/CA x 100)?
    a.   William Stern
    b.   Theophile Simon
    c.   Alfred Binet
    d.   David Wechsler

22. Which of the following is NOT one of Howard Gardner's eight types of intelligence?
    a.   verbal skills
    b.   musical skills
    c.   cooking skills
    d.   naturalist skills

23. Who is credited with proposing the concept of emotional intelligence?
    a.   Robert Sternberg
    b.   Daniel Goleman
    c.   Howard Gardner
    d.   Robert Selman

24. Which of the following is NOT one of the initial four main areas of emotional intelligence proposed by Salovey and Mayer?
    a. perceiving and expressing emotion accurately and adaptively
    b. understanding emotion and emotional knowledge
    c. controlling anger
    d. managing emotions

25. Your adolescent sister says that people with red hair cannot be trusted. You recognize that she is developing
    a. an inability to take another person's perspective.
    b. a dangerous form of prejudice.
    c. an implicit personality theory.
    d. a personal fable.

26. Which of the following is NOT one of the four content areas measured by the Stanford-Binet?
    a. short-term memory
    b. verbal reasoning
    c. long-term memory
    d. quantitative reasoning

27. Which of the following is generally considered to be a culture-fair test?
    a. the Stanford-Binet test
    b. the Wechsler test
    c. the Raven Progressive Matrices test
    d. the Kaufman Assessment Battery for Children

28. While taking an IQ test, a series of numbers is read aloud to a student, with the student being asked to repeat them as quickly as possible. Which kind of memory is being assessed?
    a. long-term
    b. short-term
    c. digital
    d. conceptual

29. Which term includes the ability to learn from and adapt to our everyday lives?
    a. self
    b. intelligence
    c. knowable self
    d. learned personality

30. Alfred Binet developed intelligence tests to
    a. show that intelligence is largely the result of heredity.
    b. identify students who would not profit from typical schooling.
    c. identify students who were gifted, and needed extra challenges in their schooling.
    d. distinguish convergent thinkers from divergent thinkers.

31. One of the main advantages of the Wechsler scales over the Binet test is that the Wechsler scales include measures that are
    a. progressive.
    b. culturally specific.

c.   not verbal.

d.   screen for brain damage.

32.   In Spearman's *two-factor theory*, g stands for _____ and *s* stands for _____.

a.   generality; specialization

b.   general intelligence; specific abilities

c.   gestalt; Spearman

d.   goodness of fit; special traits

33.   Which of the following individuals did NOT propose a theory of intelligence?

a.   L.L. Thurstone

b.   Lewis Terman

c.   Charles Spearman

d.   Howard Gardner

34.   The type or aspect of intelligence measured by the Binet and Wechsler tests is most closely matched to the aspect Sternberg calls

a.   componential intelligence.

b.   experiential intelligence.

c.   contextual intelligence.

d.   tacit knowledge.

35.   According to Howard Gardner,

a.   it is better to administer intelligence tests to individuals than to groups.

b.   intelligence is best defined in terms of eight types.

c.   individuals have a general intelligence rather than various specific intelligences.

d.   intelligence is best defined in terms of three main components.

36.   In addition to the question of whether intelligence is primarily inherited, another important question about intelligence concerns

a.   the arbitrary distinction between aptitude and achievement tests.

b.   cultural and ethnic differences in test scores.

c.   using the computer as a model for information processing.

d.   the emotional and social adjustment of gifted individuals.

37.   Intelligence tests that are explicitly designed to minimize the differences between ethnic groups are called

a.   bias liberated.

b.   culture fair.

c.   socially equitable.

d.   psychometrically equivalent.

38.   A psychology professor asks his students to think of as many uses as possible for a paper clip. The professor is encouraging

a.   brainstorming.

b.   divergent thinking.

c.   convergent thinking.

d.   ideational originality.

ADOLESCENCE ON THE SCREEN

- *Phenomenon* explores the problems that come with high levels of intelligence.

- *Little Man Tate* depicts the education of a young child prodigy.

- *Searching for Bobby Fischer* depicts parents facing the dilemma of raising a gifted chess prodigy.

ADOLESCENCE IN BOOKS

- *Teaching and Learning Through Multiple Intelligences (Second Edition)*, by Linda Campbell, Bruce Campbell, and Dee Dickonson (Allyn & Bacon, 1999), provides applications of Gardner's eight intelligences to classrooms.

- *How People Learn*, by Committee on Developments in the Science of Learning (National Academy Press, 1999), describes the current state of knowledge about how children and youth think and learn.

- *Creating Minds*, by Howard Gardner (New York: Basic Books, 1993), proposes that intelligence can be divided into seven basic forms.

Answer Key

KEY TERMS

1. **schema** Piaget's theory of a concept or framework that exists in the individual's mind to organize and interpret information.

2. **assimilation** Occurs when individuals incorporate new information into existing knowledge.

3. **accommodation** Occurs when individuals adjust to new information.

4. **equilibration** A mechanism in Piaget's theory that explains how children or adolescents shift from one stage of thought to the next. The shift occurs as they experience cognitive conflict or a disequilibrium in trying to understand the world. Eventually, the child or adolescent resolves the conflict and reaches a balance or equilibrium.

5. **sensorimotor stage** Piaget's first stage of development, lasting from birth to about 2 years of age. In this stage, infants construct an understanding of the world by coordinating sensory experiences with physical, motoric actions.

6. **preoperational stage** Piaget's second stage, which lasts from about 2 to 7 years of age. In this stage children begin to represent their world with words, images, and drawings.

7. **concrete operational thought** Piaget's third stage, which lasts from about 7 to 11 years of age. In this stage, children can perform operations. Logical reasoning replaces intuitive thought as long as the reasoning can be applied to specific or concrete examples.

8. **formal operational thought** Piaget's fourth and final stage of cognitive development, which he believes emerges between 11 to 15 years of age. It is characterized by abstract, idealistic, and logical thought.

9. **hypothetical-deductive reasoning** Piaget's term for adolescents' ability, in the formal operational stage, to develop hypotheses, or best guesses, about ways to solve problems; they then systematically deduce, or conclude the best path to follow in solving the problem.

10. **neo-Piagetians** They argue that Piaget got some things right, but that his theory needs considerable revisions. In their revision, they give more emphasis to information processing that involves attention, memory, and strategies; they also seek to provide more precise explanations of cognitive changes.

11. **postformal thought** Postformal thought involves understanding that the correct answer to a problem requires reflective thinking and can vary from one situation to another, and that the search for truth is often an ongoing, never-ending process.

12. **zone of proximal development (ZPD)** Vygotsky's concept that refers to the range of tasks that are too difficult for individuals to master alone, but that can be mastered with the guidance or assistance of adults or more skilled peers.

13. **social constructivist approach** Emphasizes the social contexts of learning and the construction of knowledge through social interaction.

14. **critical thinking** Thinking reflectively, productively, and evaluating the evidence.

15. **creativity** The ability to think about something in novel and unusual ways and come up with unique solutions to problems.

16. **convergent thinking** According to Guilford, a pattern of thinking in which individuals produce one correct answer; characteristic of the terms on conventional intelligence tests.

17. **divergent thinking** According to Guilford, a pattern of thinking in which individuals produce many answers to the same question; more characteristic of creativity than convergent thinking.

18. **metacognition** Cognition about cognition, or "knowing about knowing."

19. **self-regulatory learning** Consists of the self-generation and self-monitoring of thoughts, feelings, and behaviors to reach a goal.

20. **psychometric/intelligence view** Emphasizes the importance of individual differences in intelligence. Many advocates of this view also argue that intelligence should be assessed with intelligence tests.

21. **intelligence** Mental ability related to verbal and problem-solving skills, and the ability to adapt to and learn from life's everyday experiences. Not everyone agrees on what constitutes intelligence.

22. **mental age (MA)** Developed by Binet, an individual's level of mental development relative to others.

23. **intelligent quotient (IQ)** A person's tested mental age divided by chronological age, multiplied by 100.

24. **normal distribution** A symmetrical distribution of values or scores with a majority of scores falling in the middle of the possible range of scores and few scores appearing toward the extremes of the range; a distribution that yields what is called a "bell-shaped curve."

25. **emotional intelligence** A form of social intelligence that involves the ability to monitor one's own and others' feelings and emotions, to discriminate among them, and to use this information to guide one's thinking and action.

26. **Heritability** The fraction of the variance in a population that is attributed to genetics.

27. **culture-fair tests** Tests of intelligence that attempt to be free of cultural bias.

28. **adolescent egocentrism** The heightened self-consciousness of adolescents, which is reflected in their belief that others are as interested in them as they are in themselves.

29. **implicit personality theory** The layperson's conception of personality.

KEY PEOPLE IN THE STUDY OF ADOLESCENCE

1. c	7. l	13. u	19. p
2. f	8. t	14. o	20. q
3. g	9. k	15. d	21. r
4. i	10. m	16. n	22. s
5. h	11. v	17. e	
6. j	12. b	18. a	

"DR. DETAIL'S" TERM MATCHING EXERCISE

1. g	7. b	13. c	19. p
2. k	8. l	14. h	20. u
3. n	9. f	15. q	21. t
4. m	10. i	16. r	
5. e	11. d	17. o	
6. a	12. j	18. s	

PIAGET'S THEORY
SECTION REVIEW

1.   No answer provided—personal reflection. However, the answer should describe the preexisting schema, the disequilibrium that resulted as the result of the new information or experience, indicate the new information that was assimilated, and state how the old schema accommodated the new information.

2.   Assimilation occurs when individuals incorporate new information into existing knowledge. Accommodation occurs when individuals adjust to new information.

3.   Equilibration is a mechanism in Piaget's theory that explains how children or adolescents shift from one state of thought to the next. The shift occurs as they experience cognitive conflict or a disequilibrium in trying to understand the world. Eventually, the child or adolescent resolves the conflict and reaches a balance, or equilibrium of thought.

4.   Sensorimotor stage—infants construct an understanding of the world by coordinating sensory experiences with physical, motoric actions.
        Preoperational stage—children begin to represent their world with words, images, and drawings.
        Concrete operational thought—children can perform operations. Logical reasoning replaces intuitive thought as long as the reasoning can be applied to specific or concrete examples.
        Formal operational stage—characterized by abstract, idealistic, and logical thought.

5.   Conservation is Piaget's term for an individual's ability to recognize that the length, number, mass, quantity, area, weight, and volume of objects and substances do not change through transformations that alter their appearance.
        Classification is Piaget's concept of concrete operational thought, in which children systematically organize objects into hierarchies of classes and subclasses.

6.   Piaget was the foundation for much of the current field of cognitive development.

7.   Piaget's theory has withstood the test of time quite well. However, it has not gone unchallenged, in particular by those with specific criticisms (neo-Piagetions).

8.   Questions have been raised regarding these areas: *Estimates of children's competence* — abilities are probably too fluid to be measured in Piaget's fashion; *Stages* — Piaget's theory assumes developmental synchrony, which is not consistent; *Training children to reason at a higher level* — it would appear that if properly trained, children can skip whole stages; *Culture and education* — these exert more influence on development than Piaget envisioned.

9.   Evidence for the fifth, postformal stage has yet to be documented that would clearly show a more advanced stage than formal operational thought.

KEY PEOPLE IN SECTION

David Elkind—proposed communication and interaction with the environment in applying cognitive development to education.

Robbie Case— Canadian developmental psychologist that believes more precise description of changes within each stage needs to be carried out.

K. Warner Schaie—concluded that it is unlikely that adults go beyond the powerful methods of scientific thinking characteristic of the formal operations stage.

William Perry—said that younger adolescents tend to view the world in terms of polarities (i.e., right.wrong, or good/bad).

VYGOTSKY'S THEORY
SECTION REVIEW

1.

Topic	Vygotsky	Piaget
Constructivism	Social constructivist	Cognitive constructivist
Stages	No general stages of development proposed	Strong emphasis on stages—sensorimotor, preoperational, concrete operational, and formal operational
View on Education	Education plays a central role in helping children learn the tools of the culture	Education merely refines the child's cognitive skills that already have emerged.
Teaching Implications	Teacher is facilitator and guide, not director; establishes learning opportunities for children to learn with teacher and more skilled peers	Teacher is facilitator and guide, but not director; teacher provides support for children to explore their world and discover knowledge

2.   Zone of proximal development refers to the range of tasks that are too difficult for an individual to master alone, but can be mastered with the guidance of adults or skilled peers.

3.   a.   Scaffolding involves direct teaching, with less guidance provided by teacher or more advanced peer as student learns more.
    b.   Cognitive apprenticeship involves an adult or expert modeling thinking strategies and allowing students to anticipate or complete the expert's next step or idea.
    c.   Tutoring involves a cognitive apprenticeship between an adult or more skilled adolescent. Fellow students are more effective tutors, and peer tutoring also benefits the tutor.
    d.   Cooperative learning involves working and learning in small groups.
    e.   Reciprocal teaching involves students taking turns leading a small group discussion. The teacher gradually assumes a less active role, letting the student assume more initiative.

4.   In a cognitive constructivist approach, emphasis is on the individual's cognitive construction of knowledge and understanding. In a social constructivist approach emphasis is on collaboration with others to produce knowledge and understanding.

KEY PEOPLE IN SECTION

Barbara Rogoff—felt that cognitive development occurs as new generations collaborate with older generations in varying forms of interpersonal engagement.

Ann Brown and Annemarie Palincsar—used reciprocal teaching to improve students' abilities to enact certain strategies to improve their reading comprehension.

THE INFORMATION-PROCESSING VIEW
SECTION REVIEW

1. Thinking, change mechanisms, and encoding.

2. Short-term memory — is a limited-capacity memory system in which information is retained for as long as 30 seconds.
    Working memory — is a kind of "mental workbench" where information is manipulated and assembled to help make decisions, solve problems, and comprehend written and spoken language.
    Long-term memory — is a relatively permanent memory system that holds huge amounts of information for a long period of time.

3. Compared to children, young adolescents are more likely to generate options that will lead to appropriate decisions.

4. Increased speed and capacity of information processing, which free cognitive resources for other purposes. More breadth of content knowledge in a variety of domains. Increased ability to construct new combinations of knowledge. A greater range and more spontaneous use of strategies or procedures for applying or obtaining knowledge.

5. Convergent thinking produces one correct answer and is characteristic of the kind of thinking required on a conventional intelligence test. Divergent thinking produces many answers to the same question and is more characteristic of creativity.

6. a. Have adolescents engage in brainstorming and come up with as many meaningful ideas as possible.
    b. Provide adolescents with environments that stimulate creativity.
    c. Don't overcontrol.
    d. Encourage internal motivation.
    e. Foster flexible and playful thinking.
    f. Introduce adolescents to creative people.
    g. Talk with adolescents about creative people or have them read about them.

7. Self regulatory learners (1) set goals for extending their knowledge and sustaining their motivation;
    (2) are aware of their emotional make-up and have strategies for managing their emotions;
    (3) periodically monitor their progress toward a goal; (4) fine tune or revise their strategies based on the progress they are making; and (5) evaluate obstacles that may arise and make the necessary adaptations.

KEY PEOPLE IN SECTION

Robert Siegler—developed views related to information processing.

Robbie Case—believed adolescents process information differently than children.

Robert Sternberg—developed the triarchic theory of intelligence.

J.P. Guilford—made the distinction between convergent and divergent thinking in creativity.

Mark Strand—a Poet Laureate who said that his most creative moments come when he loses a sense of time and is absorbed in what he is doing.

Michael Pressley—felt the key to education is helping students learn a rich repertoire of strategies that result in solutions to problems.

Barry Zimmerman, Sebastian Bonner, and Robert Kovach—developed a model of turning low-self-regulatory students into students who engaged in adopting specific, positive learning goals.

PSYCHOMETRIC/INTELLIGENCE VIEW
SECTION REVIEW

1.   a.   125
        b.   55
        c.   125

2. Wechsler has both verbal and performance subscales, whereas the tests developed by Binet are predominantly verbally loaded.

3. A normal distribution is a symmetrical bell-shaped curve with a majority of the focus cases falling in the middle of the range of possible scores.

4. **1.** C; **2.** D; **3.** F; **4.** G; **5.** H; **6.** B; **7.** A; **8.** E.

5. Analytical—Analyze the book's main themes.
   Creative—Generate new ideas about how the book might have been written better.
   Practical—Think about how the book's themes can be applied to real life.

6. Developing emotional self-awareness; managing emotions; reading emotions; and, handling relationships.

7.   a.   Nature and nurture—Heredity is an important part of intelligence.
        b.   Ethnicity and culture—There are ethnic differences in the average scores on standardized intelligence tests between African American and White American adolescents, but the differences are believed to be the result of environmental factors such as social, economic, and educational opportunities.
        c.   Use and misuse of intelligence tests—Intelligence tests can lead to stereotypes and expectations about adolescents and should not be used as the main or sole characteristic of competence. Further, intelligence tests do not take into account the many domains of intelligence, such as those described by Sternberg and Gardner.

KEY PEOPLE IN SECTION

Aldous Huxley—said that children are remarkable for their curiosity and intelligence.

Alfred Binet developed the concept of mental age (MA).

Theophile Simon—Binet's student and collaborator in developing the 1905 test.

Lewis Terman—was involved in forming and revising Binet's test.

William Stern—created the concept of the intelligence quotient (IQ).

David Wechsler—developed several IQ tests with multiple subscales.

Charles Spearman—said that people have both a general intelligence (*g*), and a specific types of intelligence (*s*).

L.L. Thurstone—identified primary mental abilities: verbal comprehension, number ability, word fluency, spatial visualization, associative memory, reasoning, and perceptual speed.

Robert Sternberg—developed the triarchic theory of intelligence.

Howard Gardner—identified eight types of intelligence.

Daniel Goleman—feels that emotional intelligence is more important than IQ when predicting an adolescent's competence.

Nathan Brody—argued that people who excel at one type of intellectual task are likely to excel in other intellectual tasks.

John Carroll—conducted an extensive examination of intellectual abilities and concluded that they are all related to each other.

Robert Serpell—studied concepts of intelligence in African communities since the 1970s.

Elena Grigorenko—studied the concept of intelligence in rural African people.

Richard Herrnstein and Charles Murray—sparked controversy by publishing the controversial book on intelligence, *The Bell Curve*.

SOCIAL COGNITION
SECTION REVIEW

1. No answer provided—personal reflection.

2. Yes. Popular examples suggest that they may lead to acts of violence, among other things.

3. The link between perspective taking and adolescent egocentrism likely occurs because advances in perspective taking cause young adolescents to be acutely concerned about what others think.

4. Adolescents are more likely to interpret an individual's personality in the way that many personality theorists do, as opposed to children.

5. 1.) When adolescents are given information about another person, they are more likely to consider both previously acquired information and current information, rather than relying only on the information at hand — as children do. 2.) Adolescents are more likely to detect the situational or contextual variability in personality, rather than thinking that personality is always stable. 3.) Rather than merely accepting surface traits as a valid description of someone's personality, adolescents are more likely than children to look for deeper causes of personality.

KEY PEOPLE IN SECTION

David Elkind—believes that adolescent egocentrism can be dissected into two types of social thinking — imaginary audience and personal fable.

EXPLORATIONS IN ADOLESCENCE

No answer provided—personal reflection.

COGNITIVE CHALLENGE

No answer provided—personal reflection.

ADOLESCENCE IN RESEARCH

The hypothesis, thinking is very flexible allowing individual's to adapt and adjust to many changes in their circumstances. He described three main characteristics of the information-processing view. 1. An emphasis on thinking as information processing. 2. An emphasis on mechanisms of change (encoding, automaticity, strategy construction, and generalization). 3. An emphasis on self-modification (i.e., prior knowledge is a base built upon).

⊠ COMPREHENSIVE REVIEW

1. d	**14.** b	**27.** c
2. b	**15.** c	**28.** b
3. c	**16.** a	**29.** b
4. d	**17.** a	**30.** b
5. b	**18.** d	**31.** c
6. b	**19.** c	**32.** b
7. d	**20.** c	**33.** b
8. d	**21.** a	**34.** a
9. b	**22.** c	**35.** b
10. b	**23.** b	**36.** b
11. a	**24.** c	**37.** b
12. d	**25.** c	**38.** b
13. d	**26.** c	

⌘

Chapter 5   The Self, Identity, Emotions, and Personality

Learning Goals with Key Terms and Key People in Boldface

1.0   DESCRIBE THE DEVELOPMENT OF THE SELF IN ADOLESCENCE

    A.   The Self

        1.1   How is **self-understanding** defined?

        1.2   What causes contradictions within the self?

        1.3   What are the dimensions of adolescents' **self-understanding?**

        1.4   What is the difference between the real and ideal self, and the true and false self?

        1.5   What is meant by **possible self?**

        1.6   What is social comparison?

        1.7   What does it mean to be self-conscious and self-protective?

        1.8   What is self-integration?

        1.9   What is meant by adolescents having multiple selves?

    B.   Self-Esteem and Self-Concept

        1.10   What is **self-esteem?**

        1.11   What is **self-concept?**

        1.12   How do you measure an adolescent's self-esteem?

        1.13   What is Harter's Self-Perception Profile for Adolescents?

        1.14   Why is it good to use multiple measures to assess self-esteem?

        1.15   Does self-esteem change during the life span?

        1.16   Are some domains more salient than others to the adolescent's self esteem?

        1.17   How important is perceived physical appearance to an adolescent's self-esteem?

        1.18   What role does peer acceptance play in the self-esteem of adolescents?

        1.19   What parental influences and behaviors are associated with boys' self-esteem?

        1.20   What role do peer judgments play in self-esteem?

        1.21   Is classmate support more strongly linked to self-esteem than close-friend support?

        1.22   What is the consequence of low self-esteem for most adolescents?

        1.23   What are the ramifications for some adolescents when low self-esteem persists?

        1.24   What can happen if self-esteem is compounded by difficult school transitions?

        1.25   What are four ways that adolescents' self-esteem can be improved?

        1.26   Why should adolescents be taught to value competence?

2.0   IDENTITY

    A.   Erikson's Ideas on Identity

        2.1   What is the meaning and significance of Erikson's fifth stage, **identity versus identity confusion?**

        2.2   What is **psychosocial moratorium** as it relates to identity development?

        2.3   What is revealed by Erikson's insights?

2.4   According to Erikson, what do personality and role exploration have to do with identity development?

2.5   What are some contemporary views of identity development?

2.6   How long does identity development take?

2.7   Is identity development complex?

B.   **The Four Statuses of Identity**

2.8   What is Marcia's view of identity?

2.9   What are the four statuses of identity?

2.10   What are the characteristics of **identity diffusion** and **identity foreclosure?**

2.11   How is **crisis** identified?

2.12   How is **commitment** identified?

2.13   What is **identity moratorium?**

2.14   What does Marcia mean by **identity achievement?**

2.15   What is the role of crisis and **commitment** in Marcia's theory of identity statuses?

2.16   What are the criticisms of Marcia's identity statuses?

C.   **Developmental Changes in Identity**

2.17   What three aspects of the young adolescent's development are important in identity formation?

2.18   What are "MAMA" cycles?

D.   **Family Influences on Identity**

2.19   How do parents influence adolescents' identity development?

2.20   What is **individuality?**

2.21   What is **connectedness?**

2.22   What family processes promote adolescent identity development?

2.23   What do adolescent **individuality** and **connectedness** have to do with identity development?

E.   **Cultural and Ethnic Identity**

2.24   What emphasis did Erikson place on the role of culture in identity development?

2.25   What is meant by **ethnic identity?**

2.26   Why is adolescence a special juncture in the identity development of ethnic minority individuals?

2.27   How does identity change across generations?

2.28   What is Helms' Model of Ethnic Identity Development?

F.   **Gender and Identity**

2.29   Do ethnic minority individuals have bicultural gender identities?

2.30   Do adolescent males have a stronger vocational identity than females?

2.31   Do female adolescents have a stronger social identity than males?

G.   **Identity and Intimacy**

2.32   What are the features of Erikson's sixth stage, **intimacy versus isolation?**

2.33   What are the characteristics of Orlofsky's **intimate style, preintimate style, stereotyped style, pseudointimate style,** and **isolated style** of intimate interaction?

2.34   When are adolescents most likely to feel lonely?

2.35   What is loneliness associated with?

2.36   According to Weiss, what is the difference between **emotional isolation** and **social isolation?**

2.37   How can individuals reduce their loneliness?

3.0   EMOTIONS

    A.   The Emotions of Adolescence

        3.1   What is **emotion?**

        3.2   Why is it important for adults to realize that moodiness is normal in adolescence?

    B.   Hormones, Experience, and Emotions

        3.3   What is the relationship between puberty and emotionality?

    C.   Emotional Competence

        3.4   What role does awareness of emotional cycles play in adolescence?

        3.5   Which emotional competencies are important for adolescents to develop?

4.0   PERSONALITY DEVELOPMENT

    A.   Personality Traits

        3.6   What are the **big five factors of personality?**

        3.7   Why is it good to view personality not only in terms of traits, but also in terms of contexts and situations?

    B.   Temperament

        3.8   How is **temperament** defined?

        3.9   What are the three basic types of temperament?

        3.10   How did Mary Rothbart and John Bates revise Thomas and Chess's framework for classifying temperament?

        3.11   Is temperament in childhood linked to adjustment in adolescence and adulthood?

        3.12   What is meant by **goodness of fit?**

Exercises

KEY TERMS COMPLETION EXERCISE

Each key term is presented in the form of an incomplete sentence. Complete each sentence by either defining the term or giving an example. Compare your definitions with those given at the end of the study guide chapter.

1.   **Self-understanding** is seen in the

    _____

    _____

2.   Jacob is pondering his **possible self.** This means he is

    _____

    _____

3.   **Self-esteem** is presented as a measure of

    _____

    _____

4.   A person's **self-concept** is

_____

_____

5.   In proposing **identity versus identity confusion,** Erikson was suggesting

_____

_____

6.   **Psychosocial moratorium** is Erikson's term for

_____

_____

7.   **Crisis** is represented by

_____

_____

8.   Fred is showing **commitment** to his schoolwork as evidenced by

_____

_____

9.   According to James Marcia, **identity diffusion** is when

_____

_____

10.   **Identity foreclosure** is an adolescent state in which

_____

_____

11.   While in **identity moratorium,** a person is likely

_____

_____

12.   **Identity achievement** suggests

_____

_____

13.   Evidence of expressing **individuality** is seen in

_____

_____

14.   **Connectedness** consists of two dimensions:

_____

_____

15.   A sense of **ethnic identity** is seen

_____

_____

16.   **Intimacy versus isolation,** according to Erikson, is

_____

_____

17.   Jerry and Amanda have a relationship that reflects **intimate style** because

_____

_____

18.   **Preintimate style** is evidenced by

_____

_____

19.   **Stereotyped style** is marked by relationships that are

_____

_____

20. **Pseudointimate style** suggests a lack of

_____

_____

21. People with an **isolated style**

_____

_____

22. **Emotional isolation** is a type of

_____

_____

23. **Social isolation** is a type of

_____

_____

24. Phil shows his **emotion** by

_____

_____

25. These are the **big five factors of personality:**

_____

_____

26. **Temperament** is defined as

_____

_____

27. Suzy's mom considers her an **easy child** because

_____

_____

28.   Troy's teacher considers him to be a **difficult child** because

_____

_____

29.   Laurie is considered to be a **slow-to-warm-up child** because

_____

_____

30.   **Goodness of fit** means

_____

_____

KEY PEOPLE IN THE STUDY OF ADOLESCENCE

Match the person with the concept of adolescent development with which they are associated.

_____	1. Susan Harter	A.	Most famous for his theory of identity development
_____	2. Robert Weiss	B.	Developed an assessment for adolescent self-esteem
_____	3. Erik Erikson	C.	Expanded on Erikson's identity development theory
_____	4. James Marcia	D.	Distinguished two forms of loneliness
_____	5. Alan Waterman	E.	Proposed a four-stage model of ethnic identity development
_____	6. Catherine Cooper	F.	Conducted research on ethnic identity
_____	7. Stuart Hauser	G.	Believes that ethnic minority youth must bridge multiple worlds in constructing identity
_____	8. Jean Phinney	H.	Developed a classification of five styles of intimate interaction
_____	9. Jacob Orlofsky	I.	Illuminated family processes that promote adolescent identity development
_____	10. Janet Helms	J.	Conducted research on timing of identity achievement
_____	11. Reed Larson and Maryse Richards	K.	Argued that personality varies according to the situation
_____	12. Walter Mischel	L.	Proposed three basic types or clusters of temperament
_____	13. Alexander Thomas and Stella Chess	M.	Found that adolescents reported more extreme emotions than did their parents

"DR. DETAIL'S" IDENTITY STATUS EXERCISE

What is your identity status? Think about your exploration and commitment in the areas listed below. For each area, check whether your identity status is diffused, foreclosed, moratorium, or achieved. If you check "diffused" or "foreclosed" for any areas, take some time to think about what you need to do to move into a moratorium identity status in those areas.

Identity Component	Diffused	Foreclosed	Moratorium	Achieved
Vocational (career)				
Political				
Religious				

Relationship				
Achievement				
Sexual				
Gender				
Ethnic/Cultural				
Interests				
Personality				
Physical				

THE SELF
SECTION REVIEW

1. List and give an example or explanation for Harter's five ways an adolescent's sense of self differs from that of a child.

    a. _____

    _____

    b. _____

    _____

    c. _____

    _____

    d. _____

    _____

    e. _____

    _____

2. What are the dimensions of adolescents' self-understanding?

    _____

    _____

3. What is meant by possible self?

    _____

    _____

4.   What is social comparison?

        _____

        _____

5.   What is self-integration?

        _____

        _____

6.   Complete the chart by filling in the positive and negative behavioral indicators of self-esteem

Positive Indicators	Negative Indicators

7.   What is self-esteem?

        _____

        _____

8.   What is self-concept?

        _____

        _____

9.   What is Harter's Self-Perception Profile for adolescents?

        _____

        _____

10.   How important is perceived physical appearance to an adolescent's self-esteem?

_____

_____

11.   What role does peer judgments play in self-esteem?

_____

_____

12.   What are four ways that adolescents' self-esteem can be improved?

_____

_____

IDENTITY
SECTION REVIEW

1.   What is the meaning and significance of Erikson's fifth stage, identity versus identity confusion?

_____

_____

2.   What is psychosocial moratorium as it relates to identity development?

_____

_____

3.   How long does identity development take?

_____

_____

4.   What are the four statuses of identity?

_____

_____

5.   What are some characteristics of identity diffusion and identity foreclosure?

_____

_____

6.   Differentiate between crisis and commitment.

_____

_____

7.   What three aspects of the young adolescent's development are important in identity formation?

_____

_____

8.   What are "MAMA" cycles?

_____

_____

9.   What is individuality?

_____

_____

10.   What is connectedness?

_____

_____

11.   What family processes promote adolescent identity development?

_____

_____

12.   What is meant by ethnic identity?

_____

_____

13.   What is Helms' Model of Ethnic Identity Development?

_____

_____

14.   Contrast the vocational identity and social identity of males versus females.

_____

_____

15.   What are the features of Erikson's sixth stage, intimacy versus isolation?

_____

_____

16.   What are the characteristics of Orlofsky's intimate style, preintimate style, stereotyped style, pseudointimate style, and isolated style of intimate interaction?

_____

_____

17.   According to Weiss, what is the difference between emotional isolation and social isolation?

_____

_____

EMOTIONAL DEVELOPMENT
SECTION REVIEW

1.   What is emotion?

_____

_____

2.   Why is it important for adults to realize that moodiness is normal in adolescence?

_____

_____

3.   What is the relationship between puberty and emotionality?

_____

_____

4.   What role does awareness of emotional cycles play in adolescence?

_____

_____

5.   Which emotional competencies are important for adolescents to develop?

_____

_____

PERSONALITY DEVELOPMENT
SECTION REVIEW

1.   What are the big five factors of personality?

_____

_____

2.   Why is it good to view personality in terms of contexts and situations?

_____

_____

3.   How is temperament defined?

_____

_____

4.   What are the three basic types of temperament?

_____

_____

5.   How did Rothbart and Bates classify temperament?

_____

_____

COGNITIVE CHALLENGE

1.   Think about what your future selves might be. Which of your prospective selves do you think
      will make you the happiest? Which of your prospective selves might have negative possibilities?

      _____

      _____

      _____

      _____

      _____

ADOLESCENCE IN RESEARCH

Concerning the research about boys' self-esteem by Coopersmith (1967), state the hypothesis, the
research methods (if known), the research conclusions, and the implications and applications for
adolescent development.

      _____

      _____

COMPREHENSIVE REVIEW

1.   Bernie describes himself as in control, masculine, and intelligent when he is with his girlfriend;
      but when he is with his buddies, he describes himself as fun loving and spontaneous. Bernie is
      a.   two-faced.
      b.   differentiated.
      c.   schizophrenic.
      d.   lacking an identity.

2.   _____ felt that when the real and ideal selves are too discrepant; it is a sign of maladjustment.
      a.   Susan Harter
      b.   Erik Erikson
      c.   Carl Rogers
      d.   Jean Phinney

3.   Adolescents are more likely than children to
      a.   use social comparison.
      b.   be self-conscious.
      c.   be preoccupied with understanding.
      d.   do all of the above.

4.   Which of the following is NOT one of Marcia's phases describing changes in adolescence?
      a.   reconstruction
      b.   deconstruction
      c.   self-understanding
      d.   consolidation

5.   Joyce is on a date with someone she wants to impress. She uses large words that she does not normally use and exaggerates her intellectual ability. She is exhibiting her
       a.   negative possible self.
       b.   positive possible self.
       c.   ideal self.
       d.   false self.

6.   _____ involves domain-specific evaluations of the self.
       a.   Self-esteem
       b.   Self-concept
       c.   Positive possible self
       d.   Negative possible self

7.   _____ is the global evaluative dimension of the self.
       a.   Self-esteem
       b.   Self-concept
       c.   Positive possible self
       d.   Negative possible self

8.   _____ refers to an individuals' beliefs that they can master a situation and produce positive outcomes.
       a.   Self-esteem
       b.   Self-concept
       c.   Self-efficacy
       d.   Self-reference

9.   Adolescents understand that there may be an unconscious aspect of the self because they have
       a.   formal operations.
       b.   concrete knowledge of the unconscious.
       c.   better education about unconscious influences.
       d.   a broad world-view.

10.   An adolescent who starts to admit inconsistencies in his or her behavior is achieving
       a.   his ideal self.
       b.   egocentrism.
       c.   self-reference
       d.   self-integration.

11.   Using two instruments to measure self-esteem is considered by developmental psychologists as
       a.   likely to lead to confusion.
       b.   likely to give inconsistent results.
       c.   likely to reflect the richness of the self.
       d.   unethical.

12.   Which of the following parental characteristics is associated with self-esteem in children?
       a.   expression of affection
       b.   setting permissive rules
       c.   conflicted family environments
       d.   parental intelligence

13. Rodney's parents don't set any limits on his behavior. The family seems to always be in a state of chaos. Research indicates that Rodney's self-esteem will likely be
    a. low.
    b. high.
    c. unconscious.
    d. differentiated.

14. Programs that emphasize both academic and social skills are likely to enhance
    a. identity achievement.
    b. patience.
    c. self-esteem.
    d. harmonious family relationships.

15. Which is the most accurate statement of Erikson's views on identity development?
    a. Losing your identity in a crowd is a form of identity confusion.
    b. Running away and dropping out of school indicates moratorium.
    c. The identity crisis is unrelated to earlier psychosocial stages.
    d. Experimenting with different roles and personalities indicates a negative identity.

16. According to James Marcia and others, identity formation
    a. is a lifetime activity.
    b. should occur after intimacy.
    c. is much easier than Erikson made it out to be.
    d. does not require advanced thinking skills.

17. Karyn, who is in a state of identity foreclosure,
    a. has not experienced any crisis or made any commitment.
    b. has made a commitment but has not experienced a crisis.
    c. is in the midst of a crisis.
    d. has undergone a crisis and made a commitment.

18. Jackson came home with green spiked hair. Of the following explanations for his behavior, _____ is the LEAST adequate.
    a. identity moratorium
    b. negative identity
    c. identity confusion
    d. identity foreclosure

19. Which of the following is NOT one of Helms's stages of Ethnic Development?
    a. pre-encounter
    b. immersion
    c. encounter
    d. conversation

20. Which of the following is NOT one of Marcia's four statuses of identity?
    a. identity moratorium
    b. negative identity
    c. identity diffusion
    d. identity foreclosure

21. According to Cooper and her colleagues, the two dimensions of connectedness are
    a. bonding and respect.
    b. mutuality and sensitivity.
    c. self- and other-connectedness.
    d. mutuality and permeability.

22. Adolescence may be a particularly difficult time for minority individuals because this is the time they
    a. are subject to the most intense discrimination.
    b. also confront their own ethnicity.
    c. have the fewest resources to achieve identity.
    d. become aware of other people's resources.

23. Gender differences in identity formation
    a. are a backlash against the women's movement.
    b. are greater now because of the New Age movement.
    c. have decreased in the last twenty years.
    d. are the same as they have always been.

24. Erikson believed that intimacy should come after one has established
    a. identity.
    b. trust.
    c. generativity.
    d. industry.

25. Jacob Orlofsky discovered that college students who had a stable sense of identity were more likely to achieve _____ status.
    a. stereotyped
    b. preintimacy
    c. pseudointimacy
    d. intimacy

26. In a study of unmarried college students (male and female) it was found that a strong sense of _____ was an important factor in forming intimate relationships.
    a. confidence
    b. self
    c. humor
    d. achievement

27. Robert Weiss distinguished between
    a. emotional and social isolation.
    b. individuation and connectedness.
    c. intimate and isolated relationships.
    d. situational and chronic loneliness.

28. Which of the following is NOT a stage in Helms's model of ethnic identity development?
    a. pre-encounter
    b. encounter
    c. immersion/emersion
    d. externalization/concommitant

29. Which of the following is loneliest?
    a. adults
    b. elderly
    c. late adolescence
    d. childhood

30. This arises when a person lacks an intimate relationship.
    a. social isolation
    b. emotional isolation
    c. immersion/emersion
    d. laconic malaise

31. Which of the following is NOT one of the big five factors of personality?
    a. neuroticism
    b. conscientiousness
    c. agreeableness
    d. externalization

32. Five-year-old Teddy seems to be always in a good mood and is considered happy-go-lucky. Which of Chess and Thomas's three basic types of temperament does he best fit?
    a. difficult child
    b. positive affect and approach
    c. easy child
    d. fast-to-warm-up child

ADOLESCENCE ON THE SCREEN

- *The Cider House Rules* A young boy born and raised in an orphanage charts his own course in life, breaking away from his surrogate father who runs the orphanage.

- *King Gimp* Two University of Maryland professors won the Academy Award in 2000 for best documentary short subject with this film spanning the adolescence and young adulthood of Dan Keplinger, a young man suffering from a highly disabling form of cerebral palsy, as he searches for identity in a world that shuns him.

- *Shine* Based on the true story of Australian pianist David Helfgott, the movie chronicles Helfgott's search for an identity. He has to overcome an abusive childhood, loss of his family in concentration camps, and mental illness before he finds himself and achieves success as a concert pianist.

- *Simon Birch* Simon Birch, age 12, believes that God made him for a special purpose. The movie presents his quest to fulfill the destiny he believes in.

ADOLESCENCE IN BOOKS

- *Gandhi*, by Erik Erikson (Norton: NY, 1966), the Pulitzer Prize-winning biography of Mahatma Gandhi, emphasizes Gandhi's identity crisis.

- *Identity's Architect: A Biography of Erik H. Erikson*, by Lawrence J. Friedman (Scribner: NY, 1999), traces Erik Erikson's own identity crises, which contributed to the development of his psychosocial theory.

- *Intimate Connections*, by David D. Burns (William Morrow: NY, 1985), presents a program for overcoming loneliness.

Answer Key

KEY TERMS

1. **self-understanding** The adolescent's cognitive representation of the self, the substance and content of the adolescent's self-conceptions.

2. **possible self** What individuals might become, what they would like to become, and what they are afraid of becoming.

3. **self-esteem** The global evaluative dimension of the self. Self-esteem is also referred to as self-worth or self-image.

4. **self-concept** Domain-specific evaluations of the self.

5. **identity versus identity confusion** Erikson's fifth developmental stage, which individuals experience during the adolescent years. At this time, individuals are faced with finding out who they are, what they are all about, and where they are going in life.

6. **psychosocial moratorium** Erikson's term for the gap between childhood security and adult autonomy that adolescents experience as part of their identity exploration.

7. **crisis** A period of identity development during which the adolescent is choosing among meaningful alternatives.

8. **commitment** The part of identity development in which adolescents show a personal investment in what they are going to do.

9. **identity diffusion** Marcia's term for the state adolescents are in when they have not yet experienced a crisis or made any commitments.

10. **identity foreclosure** Marcia's term for the state adolescents are in when they have made a commitment but have not experienced a crisis.

11. **identity moratorium** Marcia's term for the state of adolescents who are in the midst of a crisis, but whose commitments are either absent or are only vaguely defined.

12. **identity achievement** Marcia's term for having undergone a crisis and made a commitment.

13. **individuality** An important element in adolescent identity development. It consists of two dimensions: self-assertion, the ability to have and communicate a point of view; and separateness, the use of communication patterns to express how one is different from others.

14. **connectedness** An important element in adolescent identity development. It consists of two dimensions: mutuality, sensitivity to and respect for others' views; and permeability, openness to others' views.

15. **ethnic identity** An enduring, basic aspect of the self that includes a sense of membership in an ethnic group and the attitudes and feelings related to that membership.

16. **intimacy versus isolation** Erikson's sixth developmental stage, which individuals experience during the early adulthood years. At this time, individuals face the developmental task of forming intimate relationships with others.

17. **intimate style** The individual forms and maintains one or more deep and long-lasting love relationships.

18. **preintimate style** The individual shows mixed emotions about commitment, an ambivalence reflected in the strategy of offering love without obligations.

19. **stereotyped style** The individual has superficial relationships that tend to be dominated by friendship ties with same-sex rather than opposite-sex individuals.

20. **pseudointimate style** The individual maintains a long-lasting sexual attachment with little or no depth or closeness.

21. **isolated style** The individual withdraws from social encounters and has little or no attachment to same or opposite-sex individuals.

22. **emotional isolation** A type of loneliness that arises when a person lacks an intimate attachment relationships; single, divorced, and widowed adults often experience this type of loneliness.

23. **social isolation** A type of loneliness that occurs when a person lacks a sense of integrated involvement. Being deprived of participation in a group or community involving companionship, shared interests, organized activities, and meaningful roles causes a person to feel alienated, bored, and uneasy.

24. **emotion** Feeling or affect that involves physiological arousal, behavioral expression, and sometimes conscious experience.

25. **big five factors of personality** Five core traits of personality: openness to experience, conscientiousness, extraversion, agreeableness, and neuroticism.

26. **temperament** An individual's behavioral style and characteristic way of responding.

27. **easy child** Generally in a positive mood, quickly establishes regular routines, and adapts easily to new experiences.

28. **difficult child** This child reacts negatively to many situations and is slow to accept new experiences.

29. **slow-to-warm-up child** This child has a low activity level, is somewhat negative, and displays a low intensity of mood.

30. **goodness of fit** The match between an individual's temperament style and the environmental demands the individual must cope with.

KEY PEOPLE IN THE STUDY OF ADOLESCENCE

1.	B	**2.**	D	**3.**	A	**4.**	C	**5.**	J
6.	G	**7.**	I	**8.**	F	**9.**	H	**10.**	E
11.	M	**12.**	K	**13.**	L					

"DR. DETAIL'S" IDENTITY STATUS EXERCISE

Individual answers may vary.

THE SELF
SECTION REVIEW

1. Individual answers may vary.
   a. **Abstraction and idealism:** A teenager is more apt to describe himself/herself in abstract terms, such as saying that he/she is compassionate and caring.
   b. **Differentiation:** An adolescent is likely to describe himself/herself as having one set of characteristics in relationship to his/her families and another in relationship to his/her peers and friends.
   c. **The fluctuating self:** Adolescents' sense of themselves changes over short periods of time. They can be self-confident one moment and anxious the next.
   d. **Contradictions within the self:** Adolescents' self-descriptions show contradictions. They may think of themselves as both attractive and unattractive.
   e. **Real versus ideal, true versus false selves:** Depression and self-doubt can arise when an adolescent feels that they are not living up to their ideal sense of self.

2. (a) abstract and idealistic, (b) differentiated, (c) the fluctuating self, (d) contradictions within the self, (e) real and ideal, true and false selves.

3. What individuals might become, what they would like to become, and what they are afraid of becoming.

4. They ways in which adolescents evaluate themselves.

5. In adolescence, self-understanding becomes more integrative, with the disparate parts of the self more systematically pieced together, especially in late adolescence.

6.

Positive Indicators	**Negative Indicators**
Gives others directives or commands	Puts down others by teasing, name-calling, or gossiping
Uses voice quality appropriate for situation	Uses gestures that are dramatic or out of context
Expresses opinions	Engages in inappropriate touching or avoids physical contact
Sits with others during social activities	Gives excuses for failures
Works cooperatively in a group	Glances around to monitor others
Faces others when speaking or being spoken to	Brags excessively about achievements, skills, appearance
Maintains eye contact during conversation	Verbally puts self down; self-deprecation
Initiates friendly contact with others	Speaks too loudly, abruptly, or in a dogmatic tone

Maintains comfortable space between self and others	Does not express views or opinions, especially when asked
Little hesitation in speech, speaks fluently	Assumes a submissive stance

7.   Self-esteem is the global evaluative dimension of the self.

8.   Self-concept involves domain-specific evaluations of the self.

9.   Scholastic competence, athletic competence, social acceptance, physical appearance, behavioral conduct, close friendship, romantic appeal, and job competence.

10.   Very important. It's the foundation of adolescent self-perception.

11.   Peer judgments gain greater importance among older children and adolescents.

12.   (a) identifying the causes of low esteem and the domains of competence important to the self, (b) emotional support and social approval, (c) achievement, and (d) coping.

IDENTITY
SECTION REVIEW

1.   It is Erikson's fifth developmental stage, which individuals experience during the adolescent years. Adolescents examine who they are, what they are all about, and where they are going in life.

2.   Erikson's term for the gap between childhood security and adult autonomy that adolescents experience as part of their identity exploration.

3.   It is a lengthy process that neither begins nor ends in adolescence.

4.   (a) identity diffusion, (b) identity foreclosure, (c) identity moratorium, and (d) identity achievement.

5.   Identity diffusion is Marcia's term for the state adolescents are in when they have not yet experienced a crisis or made any commitments. Identity foreclosure is Marcia's term for the state adolescents are in when they have made a commitment but have not experienced a crisis.

6.   Crisis is defined as a period of identity development during which the adolescent is choosing among meaningful alternatives. Commitment is a part of identity development in which adolescents show a personal investment in what they are going to do.

7.   Young adolescents must be confident that they have parental support, must have an established sense of industry, and must be able to adopt a self-reflective stance toward the future.

8.   "MAMA" cycles are moratorium-achievement-moratorium-achievement.

9.   Individuality consists of two dimensions: self-assertion, the ability to have and communicate a point of view; and separateness, the use of communication patterns to express how one is different from others.

10.   Connectedness consists of mutuality, sensitivity to and respect for others' views; and permeability, openness to others' views.

11.   Parents who explain, accept, and give empathy foster development.

12.   An enduring, basic aspect of the self that includes a sense of membership in an ethnic group and the attitudes and feelings related to that membership.

13.   Helm's model consists of four stages: (a) pre-encounter, (b) encounter, (c) immersion/emersion, and (d) internalization/commitment.

14.   In recent decades, differences that once existed have now begun to disappear as females close the gap.

15.   In Erikson's sixth stage, individuals experience during early adulthood. At this time, individuals face the task of forming intimate relationships with others.

16.   Intimate style — the individual forms and maintains one or more deep and long-lasting love relationships. Preintimate style — the individual shows mixed emotions about commitment. Stereotyped style — the individual has superficial relationships that tend to be dominated by friendship ties with same-sex rather than opposite-sex individuals. Pseudointimate style — the individual maintains a long-lasting sexual attachment with little depth. Isolated style — the individual withdraws from social encounters and has little or no attachment to same- or opposite-sex individuals.

17.   Emotional isolation is a type of loneliness that arises when a person lacks an intimate attachment relationship. Social isolation is a type of loneliness that occurs when a person lacks a sense of integrated involvement.

EMOTIONAL DEVELOPMENT
SECTION REVIEW

1.   Emotion is feeling or affect that involves physiological arousal, behavioral expression, and sometimes conscious experience.

2.   It is normal for adolescents to behave this way, and eventually they emerge from it.

3.   Puberty is associated with an increase in negative emotions.

4.   Awareness of emotional cycles will allow an adolescent to better control his/her ability to cope with those emotions.

5.   Being aware that the expression of emotions plays a major role in relationships; adaptively coping with negative emotions by using self-regulatory strategies that reduce the intensity and duration of such emotional states. Understanding that inner emotional states do not have to correspond to outer expressions. Being aware of one's emotional states without becoming overwhelmed by them.

PERSONALITY DEVELOPMENT
SECTION REVIEW

1.   Openness to experience, conscientiousness, extraversion, agreeableness, and neuroticism.

2.   Because the trait approach alone ignores environmental factors and places too much emphasis on stability and lack of change.

3.   An individual's behavioral style and characteristic way of responding.

4.   According to Thomas and Chess, they are: easy child, difficult child, and slow-to-warm-up child.

5.   Their framework focuses more on: positive affect and approach; negative affectivity; effortful control.

COGNITIVE CHALLENGE

1.   No answers provided. Individual activity

ADOLESCENCE IN RESEARCH

The hypothesis was that relationships with parents and peers contribute to adolescents' self-esteem. Coopersmith administered a self-esteem assessment to boys, and also interviewed boys and their mothers about their family relationships. The methods were assessment instrument and interviews. The study was correlational. The conclusions were that the following parenting attributes were associated with high self esteem: expression of affection, concern about the boys' problems, harmony in the home, participation in joint family activities, giving boys competent, organized help when needed, setting and abiding by clear and fair rules, and allowing boys freedom within prescribed limits. The research is important because it establishes parenting factors that may be related to self-esteem.

⊠ COMPREHENSIVE REVIEW

1	b	9.	a	17.	b	25.	d
2.	c	10.	d	18.	d	26.	b
3.	d	11.	c	19.	d	27.	a
4.	c	12.	a	20.	b	28.	d
5.	d	13.	a	21.	d	29.	c
6.	b	14.	c	22.	b	30.	b
7.	a	15.	a	23.	c	31.	d
8.	c	16.	a	24.	a	32.	c

⌘

Chapter 6   Gender

Learning Goals with Key Terms and Key People in Boldface

1.0   DESCRIBE THE BIOLOGICAL, SOCIAL, AND COGNITIVE INFLUENCES ON GENDER

A.   What is Gender?

    1.1   What is the nature of gender?

    1.2   What is meant by one's **gender role?**

B.   Biological, Social, and Cognitive Influences on Gender

    1.3   How strong are the biological influences on gender?

    1.4   What is the role of sexuality in adolescent gender development?

    1.5   How do Freud and Erikson's ideas promote the premise that anatomy is destiny?

    1.6   How do today's developmentalists believe that biological and environmental influences affect gender?

    1.7   What are some criticisms of the anatomy-is-destiny view?

    1.8   What is the evolutionary psychology view of gender development?

C.   Social Influences on Gender

    1.9   What impact do social roles have on gender development?

    1.10   What roles do gender hierarchy and sexual division of labor play in sex-differentiated behavior?

    1.11   According to the **social cognitive theory of gender**, what role do parents play in the development of gender-appropriate behavior?

    1.12   How do peers reward gender-appropriate behavior?

    1.13   How has the increase in the number of working mothers in recent years impacted adolescents?

    1.14   What evidence suggests that gender inequity still exists in education?

    1.15   What evidence is there that the classroom is biased against boys?

    1.16   How does television program to specifically male and females audiences, and what impact does it have?

    1.17   How are men portrayed on television?

D.   Cognitive Influences on Gender

    1.18   What was **Kohlberg's** theory of gender development?

    1.19   What is a schema?

    1.20   What does the **gender schema theory** state about individual gender development?

    1.21   According to the **cognitive development theory of gender,** when does gender typing occur?

2.0   GENDER STEREOTYPES, SIMILARITIES, AND DIFFERENCES

    A.   Gender Stereotyping

        2.1   What is the nature of **gender stereotypes** today?

        2.2   How common is stereotyping?

        2.3   How widespread is feminine and masculine stereotyping?

        2.4   What is **sexism?**

    B.   Gender Similarities and Differences

        2.5   What are the physical and biological differences that characterize male and female comparisons?

        2.6   Have male/female differences been exaggerated?

        2.7   How is modern **sexism** different from that in the past?

        2.8   What distinguishes **rapport talk** from **report talk?**

    C.   Gender Controversy

        2.9   What is the current nature of the controversy over the differences between males and females?

    D.   Gender in Context

        2.10   Why is context an important factor in understanding gender?

3.0   GENDER-ROLE CLASSIFICATION

    A.   Masculinity, Femininity, and Androgyny

        3.1   According to past tradition, what were the characteristics of a well-adjusted male?

        3.2   According to past tradition, what were the characteristics of a well-adjusted female?

        3.3   When did alternatives to traditional masculinity and femininity begin to be explored?

        3.4   What is meant by **androgyny?**

        3.5   How do androgynous individuals compare with either masculine or feminine individuals?

    B. Context, Culture, and Gender Roles

        3.6   Do gender roles vary around the world?

        3.7   How do males and females differ on how they show anger?

    C.   Androgyny and Education

        3.8   Should **androgyny** be taught to students?

        3.9   What is meant by the "boy code?"

    D.   Gender-Role Transcendence

        3.10   What do critics of androgyny suggest as an alternative?

        3.11   What are some concerns regarding teaching children and adolescents to depart from socially approved behavior patterns?

4.0   SUMMARIZE DEVELOPMENTAL CHANGES AND JUNCTURES

    A.   Early Adolescence and Gender Intensification

        4.1   What is the **gender intensification hypothesis?**

        4.2   Do all researchers consider the **gender intensification hypothesis** valid?

    B.   Is Early Adolescence a Critical Juncture for Females?

        4.3   Is early adolescence a critical juncture for females?

        4.4   What is Gillian's belief about the critical juncture for adolescent females?

        4.5   What are some criticisms about Gillian's beliefs about male and female differences in intimacy and connectedness?

Exercises

KEY TERMS COMPLETION EXERCISE

Each key term is presented in the form of an incomplete sentence. Complete each sentence by either defining the term or giving an example. Compare your definitions with those given at the end of the study guide chapter.

1. Simply put, **gender** refers to

    _____

    _____

2. **Gender role** refers to one's

    _____

    _____

3. **Cognitive developmental theory of gender** states

    _____

    _____

4. **Social cognitive theory of gender** states

    _____

    _____

5. A good example of a **schema** is

    _____

    _____

6. A **gender schema** is a

    _____

    _____

7. **Gender schema theory** suggests that

    _____

    _____

8.   **Gender stereotypes** can be seen in

_____

_____

9.   **Sexism** is seen in situations where

_____

_____

10.   Jill uses **rapport talk** when she is

_____

_____

11.   Bart uses **report talk** because

_____

_____

12.   A sure sign of **androgyny** is when

_____

_____

13.   **Gender-role transcendence** is a belief that

_____

_____

14.   The **gender intensification hypothesis** states that

_____

_____

KEY PEOPLE IN THE STUDY OF ADOLESCENCE

Match the person with the concept of adolescent development with which they are associated.

_____   1. Sigmund Freud   A. An evolutionary psychologist
_____   2. Erik Erikson   B. Proposed the cognitive developmental theory of gender
_____   3. Alice Eagly   C. Developed an assessment instrument for androgyny
_____   4. Eleanor Maccoby   D. Finds that males and females have different styles of "talk"
_____   5. Myra Sadker and   E. Worked with Eleanor Maccoby and concluded that males have better

		David Sadker		math and visuospatial abilities
_____	6.	Lawrence Kohlberg	F.	Proposes that women have a different "voice"
_____	7.	Carol Jacklin	G.	Argued that male and female psychological differences are related to genital structure
_____	8.	Janet Shibley Hyde	H.	Argued that gender and sexual behavior are unlearned and instinctual
_____	9.	Deborah Tannen	I.	Proponent of the male role-strain perspective
_____	10.	David Buss	J.	Studied gender discrimination in schools
_____	11.	Sandra Bem	K.	Says that psychological sex differences arise from social roles of men and women
_____	12.	Joseph Pleck	L.	Argues that cognitive differences between females and males have been exaggerated
_____	13.	Carol Gilligan	M.	Proposes that differences in male and female verbal ability have now virtually disappeared

BIOLOGICAL, SOCIAL, AND COGNITIVE INFLUENCES ON GENDER SECTION REVIEW

1.   What is gender?

_____

_____

2.   What is meant by one's gender role?

_____

_____

3.   How strong are biological influences on gender?

_____

_____

4.   Compare Freud's and Erikson's theories related to gender, and explain how they promote the notion that anatomy is destiny.

_____

_____

5.   To what extent do hormones play a role in the sexual activities of boys and girls?

_____

_____

6.   What is the evolutionary view of gender development?

_____

_____

7.   What roles do gender hierarchy and sexual division of labor play in sex-differentiated behavior?

_____

_____

8.   According to the social cognitive theory of gender, what role do parents play in the development of gender-appropriate behavior?

_____

_____

9.   How does television programming appeal specifically to male and female audiences, and what impact does it have?

_____

_____

10.   How are men typically portrayed on television?

_____

_____

11.   What was Kohlberg's theory of gender development?

_____

_____

12.   What is a schema?

_____

_____

13.   What does gender schema theory state about individual gender development?

_____

_____

GENDER STEREOTYPES, SIMILARITIES, AND DIFFERENCES
SECTION REVIEW

1.   What is the nature of gender stereotypes today?

_____

_____

2.   How common is gender stereotyping?

_____

_____

3.   How widespread is feminine and masculine stereotyping?

_____

_____

4.   What is sexism?

_____

_____

5.   Differentiate between "old fashioned" and "modern" sexism.

_____

_____

6.   Using Tannen's model, distinguish between rapport talk and report talk.

_____

_____

7.   What is David Buss's hypothesis regarding how gender differences develop?

_____

_____

8.   Why is context an important factor in understanding gender?

_____

_____

GENDER-ROLE CLASSIFICATION
SECTION REVIEW

1.   Do gender roles vary around the world?

_____

_____

2.   When did alternatives to traditional masculinity and femininity begin to develop?

_____

_____

3.   How do androgynous individuals compare with either masculine or feminine individuals?

_____

_____

4.   What are some concerns associated with teaching children and adolescents to depart from socially approved behavior patterns?

_____

_____

SUMMARIZE DEVELOPMENTAL CHANGES AND JUNCTURES
SECTION REVIEW

1.   What is the gender intensification hypothesis?

_____

_____

2.   Is early adolescence a critical juncture for females?

_____

_____

3.   What is Gillian's belief about the critical juncture for adolescent females?

_____

_____

4.   What are some criticisms of Gillian's beliefs and theories?

_____

_____

EXPLORATIONS IN ADOLESCENCE DEVELOPMENT

How widespread is gender stereotyping today? Generate two lists; one for males and one for females, of all of the current gender stereotypes you can think of.

_____

_____

_____

COGNITIVE CHALLENGE

1.   Make up a list of words that you associated with masculinity and femininity. Identify those words that have negative connotations for males and/or females. Then replace them with words that have more positive connotations.

_____

_____

2.   Suppose you have children: How will you attempt to raise them in terms of gender roles? Will you try to raise gender-neutral children? Or will you encourage more traditional gender distinctions?

_____

_____

3.   What factors during your childhood led you to develop your gender role?

_____

_____

ADOLESCENCE IN RESEARCH

Describe the attitudes towards masculinity as given by Pleck and colleagues.

⊠ COMPREHENSIVE REVIEW
---

1. _____ refers to a set of expectations about sex-appropriate behavior.
   a. Stereotype
   b. Gender role
   c. Gender intensification
   d. Sexism

2. According to Udry, which of the following has the greatest impact on sexual activity for adolescent girls?
   a. levels of the hormone estrogen
   b. levels of the hormone androgen
   c. the type of friends they affiliate with
   d. the SES of their family

3. According to Freud and Erikson, this is a largest single factor regarding gender behavior of adolescents.
   a. temperament
   b. religion
   c. attitudes of the parents
   d. genitals they are born with

4. Erik Erikson and Sigmund Freud believed that the differences between males and females
   a. were the result of females' ability and males' inability to articulate their feelings.
   b. resulted from prenatal hormonal influences.
   c. resulted from anatomical differences.
   d. were gender stereotypes rather than gender differences.

5. An adolescent mother can reduce the sex-role stereotypes of her children by
   a. dressing them all the same.
   b. withholding praise for their physical appearance.
   c. holding a job outside the home.
   d. divorcing their father.

6. According to contemporary views of evolutionary psychology, which of the following is NOT an evolved disposition of men?
   a. violence
   b. competition
   c. risk taking
   d. compassion

7. On the playground, girls teach girls and boys teach boys about their gender behaviors. This is known as
   a. gender socialization.
   b. gender intensification.
   c. peer socialization.
   d. peer generalization.

8.   DeZolt and Hull (2001) noted that in some ways boys might not receive a fair education. Which is NOT one of their listed concerns?
    a.   Boys are more likely than girls to be identified as having learning problems.
    b.   Boys are more likely than girls to be criticized.
    c.   School personnel tend to stereotype boys' behavior as problematic.
    d.   A large majority of teachers are males who inherently distrust boys, based on past experiences.

9.   Sadker and Sadker (1994) noted that in some ways both boys and girls might not receive a fair education. Which is NOT one of their listed concerns?
    a.   Girls' learning problems are not identified as often as boys' learning problems.
    b.   Boys are given the lion's share of attention in school.
    c.   Pressure to achieve is more likely to be heaped on boys than on girls.
    d.   More girls than boys come from families living in poverty.

10.   School curriculum planners decide in which grades algebra, history, and science are to be taught. These decisions are based mainly upon the
    a.   cognitive developmental norms for children.
    b.   social-emotional developmental norms for children.
    c.   developmental norms for males.
    d.   developmental norms for females.

11.   Adolescent females watching television are likely to find
    a.   fewer role models than their brothers will.
    b.   accurate representations of women's roles.
    c.   important lessons on managing relationships.
    d.   little to identify with in terms of sexual intimacy.

12.   A boy recognizes that he is a male and then starts doing "male" things. This description is consistent with the _____ theory of gender.
    a.   socialization
    b.   genderization
    c.   cognitive-developmental
    d.   intensification

13.   Television directed at adolescents might be the most extreme in its portrayal of
    a.   violence.
    b.   sexual behavior.
    c.   teenage girls.
    d.   teenage boys.

14.   According to Kohlberg, the main changes in gender development occur
    a.   in infancy.
    b.   in adolescence.
    c.   in childhood.
    d.   as young adults.

15.   Gender schema theory predicts that adolescents are drawn to sources of information that enable them to
        a.   conform to stereotypes.
        b.   learn about sexuality.
        c.   learn about relationships.
        d.   think idealistically.

16.   Which of the following is NOT part of Pollack's "boy code"?
        a.   Boys are taught to express their anxieties.
        b.   Boys should show little if any emotion.
        c.   Bottling emotions is a way to regulate aggression.
        d.   Boys adopt a masculine role in adolescence.

17.   Pat gets embarrassed when making a mistake in public and experiences episodes of jealousy and passion. What gender is Pat likely to be?
        a.   male
        b.   female
        c.   equally likely to be male or female
        d.   There is no research on which to base an answer.

18.   According to the Bem's Sex-Role Inventory, an adolescent is androgynous if she scores
        a.   high on masculinity and high on femininity.
        b.   high on masculinity and low on femininity.
        c.   low on femininity and low on masculinity.
        d.   half-way between masculinity and femininity.

19.   The concept of _____ involves the notion that an individual's competence should not be conceptualized along the lines of gender orientation, but rather, the emphasis should be on the individual.
        a.   gender-neutrality
        b.   humanism
        c.   gender-role transcendence
        d.   critical feminism

20.   The gender intensification hypothesis indicates that behavioral differences between males and females become greater during adolescence as a result of
        a.   hormones.
        b.   pressures to conform to stereotypes.
        c.   television commercials.
        d.   the development of a new schema.

21.   The concept of _____ refers to the fact that the amount, timing, and intensity of gender socialization are different for girls and boys.
        a.   gender intensification
        b.   asymmetric gender socialization
        c.   gender role transcendence
        d.   sex difference

22. According to Tannen, which of the following is NOT an example of "report talk"?
    a. joking
    b. storytelling
    c. lecturing
    d. relationship oriented conversation

23. According to Tannen, which of the following is an example of "rapport talk"?
    a. joking
    b. story telling
    c. lecturing
    d. relationship oriented conversation

24. Carol Gilligan has suggested that girls
    a. are better than boys.
    b. are equal to boys.
    c. are different than boys.
    d. are none of the above.

25. According to many studies, adolescent girls are likely to suffer from declines in
    a. intelligence.
    b. self-esteem.
    c. verbal fluency.
    d. social skills.

ADOLESCENCE IN RESEARCH

Concerning Pleck and colleagues' 1994 National Survey of Adolescent Males, state the hypothesis, the research methods (if known), the research conclusions, and the implications and applications for adolescent development.

_____

_____

ADOLESCENCE ON THE SCREEN

■   *Boys Don't Cry* Hilary Swank won an academy award for her portrayal of the true story of a boy with gender identity disorder who was murdered when his biological sex was revealed.

■   *The Crying Game* A shocking ending reveals that one of the main characters is a transsexual.

■   *Mr. and Mrs. Bridges* Joanne Woodward and Paul Newman as an upper-class couple in the American Midwest of the 1940s who embody the male and female stereotypical roles of the time.

■   *Ma Vie En Rose (My Life in Pink)* A French movie (with English subtitles) about a boy with gender identity disorder who dresses and lives as a girl.

■   *Antonia's Line* A longitudinal portrayal of the transformation from adolescence to womanhood and the life decisions involved.

- *The Body Beautiful* This film is a generative example of how our various bodily and social identities are built and given meaning concurrently.

- *Daughters of the Dust* Life and development on a barrier island amongst the Gullah Subculture. An isolated African-American culture off the coast of South Carolina.

ADOLESCENCE IN BOOKS

- *A New Psychology of Men*, by Ronald Levant and William Pollack (Basic Books, 1995), is a collection of essays on men's issues and male gender roles.

- *As Nature Made Him*, by John Colapinto (HarperCollins: NY, 2000), is the true story of one of identical twins whose penis was accidentally severed during circumcision and who was given female hormones and raised as a girl until his parents revealed the accident. He then had penile reconstructive surgery and hormone treatments and resumed life as a man.

- *Stiffed: The Betrayal of the American Man*, by Susan Faludi (William Morrow: NY, 1999), examines the problems of men in modern life, emphasizing the stress and strain of male sex roles.

- *You Just Don't Understand*, by Deborah Tannen (Ballantine: NY, 1990), explores the differences in male and female communication styles.

Answer Key

KEY TERMS

1. **gender** The sociocultural dimension of being male or female.

2. **gender role** A set of expectations that prescribes how females and males should think, act, and feel.

3. **social cognitive theory of gender** This theory emphasizes that children's and adolescents' gender development occurs through observation and imitation of gender behavior, and through rewards and punishments they experience for gender-appropriate and -inappropriate behavior.

4. **cognitive developmental theory of gender** In this view, children's gender-typing occurs after they have developed a concept of gender. Once they begin to consistently conceive of themselves as male or female, children often organize their world on the basis of gender.

5. **schema** A cognitive structure of network of associations that organizes and guides an individual's perception.

6. **gender schema** A cognitive structure that organizes the world in terms of male and female.

7. **gender schema theory** According to this theory, an individual's attention and behavior are guided by an internal motivation to conform to gender-based sociocultural standards and stereotypes.

8. **gender stereotypes** Broad categories that reflect our impressions and beliefs about females and males.

9. **sexism** Prejudice and discrimination against an individual because of his or her sex.

10. **rapport talk** Is the language of conversation and a way of establishing connections and negotiating relationships.

11. **report talk** Is talk that gives information. Public speaking would be an example.

12. **androgyny** The presence of a high degree of desirable feminine and masculine characteristics in the same individual.

13. **gender-role transcendence** The belief that, when an individual's competence is at issue, it should be conceptualized not on the basis of masculinity, femininity, or androgyny but, rather, on a person basis.

14. **gender intensification hypothesis** This hypothesis states that psychological and behavioral differences between boys and girls become greater during early adolescence because of increased socialization pressures to conform to masculine and feminine gender roles.

KEY PEOPLE IN THE STUDY OF ADOLESCENCE

1.	H	5.	J	9.	D	13.	F
2.	G	6.	B	10.	A		
3.	K	7.	E	11.	C		
4.	M	8.	L	12.	I		

BIOLOGICAL, SOCIAL, AND COGNITIVE INFLUENCES ON GENDER SECTION REVIEW

1. Gender refers to the psychological and sociocultural dimensions of being male or female.

2. Gender role is a set of expectations that prescribes how females or males should think, act, and feel.

3. Hormones and pubertal change contribute to an increased incorporation of sexuality in the gender attitudes and behavior of adolescents.

4. Both felt that genitals were the primary source of influence on gender behavior.

5. Androgen levels are related to sexual activity in boys, but girls were more likely to be influenced by the kinds of friends they hung out with.

6. Evolutionary psychologists argue that men and women faced different evolutionary pressures in primeval environments, and adapted to these.

7. From the perspective of social influences, gender hierarchy and sexual division of labor are important causes of sex-differentiated behavior.

8. Emphasizes that childrens' and adolescents' gender development occurs through observation and imitation of gender behavior, and through rewards and punishments they experience for gender-appropriate and -inappropriate behavior.

9. Television targets teens, in particular teenage girls in its depiction of females on TV.

10. Males are more often seen in work roles, cars, or in sports. Females get much less TV time and are more likely to be seen in the home.

11. Children's gender typing occurs after they have developed a concept of gender. Once they begin to consistently conceive of themselves as male or female, children often organize their world on the basis of gender.

12. A schema is a cognitive structure, a network of associations that organizes and guides an individual's perceptions.

13. Gender Schema Theory state that an individual's attention and behavior are guided by an internal motivation to conform to gender-based sociocultural standards and stereotypes.

GENDER STEREOTYPES, SIMILARITIES, AND DIFFERENCES
SECTION REVIEW

1. These are broad categories that reflect our impressions and beliefs about females and males.

2. They are so general that they are often ambiguous.

3. According to college students in 30 countries, it is very common.

4. Sexism is prejudice and discrimination against an individual because of her or his sex.

5. Old-fashioned is characterized by endorsement of traditional gender roles, differential treatment for men and women with the assumption that women are less competent then men. Modern sexism is characterized by the denial that there is still discrimination and lack of support for policies designed to help women.

6. Rapport talk is the language of conversation and a way of establishing connections and negotiating relationships. Report talk is talk that gives information (e.g., public speaking).

7. Buss argues that men and women differ psychologically in those domains in which they have faced different adaptive problems across their evolutionary history.

8. Context determines what males and females are likely to do in particular circumstances when they encounter specific problems.

GENDER-ROLE CLASSIFICATION
SECTION REVIEW

1. Yes. Many cultures have quite different views regarding the roles of men and women.

2. Alternatives were introduced in the 1960s and 1970s.

3. Androgynous individuals are described as more flexible and more mentally healthy.

4. Ethical concerns are raised when the program involves teaching children and adolescents to depart from socially approved behavior patterns.

SUMMARIZE DEVELOPMENTAL CHANGES AND JUNCTURES
SECTION REVIEW

1. This states that psychological and behavioral differences between boys and girls become greater during early adolescence because of increased socialization pressures to conform to traditional masculine and feminine gender roles.

2. Yes. Much is learned from the age of 6 through 18.

3. Gilligan suggests that the critical juncture for the development of little girls is around 11–12 years of age.

4. Critics argue that Gilligan overemphasized differences in gender.

EXPLORATIONS IN ADOLESCENCE DEVELOPMENT

No answers provided. Individual activity.

COGNITIVE CHALLENGE

1. No answers provided. Individual activity.
2. No answers provided. Individual activity.
3. No answers provided. Individual activity.

ADOLESCENCE IN RESEARCH

Pleck and colleagues hypothesized that problem behaviors in adolescent males are associated with their attitudes toward masculinity. They also examined the risk and protective influences for problem behaviors. They studied 1,680 15- to 19-year-old males. Their findings supported their hypothesis. Males who had traditional beliefs about masculinity were more likely to have difficulty in school, use drugs and alcohol, be sexually active, and participate in delinquent activities. Risk factors for problem behaviors included low parental education, being the son of a teenage mother, living in a mother-headed household or having no nonmaterial family member in the home, lenient family rules, and infrequent church attendance. Protective factors included strict family rules and frequent church attendance.

⊠ COMPREHENSIVE REVIEW

1.	b	8.	c	15.	a	22.	d
2.	c	9.	d	16.	b	23.	d
3.	d	10.	a	17.	c	24.	c
4.	c	11.	a	18.	a	25.	b
5.	c	12.	c	19.	a		
6.	d	13.	c	20.	b		
7.	c	14.	c	21.	a		

⌘

Chapter 7   Sexuality

Learning Goals with Key Terms and Key People in Boldface

1.0 **DISCUSS SEXUALITY AS A NORMAL ASPECT OF ADOLESCENCE AND SUMMARIZE THE NATURE OF ADOLESCENT SEXUAL ATTITUDES AND BEHAVIOR**

    A. **A Normal Aspect of Development**

        1.1   Do cultures differ in how they view adolescent sexuality?

        1.2   What other chapters in the text serve as a backdrop for understanding adolescent sexuality?

        1.3   What is the nature of adolescent sexuality in today's culture?

        1.4   Is there more tension related to sexuality between adolescents and parents in the United States than in other cultures?

        1.5   What is involved in forming a sexual identity?

        1.6   What is an adolescent's sexual preference?

        1.7   Who is most likely to respond to a sex survey?

        1.8   Why is it difficult to obtain valid information about adolescent sexuality?

    B. **Sexual Attitudes and Behaviors**

        1.9   What is the progression of sexual behaviors?

        1.10   Are some adolescents more vulnerable to irresponsible sexual behavior than others?

        1.11   Have the number of females engaging in intercourse increased more rapidly than that of males?

        1.12   Are there ethnic and racial differences in sexual activity?

        1.13   What is the current profile of sexual activity of adolescents?

        1.14   What are the common male and female adolescent **sexual scripts?**

        1.15   What are some of the risks faced by adolescents who are sexually active?

        1.16   What are specific risk factors for sexual problems in adolescence?

        1.17   What is the attitude today about sexual orientation?

        1.18   What do we know about adolescents' same-sex attractions?

        1.19   What is the continuum of sexual orientation?

        1.20   What conclusions can be reached about adolescents who disclose their gay or lesbian identity?

        1.21   What is meant by homophobia?

        1.22   What is a harmful aspect of the stigmatization of homosexuality?

        1.23   What is the nature of sexual self-stimulation?

        1.24   How many adolescents are using contraceptives?

        1.25   Which adolescents are least likely to use contraceptives?

2.0   DESCRIBE THE MAIN SEXUAL PROBLEMS THAT CAN EMERGE IN ADOLESCENCE

    A.   Adolescent Pregnancy

        2.1   How many American adolescents become pregnant each year?

        2.2   How many adolescent females have children before their eighteenth birthday?

        2.3   Is adolescent pregnancy increasing or decreasing?

        2.4   What cultural changes have taken place in the last forty years regarding adolescent sexuality and pregnancy?

        2.5   What are the health risks for mother and offspring?

        2.6   How does adolescent pregnancy affect a mother's school and work opportunities?

        2.7   How does the personal fable impact on pregnancy prevention efforts?

        2.8   What infant risks are associated with being born to an adolescent mother?

        2.9   What kind of mothers do adolescents make?

        2.10   What is the nature of adolescent fatherhood?

        2.11   What are Congers four recommendations for reducing adolescent pregnancy?

        2.12   What programs have worked to reduce adolescent pregnancy?

        2.13   What is the Teen Outreach Program?

    B.   Sexually Transmitted Infections

        2.14   What are **sexually transmitted infections** (STIs)?

        2.15   How are STIs contracted?

        2.16   What is **AIDS?**

        2.17   What is the rate of AIDS in adolescence?

        2.18   How does the long incubation period affect adolescents who may have been infected with the AIDS virus as teenagers?

        2.19   Where is the region of most concern regarding the spread of HIV/AIDS?

        2.20   How is AIDS transmitted?

        2.21   How is AIDS prevented?

        2.22   What is **genital herpes?**

        2.23   What are genital warts?

        2.24   What is **gonorrhea?**

        2.25   What is **syphilis?**

        2.26   What is **chlamydia?**

    C.   Forcible Sexual Behavior and Sexual Harassment

        2.27   What is the nature and incidence of **rape?**

        2.28   What is **date, or acquaintance, rape?**

        2.29   Who are the victims of acquaintance rape?

        2.30   What is sexual harassment?

        2.31   How prevalent is adolescent sexual harassment?

        2.32   What is **quid pro quo sexual harassment?**

        2.33   What is the nature of **hostile environment sexual harassment?**

3.0   CHARACTERIZE THE SEXUAL LITERACY OF ADOLESCENTS AND SEX EDUCATION

    A.   Sexual Literacy

        3.1   How much do American adolescents and adults know about sex?

    B.   Sources of Sex Information

        3.2   What is the nature or source of most sex information?

        3.3   What are the sources of sex information?

C.   **Sex Education in the Schools**

    3.4   What is the incidence and nature of sex education in the schools?

    3.5   How is sex education changing?

    3.6   What are some criticisms of school-linked sex education?

4.0   EXPLAIN WHAT IS NEEDED FOR WELL-BEING AND SOCIAL POLICY IN ADOLESCENT SEXUALITY

A.   **Sexual Well-Being and Development Transitions**

    3.7   What are the five issues related to adolescent sexuality that need examination?

    3.8   What might be considered some healthy sexual pathways?

B.   **Social Policy and Adolescent Sexuality**

    3.9   What social policy initiatives do we need concerning sex education?

    3.10   What must be done to improve current policies?

Exercises

KEY TERMS COMPLETION EXERCISE

Each key term is presented in the form of an incomplete sentence. Complete each sentence by either defining the term or giving an example. Compare your definitions with those given at the end of the study guide chapter.

1.   A **sexual script** is

    _____

    _____

2.   James is **bisexual,** which means he

    _____

    _____

3.   People must learn about **sexually transmitted infections (STIs)** because

    _____

    _____

4.   The symptoms of **gonorrhea** are

    _____

    _____

5.   The symptoms of **syphilis** are

    _____

    _____

6.　The symptoms of **chlamydia** are

_____

_____

7.　The symptoms of **genital herpes** are

_____

_____

8.　The symptoms of **genital warts** are

_____

_____

9.　**AIDS** is an acronym standing for

_____

_____

10.　The description of **rape** is

_____

_____

11.　**Date, or acquaintance, rape** occurs when

_____

_____

12.　**Quid pro quo sexual harassment** occurs when

_____

_____

13.　**Hostile environment sexual harassment** occurs when

_____

_____

KEY PEOPLE IN THE STUDY OF ADOLESCENCE

Match the person with the concept of adolescent development with which they are associated.

_____　1.　Shirley Feldman　　　A.　Director of Kinsey Institute for Sex, Gender, and Reproduction
_____　2.　Alfred Kinsey　　　　B.　Views sexuality as a normal aspect of adolescent development
_____　3.　Richard Savin-Williams　C.　Studies developmental issues in adolescent sexuality

_____ 4. Simon LeVay   D. Early and famous sex researcher
_____ 5. P. Lindsay Chase-Lansdale   E. Studied the brains of gay men for clues to causes of homosexuality
_____ 6. June Reinisch   F. Researched the pattern of gay and lesbian adolescents' disclosure of sexual orientation

_____ 7. Jeanne Brooks-Gunn   G. Studies contraceptive patterns in American adolescents and adolescents in foreign countries

"DR. DETAIL'S" MATCHING EXERCISE

Match the STI with the associated features.

_____ 1. Syphilis   A. Colloquially called "the drip" or "clap"
_____ 2. Chlamydia   B. Caused by a large family of viruses with many different strains
_____ 3. Genital herpes   C. Destroys the body's immune system
_____ 4. Gonorrhea   D. Is caused by the bacterium *Treponema pallidum*
_____ 5. AIDS   E. Common sexually transmitted infection that infects genital organs of both sexes

_____ 6. Genital Warts   F. Is the most common of all sexually transmitted diseases in the U.S

EXPLORING ADOLESCENT SEXUALITY
SECTION REVIEW

1. Do cultures differ in how they view adolescent sexuality?

_____

_____

2. What other chapters in the text serve as a backdrop for understanding adolescent sexuality?

Chapter	Concept
Biological Differences	
Cognitive Differences	
Families	
Peers	
Schools	
Culture	
The Self and Identity	
Gender	

3.   What is the nature of adolescent sexuality in today's culture?

_____

_____

4.   What is involved in forming a sexual identity?

_____

_____

5.   Who is most likely to respond to a sex survey?

_____

_____

6.   What is the typical progression of sexual behaviors?

_____

_____

7.   Have the number of females engaging is intercourse increased more rapidly than males?

_____

_____

8.   Are there ethnic and racial differences in sexual activity?

_____

_____

9.   What is the current profile of sexual activity of adolescents?

_____

_____

10. What are the common male and female adolescent sexual scripts?

_____

_____

11. What are some of the risk factors faced by adolescents who are sexually active?

_____

_____

12.　　What is the attitude today about sexual orientation?

_____

_____

13.　　What is meant by homophobia?

_____

_____

14.　　What is a harmful aspect of the stigmatization of homosexuality?

_____

_____

15.　　What five conclusions did Savin-Williams (1998, 2000) make about adolescents who disclose their gay or lesbian identity?

_____

_____

16.　　What is the nature of sexual self-stimulation?

_____

_____

17.　　Which adolescents are least likely to use contraceptives?

_____

_____

KEY PEOPLE IN SECTION (describe the contributions of this individual to the study and understanding of adolescence).

Alfred Kinsey—

_____

_____

Simon LeVay—

_____

_____

ADOLESCENT SEXUAL PROBLEMS
SECTION REVIEW

1.　How many adolescent births are unintended?

_____

_____

2.　What cultural changes have taken place in the last forty years regarding adolescent sexuality and pregnancy?

_____

_____

3.　What are the health risks for mother and child of adolescent pregnancy?

_____

_____

4.　How does adolescent pregnancy affect a mother's school and work opportunities?

_____

_____

5.　How does the *personal fable* affect pregnancy prevention efforts?

_____

_____

6.　What infant risks are associated with teenage pregnancy?

_____

_____

7.　What is the nature of adolescent fatherhood?

_____

_____

8.　What are Conger's four recommendations for reducing adolescent pregnancy?

_____

_____

9.   What is the Teen Outreach Program?

_____

_____

10.   What are sexually transmitted infections?

_____

_____

11.   What is AIDS?

_____

_____

12.   Where is the region of most concern regarding the spread of HIV/AIDS?

_____

_____

13.   How is AIDS transmitted?

_____

_____

14.   How is AIDS prevented?

_____

_____

15.   What is the nature and incidence of rape?

_____

_____

16.   What is acquaintance rape?

_____

_____

17.   What is sexual harassment?

_____

_____

18.   What is quid pro quo sexual harassment?

_____

_____

19.   What is the nature of hostile environment sexual harassment?

_____

_____

KEY PEOPLE IN SECTION (describe the contributions of this individual to the study and understanding of adolescence).

John Conger—

_____

_____

SEXUAL LITERACY AND SEX EDUCATION
SECTION REVIEW

1.   How much do American adolescents and adults know about sex?

_____

_____

2.   What are the sources of most sex information?

_____

_____

3.   Why do some experts believe that school-linked sex education tied to community health centers is a promising strategy?

_____

_____

4.   What are some criticisms of school-linked sex education?

_____

_____

KEY PEOPLE IN SECTION (describe the contributions of this individual to the study and understanding of adolescence).

June Reinisch—

_____

_____

SEXUAL WELL-BEING, SOCIAL POLICY, AND ADOLESCENTS SECTION REVIEW

1.   What are the five issues related to adolescent sexuality that need examination?

_____

_____

2.   What might be considered some healthy sexual pathways?

_____

_____

3.   What initiatives are needed to reduce adolescent pregnancy?

_____

_____

4.   What did the Carnegie Foundation report emphasize?

_____

_____

KEY PEOPLE IN SECTION (describe the contributions of this individual to the study and understanding of adolescence).

Jeanne Brooks-Gunn and Roberta Paikoff—

_____

_____

COGNITIVE CHALLENGE

1.   Caroline contracted genital herpes from an old boyfriend. When she started dating Charles, she told him she had the herpes infection and he broke up with her. Now she is dating Jeff and she is afraid to tell him about the herpes because she thinks he will also break up with her. She thought maybe she should just tell him to use a condom so she won't get pregnant, and then she won't need to mention the herpes. What do you think Caroline should do?

_____

_____

2.   Based upon how you learned about sexuality, how do you expect to teach your children about sex? How do you want the schools to be involved in sex education for your children? Who other than parents and schools do you think should be involved in sex education?

_____

_____

ADOLESCENCE IN RESEARCH

Buzwell and Rosenthal (1996) conducted an investigation of an adolescent's sexual identity; state the hypothesis, the research methods (if known), the research conclusions, and the implications and applications for adolescent development.

_____

_____

☒ COMPREHENSIVE REVIEW

1.   Sexual behaviors usually progress in the following order:
      a.   kissing, oral sex, necking.
      b.   petting, necking, kissing.
      c.   intercourse, sexual adventure, oral sex.
      d.   necking, petting, intercourse.

2.   A _____ is a pattern involving stereotyped role prescriptions for how individuals should behave sexually.
      a.   sexual bias
      b.   sexual schema
      c.   sexual role
      d.   sexual script

3.   Irresponsible sexual behavior such as unprotected intercourse is probably a reflection of
      a.   cognitive immaturity.
      b.   hostility against parental limits.
      c.   vulnerability.
      d.   parental stress or divorce.

4.   An individual sexually attracted to both females and males is
      a.   bisexual.
      b.   homosexual.
      c.   heterosexual.
      d.   transsexual.

5.   The most frequent sexual outlet for an adolescent is
      a.   oral sex.
      b.   sexual fantasy.

    c.   masturbation.
    d.   sexual intercourse.

6.   As a drugstore clerk, you are not at all surprised to find that condom sales are made most often to
    a.   older adolescents.
    b.   female adolescents.
    c.   younger adolescents.
    d.   sexually inactive adolescents.

7.   Compared to those who wait to have children until they are in their mid- to late twenties, adolescent parents
    a.   have a better chance of staying married.
    b.   are less lonely.
    c.   have fewer children throughout their adult lives.
    d.   have lower incomes.

8.   Infants born to adolescent mothers are more likely to
    a.   be overweight.
    b.   have an average survival rate.
    c.   bond with their mothers.
    d.   have low birth weights.

9.   Sexually transmitted infections are defined as those contracted through
    a.   vaginal intercourse.
    b.   vaginal intercourse and oral-genital contact.
    c.   oral-genital and anal-genital contact.
    d.   oral-genital and anal-genital contact and vaginal intercourse.

10.   The most fatal sexually transmitted infection caused by a bacterium is
    a.   syphilis.
    b.   herpes.
    c.   AIDS.
    d.   gonorrhea.

11.   The most common sexually transmitted disease among adolescents is
    a.   genital warts.
    b.   herpes.
    c.   syphilis.
    d.   gonorrhea.

12.   If you come into intimate sexual contact with an infected person, your risk of contracting the disease is greatest for
    a.   gonorrhea.
    b.   syphilis.
    c.   herpes.
    d.   AIDS.

13.   According to comparative studies, the rate of AIDS among adolescents is
    a.   higher than adult rates.
    b.   about the same as adult rates.

c.   lower than adult rates.

d.   not directly compared with adult rates.

14.   Which of the following STIs is NOT a virus?

a.   genital warts

b.   HIV

c.   syphilis

d.   genital herpes

15.   _____ are usually the main source of an adolescent's sexual information.

a.   Parents

b.   Schools

c.   Peers

d.   Literature

16.   Which of the following statements concerning sex education in the schools is accurate?

a.   The majority of adults in the United States do not approve of sex education in the schools.

b.   Sex education programs are more likely to appear in high schools and junior high schools than elementary schools.

c.   The emphasis in sex education classes is on contraception and variations in sexual behavior.

d.   Most sex education programs consist of full-semester courses on human sexuality.

17.   Belinda's boyfriend used a variety of psychological and physical ploys to coerce her into having sex, even though she had said no to him. Her boyfriend's behavior is referred to as _____ rape.

a.   power

b.   sexual

c.   controlling

d.   acquaintance

18.   The factor that is most important in facilitating the recovery from rape is

a.   physical health.

b.   retaliation against the rapist.

c.   resumption of consensual sexual relations.

d.   social support.

19.   Which of the following is most indicative of sex education today in the U.S.?

a.   discussion about abstinence

b.   discussion about abortion

c.   discussion about birth control

d.   discussion about sexual orientation

20.   The purpose of sex education programs in such countries as Holland and Sweden is to _____ the experience of adolescent sexuality.

a.   promote

b.   discourage

c.   demystify

d.   simplify

ADOLESCENCE ON THE SCREEN

- *Chasing Amy* A young man is attracted to a girl who tells him that she is a lesbian. Actually, she has had a wild heterosexual past and is manipulating the boy's attraction for her.

- *Taxi Driver* A New York City taxi driver tries to save a child prostitute.

- *The Summer of '42* A young boy has his first sexual experience with a kind, older woman on whom he has a crush.

- *The Middle School Chronicles* [HBO] Startling view of sexuality and sex from very young children.

- *The Lost Kids of Rockdale County* [PBS Frontline] Chilling details regarding an epidemic of syphilis that raged through the school in this quiet town. There is also discussion on school-related violence.

- *Rain* A 13-year-girl becomes increasingly aware of problems in her parents' marriage while at the same time starting to discover her own sexuality.

ADOLESCENCE IN BOOKS

- *Boys and Sex*, by Wardell Pomery (Delacorte Press: NY, 1991), was written for adolescent boys and stresses the responsibility that comes with sexual maturity.

- *Girls and Sex*, by Wardell Pomery (Delacorte Press: NY, 1991), poses a number of questions that young girls often ask about sex and then answers them. Many myths that young girls hear about sex are also demystified.

Answer Key

KEY TERMS

1. **sexual script** A stereotypical pattern of role prescriptions for how individuals should behave sexually. Females and males have been socialized to follow different sexual scripts.

2. **bisexual** A person who is attracted to people of both sexes.

3. **sexually transmitted infections (STIs)** Infections that are contracted primarily through sexual contact. This contact is not limited to vaginal intercourse but includes oral-genital contact and anal-genital contact as well.

4. **gonorrhea** Reported to be one of the more common STIs in the United States, this sexually transmitted infection is caused by a bacterium called *gonococcus,* which thrives in the moist mucous membrane lining the mouth, throat, vagina, cervix, urethra, and anal tract. This infection is commonly called the "drip" or the "clap."

5.   **syphilis** A sexually transmitted infection caused by the bacterium *Treponema pallidum,* a spirochete.

6.   **Chlamydia** A common sexually transmitted infection, is named for Chlamydia trachomatis, an organism that infects both sexual partners.

7.   **genital herpes** A sexually transmitted infection caused by a large family of viruses of different strains. These strains produce other, nonsexually transmitted diseases such as chicken pox and mononucleosis.

8.   **genital warts** The most common STI in the United States, it is caused by the Human Papilloma Virus and is highly contagious.

9.   **AIDS** Acquired immune deficiency syndrome, primarily a sexually transmitted infection caused by the HIV virus, which destroys the body's immune system.

10.   **rape** Forcible nonconsensual sexual intercourse.

11.   **date or acquaintance rape** Coercive sexual activity directed at someone with whom the perpetrator is at least casually acquainted.

12.   **quid pro quo sexual harassment** Occurs when a school employee threatens to base an educational decision (such as a grade) on a student's submission to unwelcome conduct

13.   **hostile environment sexual harassment** Occurs when students are subjected to unwelcome sexual conduct that is so severe, persistent, or pervasive that it limits the students' ability to benefit from their education.

KEY PEOPLE IN THE STUDY OF ADOLESCENCE

1.	B		**5.**	G
2.	D		**6.**	A
3.	F		**7.**	C
4.	E			

"DR. DETAIL'S" MATCHING EXERCISE

1.	D		**4.**	A
2.	E		**5.**	C
3.	B		**6.**	F

EXPLORING ADOLESCENT SEXUALITY
SECTION REVIEW

1.   Yes. In some societies women are escorted or get married before any sexual activity. Other societies are less concerned regarding sexual exploration.

2.

Chapter	Concept
3: Biological Differences	Early pubertal maturation in girls may lead to early dating and sexual activity.
4: Cognitive Differences	Adolescent egocentrism may lead to sexual risk-taking.
5: Families	Prolonged family conflict and lack of parental monitoring can lead to problems in sexuality
6: Peers	Peers and friends influence learning about and discussing sexual behavior.
7: Schools	Schools have a big role in sex education.
8: Culture	Sexuality in the media is often presented to adolescents in an unrealistic way.
9: The Self and Identity	Sexual identity is one dimension of identity.
10: Gender	Pubertal changes may lead to boys and girls conforming to traditional masculine and feminine behaviors.

3.   Many Americans are ambivalent about sex. It is used to sell just about everything.

4.   An adolescent's sexual identity involves an indication of sexual preference (homosexual, heterosexual, bisexual).

5.   The most likely people to respond would be those least inhibited. So surveys may measure an extreme.

6.   Kissing preceded petting, which preceded sexual intercourse and oral sex.

7.   The proportion of female college students who report that they have had sexual intercourse has increased more rapidly than that of males.

8.   Male African Americans are more likely to have a less restrictive timetable for sexual behaviors than other groups, whereas Asian Americans are more likely to have a more restrictive one. Male African Americans and inner-city adolescents report being the most sexually active.

9.   Eight in 10 girls and seven in 10 boys are virgins at age 15. The probability that adolescents will have sexual intercourse increases steadily with age, but 1 in 5 individuals have not had intercourse by age 19. Initial sexual intercourse occurs in the mid- to late-adolescent years for a majority of teenagers. The majority of females' first sexual partners are similar in age.

10.   A sexual script is a stereotyped pattern of role prescriptions for how individuals should sexually behave. Females and males have been socialized to follow different sexual scripts.

11.   Pregnancy and sexually transmitted infections.

12.   Exclusively heterosexual behavior; largely heterosexual; equal amounts of heterosexual and homosexual behavior; largely homosexual; exclusively homosexual behavior.

13.   Having irrational negative feelings against homosexuals.

14.   Self-devaluation.

15. Parents are seldom the first to hear about the same-sex attraction. Mothers are usually told before fathers. Mothers are more likely than fathers to find out about a son's or a daughter's same-sex attraction. Approximately 50 to 60 percent of gay adolescents have told a sibling. The first person told about same-sex attraction is usually a friend.

16. It's a way to deal with arousal.

17. Sexually active younger adolescents.

KEY PEOPLE IN SECTION (describe the contributions of this individual to the study and understanding of adolescence).

Alfred Kinsey—described sexual orientation as a continuum on a six-point scale.

Simon LeVay—found that an area of the hypothalamus that governs sexual behavior is twice as large in heterosexual men as in homosexual men.

ADOLESCENT SEXUAL PROBLEMS
SECTION REVIEW

1. Forty-nine out of every 1000 girls.

2. More acceptance of sexual practice, contraception, and abortion.

3. Adolescent mothers often drop out of school. Children are often of low birth weight, which is associated with a variety of problems later in life.

4. She is more likely to drop out of school and have a low skilled job.

5. "It won't happen to me."

6. Low birth weight, neurological problems and illness.

7. Most are uninvolved with their children.

8. (a) Sex education and family planning, (b) access to contraceptives, (c) the life options approach, and (d) broad community involvement and support.

9. It focuses on engaging adolescents in volunteer community service and stimulates enlightening discussions.

10. Diseases that are contracted primarily through sexual contact.

11. Is a sexually transmitted infection that is caused by a virus, the human immunodeficiency virus, which destroys the body's immune system.

12. Sub-Saharan Africa.

13. Heterosexual sex, homosexual sex, blood transfusion, shared needles.

14.   Using condoms, not sharing needles, and screening blood donations.

15.   Forcible sexual intercourse with a person who does not give consent.

16.   Coercive sexual activity directed at someone with whom the perpetrator is at least casually acquainted.

17.   Unwanted touch or harassing remarks.

18.   A school employee threatens to base an educational decision, such as a grade, on a student's submission to sex.

19.   Students are subjected to unwelcomed sexual conduct that is so severe, persistent, or pervasive that it limits the student's ability to benefit from their education.

KEY PEOPLE IN SECTION (describe the contributions of this individual to the study and understanding of adolescence).

John Conger—offered four recommendations for attacking the high rate of adolescent pregnancy.

SEXUAL LITERACY AND SEX EDUCATION
SECTION REVIEW

1.   According to June Reinisch, they know more about their cars than how their bodies function sexually.

2.   Peers.

3.   The attitude is that this can be more informative and reach more children in an unintrusive environment.

4.   Some feel that the knowledge is used to experiment with sexual behaviors, as opposed to abstaining.

KEY PEOPLE IN SECTION (describe the contributions of this individual to the study and understanding of adolescence).

June Reinisch—feels that U.S. citizens know more about how their automobiles function than about how their bodies function sexually.

SEXUAL WELL-BEING, SOCIAL POLICY, AND ADOLESCENTS
SECTION REVIEW

1.   (a) Timing of behaviors associated with behavior, (b) co-occurrence of health-related behaviors, (c) the contexts of sexual behavior, (d) the timing of sexual experiences, and (e) gender and sexuality.

2. (a) practicing abstinence, but having positive sexual attitudes, (b) engaging in sexual exploration as opposed to sexual intercourse, (c) engaging in sexual intercourse within the context of a committed relationship, and (d) participating in preintercourse behaviors with another individual early in adolescence.

3. Teach kids responsibility before they become sexually active.

4. The importance of preparing adolescents for responsible parenthood.

KEY PEOPLE IN SECTION (describe the contributions of this individual to the study and understanding of adolescence).

Jeanne Brooks-Gunn and Roberta Paikoff—proposed five developmental issues that need to be examined more thoroughly in adolescent sexuality.

COGNITIVE CHALLENGE

1. Individual activity. No answer provided.

2. Individual activity. No answer provided.

ADOLESCENCE IN RESEARCH

The hypothesis was that adolescents, in choosing their sexual identity adopt different styles. They studied 470 tenth- to twelfth-grade Australian youth. Their results showed five different styles: Sexually naïve; sexually unassured; sexually competent; sexually adventurous; sexually driven.

⊠ COMPREHENSIVE REVIEW

1.	d	6.	c	11.	a	16.	b
2.	d	7.	d	12.	c	17.	d
3.	c	8.	d	13.	c	18.	d
4.	a	9.	d	14.	c	19.	a
5.	c	10.	a	15.	c	20.	c

⌘

Chapter 8   Moral Development, Values, and Religion

Learning Goals with Key Terms and Key People in Boldface

1.0   DISCUSS THEORIES AND RESEARCH ON MORAL THOUGHT, BEHAVIOR, AND FEELING

A.   **Domains of Moral Development?**

1.1   What is involved in **moral development?**

1.2   What are the dimensions of **moral development?**

B.   **Moral Thought**

1.3   What is the difference between **Piaget's heteronomous morality** and his **autonomous morality?**

1.4   What is the concept of **immanent justice?**

1.5   What does the development of formal operational thought have to do with adolescent moral reasoning?

1.6   What is **Hoffman's** proposed **cognitive disequilibrium theory** of moral development?

1.7   What is **internalization?**

1.8   What are **Kohlberg's** three levels of moral development?

1.9   What are the differences between **preconventional reasoning, conventional reasoning,** and **postconventional reasoning?**

1.10   What stage of moral reasoning is characterized by heteronomous morality?

1.11   What stage of moral reasoning is characterized by individualism, instrumental purpose and exchange?

1.12   What stage of moral reasoning is characterized by mutual interpersonal expectations, relationships, and interpersonal conformity?

1.13   What is the meaning of the social contract or utility and individual rights?

1.14   What are universal ethical principles?

1.15   What are some major criticisms of Kohlberg's theories?

1.16   What is the Defining Issues Test?

1.17   According to Richard Shweder, there are three ethical orientations or world views, what are they?

1.18   What was the basis for **Gilligan's** criticism of **Kohlberg?**

1.19   What are the **justice perspective** and **care perspective?**

1.20   Why is it important to make distinctions regarding different domains when considering adolescent's sociocognitive reasoning?

1.21   What are social-conventional concepts?

1.22   What three domains have been given the most attention?

C.   **Moral Behavior**

    1.23   How is moral behavior determined by the processes of reinforcement, punishment, and imitation?

    1.24   What situational variations are involved in moral behavior?

    1.25   What did **Hartshorne** and **May** find about situational variation in moral behavior?

    1.26   What is the nature of the **social cognitive theory of moral development**?

    1.27   What is the difference between moral competence and moral performance?

    1.28   Explain Kohlberg's conceptualization of "extra-moral" factors.

    1.29   What are the social cognitive theorists' criticisms of Kohlberg's theory of moral development?

    1.30   What is the nature of **altruism?**

    1.31   How are reciprocity and exchange involved in altruism?

    1.32   What is the role of **forgiveness** in prosocial behavior?

D.   **Moral Feelings**

    1.33   According to **Freud,** what is the moral part of personality?

    1.34   How does the process of identification affect moral development?

    1.35   Why do children conform to moral standards, according to **Freud?**

    1.36   What did **Freud** mean by the **ego ideal** and the **conscience?**

    1.37   What were **Erikson's** views regarding three stages of moral development?

    1.38   What is **empathy** and how does it contribute to moral development?

    1.39   How are emotions interwoven with moral development?

2.0   DESCRIBE HOW THE CONTEXTS OF PARENTING AND SCHOOLS CAN INFLUENCE MORAL DEVELOPMENT

A.   **Parenting**

    2.1   What do child-rearing techniques have to do with moral development?

    2.2   How do **love withdrawal, power assertion,** and **induction** affect a child's moral development?

    2.3   According to **Eisenberg,** what qualities do parents of moral children and adolescents have?

B.   **Schools**

    2.4   What is meant by the **hidden curriculum?**

    2.5   Who was **John Dewey?**

    2.6   What is **character education?**

    2.7   What is the nature of moral literacy?

    2.8   What is the nature of **values clarification?**

    2.9   What is **cognitive moral education?**

    2.10   Whose theory of moral development is the basis for many **cognitive moral education** programs?

    2.11   What is **service learning?**

3.0   EXPLAIN THE ROLES OF VALUES, RELIGION, AND CULTS IN ADOLESCENTS' LIVES

A.   **Values**

    3.1   How are **values** defined?

    3.2   How are adolescent values changing?

    3.3   What is some evidence that today's college students are shifting toward a stronger interest in the welfare of society?

B.   **Religion**

    3.4   What is the scope of religion interest in children and adolescents?

      3.5   Is adolescence a special juncture in religious development?

      3.6   What is Piaget's theory about the role of religion in development?

      3.7   What is Fowler's life-span development view of the six stages of finding meaning in life?

      3.8   Are there links between religiousness and sexuality?

C.   **Cults**

      3.9   What is the nature of cults?

      3.10   What is the difference between a cult and a church?

      3.11   Why do people join cults?

      3.12   What is a cult's potential for abuse?

Exercises

KEY TERMS COMPLETION EXERCISE

Each key term is presented in the form of an incomplete sentence. Complete each sentence by either defining the term or giving an example. Compare your definitions with those given at the end of the study guide chapter.

1.   **Moral development** influences an adolescent's

_____

_____

2.   You can tell that Mick is in the stage of **heteronomous morality** because

_____

_____

3.   As Justin passes age 10, he enters the stage of **autonomous morality,** which means

_____

_____

4.   **Immanent justice** should be used when

_____

_____

5.   **Cognitive disequilibrium theory** suggests that

_____

_____

6.   **Internalization** refers to

_____

_____

7.   In **preconventional reasoning** children

_____

_____

8.   In **conventional reasoning** children begin to

_____

_____

9.   During **postconventional reasoning** morality

_____

_____

10.   From the **justice perspective** individuals

_____

_____

11.   According to Carol Gilligan, **care perspective** is

_____

_____

12.   According to the **social cognitive theory of moral development**

_____

_____

13.   Characteristics of an act of **altruism** are

_____

_____

14. **Forgiveness** is when

_____

_____

15. Shoshana's behavior is consistent with her parent's **ego ideal** because

_____

_____

16. You can tell Peggy has a **conscience** because

_____

_____

17. Parents practicing **love withdrawal** are likely to

_____

_____

18. **Power assertion** suggests a parenting style that uses

_____

_____

19. According to Hoffman, **induction** is when parents

_____

_____

20. A good example of **empathy** is

_____

_____

21. **Hidden curriculum** in schools is

_____

_____

22.   Good **character education** begins with

_____

_____

23.   An example of **values clarification** is

_____

_____

24.   **Cognitive moral education** is based on the belief that

_____

_____

25.   **Service learning** is a form of education that

_____

_____

26.   **Values** are

_____

_____

KEY PEOPLE IN THE STUDY OF ADOLESCENCE

Match the person with the concept of adolescent moral development with which they are associated.

_____   1. Jean Piaget   A. Associated with social-cognitive perspective of moral development

_____   2. Martin Hoffman   B. Finds that parents play a role in moral development

_____   3. Lawrence Kohlberg   C. Developed a six-stage model of moral development, with three levels of moral reasoning

_____   4. James Rest   D. Proposed that there were two types of morality, depending upon the age of the child

_____   5. Robert Shweder   E. Believed that moral education was the schools' hidden curriculum

_____   6. Carol Gilligan   F. Proposed that adolescents develop an ideology as part of their identity

_____   7. Hugh Hartshorne and Mark May   G. Developed the cognitive disequilibrium theory

_____   8. Albert Bandura   H. Thought that resolution of the Oedipus complex was associated with moral development

_____   9. Sigmund Freud   I. Developed the Defining Issues Test to measure morality

_____ 10. Erik Erikson   J. Proposes that there are three types of ethical orientation

_____	11.	Nancy Eisenberg	K.	Insists that girls' need for relationships is significant factor in their sense of morality
_____	12.	John Dewey	L.	Involved in large study of situational morality
_____	13.	James Fowler	M.	Proposed a theory of religious development that focuses on the motivation to discover meaning in life

"DR. DETAIL'S" STAGE MASTERY EXERCISE

Complete the table by listing the main characteristics of each of Kohlberg's stages of moral development.

Stage	Characteristic
Preconventional Reasoning	
Heteronomous morality	
Individualism, instrumental purpose, and exchange	
Conventional Reasoning	
Mutual interpersonal expectations, relationships, and interpersonal conformity	
Social systems morality	
Postconventional Reasoning	
Social contract or utility and individual rights	
Universal ethical principles	

DOMAINS OF MORAL DEVELOPMENT
SECTION REVIEW

1.   What is moral development?

      _____

      _____

2.   What are the dimensions of moral development?

      _____

      _____

3. What is the difference between Piaget's heteronomous morality and his autonomous morality?

    _____

    _____

4. What is immanent justice?

    _____

    _____

5. What is Hoffman's proposed cognitive disequilibrium theory of moral development?

    _____

    _____

6. What is internalization?

    _____

    _____

7. What are Kohlberg's three levels of moral development?

    _____

    _____

8. What are the justice perspective and care perspective?

    _____

    _____

9. What are some major criticisms of Kohlberg's theories?

    _____

    _____

10. What is the Defining Issues Test?

    _____

    _____

11.   According to Shweder, there are three ethical orientations or world views, what are they?

_____

_____

12.   What did Hartshorne and May find about situational variation in moral behavior?

_____

_____

13.   What is the nature of the social cognitive theory of moral development?

_____

_____

14.   What is the difference between moral competence and moral performance?

_____

_____

15.   What is the nature of altruism?

_____

_____

16.   What is the role of forgiveness in altruism?

_____

_____

17.   Explain Kohlberg's conceptualization of "extra-moral" factors.

_____

_____

18.   What is the best way for parents to help children develop moral maturity, other than setting a good behavioral example?

_____

_____

19.   Why is an adolescent more likely to forgive someone if his friends encourage him to do so?

_____

_____

20.   What did Freud mean by the ego ideal and the conscience?

_____

_____

21.   What were Erikson's views regarding three stages of moral development?

_____

_____

MORAL DEVELOPMENT
SECTION REVIEW

1.   How do love withdrawal, power assertion, and induction affect a child's moral development?

_____

_____

2.   According to Eisenberg, what qualities do parents of moral children and adolescents have?

_____

_____

3.   Name two books that promote character education.

_____

_____

4.   What is meant by the hidden curriculum?

_____

_____

5.   What is character education?

_____

_____

6.   What is the nature of values clarification?

_____

_____

7.   What is cognitive moral education?

_____

_____

8.   What is service learning?

_____

_____

VALUES, RELIGION, AND CULTS
SECTION REVIEW

1.   How are values defined?

_____

_____

2.   How are adolescent values changing?

_____

_____

3.   Complete the table by filling in the name of Fowler's stage of religious development, the period of development in which it occurs, and brief descriptions of the characteristics of the stage.

Name of Stage	Developmental Period	Characteristics
1.		
2.		
3.		
4.		
5.		
6.		

4.   What is Piaget's theory about the role of religion in development?

_____

_____

5.   What is the nature of cults?

_____

_____

6.   Why do people join cults?

_____

_____

COGNITIVE CHALLENGE

1.   A man who had been sentenced to serve 10 years for selling a small amount of marijuana walked away from a prison camp after serving six months there. Twenty-five years later he was caught. He is now in his 50s and has been a model citizen. Should he be sent back to prison? Why or why not? At what Kohlberg stage is your response? Would you feel differently if he were your sibling?

_____

_____

2.   What are your five most important values? How did you get these? Did they come from your parents, friends, teachers, or some event or experience? How carefully do you stick to society's ethical standards.

_____

_____

3.   As you progressed through the first four stages of Fowler's stages of religious development, how were your experiences different from or similar to his characterizations? Are you resolved about your choice of religious practice, or do you have some doubts?

_____

_____

ADOLESCENCE IN RESEARCH

Concerning Hartshorne and May's research (1928–1930), state the hypothesis, the research methods (if known), the research conclusions, and the implications and applications for adolescent development.

_____

_____

COMPREHENSIVE REVIEW

1.   The three major aspects of moral development include
      a.   stimulus, response, and consequences.
      b.   thought, feeling, and behaving.
      c.   individual, family, and society.
      d.   id, ego, and superego.

2.   Jean Piaget indicates that the heteronomous thinker
      a.   believes that rules can be changed because they are merely conventions.
      b.   recognizes that punishment for wrongdoing is not inevitable.
      c.   judges the goodness of behavior by focusing on the consequences of the behavior.
      d.   is usually a child between the ages of 10 and 12.

3.   _____ is the idea that, if a rule is broken, punishment will be meted out immediately.
      a.   Autonomous morality
      b.   Immanent justice
      c.   Response cost
      d.   Love withdrawal

4.   Six stages of moral development were proposed by _____
      a.   Martin Hoffman.
      b.   Jean Piaget.
      c.   Sigmund Freud.
      d.   Lawrence Kohlberg.

5.   Which of the following was NOT a criticism of Kohlberg's theory of moral development?
      a.   He placed too little emphasis on moral behavior.
      b.   The research was of poor quality.
      c.   He placed too much emphasis on the development of the Superego.
      d.   He did not fully consider cultural or gender variables.

6.   Martin Hoffman indicates that going to high school is associated with a dramatic change in moral reasoning because
      a.   there is more opportunity for sexual exploitation.
      b.   parental supervision is nullified.
      c.   peer pressure to violate community standards is high.
      d.   discussions reveal the variety of moral beliefs.

7.   Which of the following is NOT a social cognitive domain noted in the chapter?
      a.   moral domain
      b.   human domain
      c.   social-conventional domain
      d.   personal domain

8.   _____ is an unselfish interest in helping another person.
      a.   Forgiveness
      b.   Conscience

    c.   Induction

    d.   altruism

9. Lawrence Kohlberg argues that the distinctions between the three levels of moral reasoning have to do with
   a. the degree of internalization.
   b. the immediacy of the consequences for moral actions.
   c. the severity of punishments experienced.
   d. the social pressure of peers.

10. An adolescent at Kohlberg's conventional level of moral reasoning
    a. obeys rules in order to meet his defined obligations.
    b. obeys rules in order to avoid punishment.
    c. will follow rules if they are in his immediate best interest.
    d. has developed a social contract involving self-chosen ethical principles.

11. Who is most likely to join a cult?
    a. someone who is psychologically unstable
    b. a person just recently released from prison
    c. a normal, average person
    d. someone with strong religious beliefs

12. James Rest developed the Defining Issues Test because
    a. there were no available measures of moral reasoning.
    b. he found Piaget's tests too hard for adolescents.
    c. Kohlberg's stories were too difficult to score.
    d. he didn't know that several other tests were available.

13. There is general agreement that Lawrence Kohlberg's theory
    a. is correct for adolescents, but not for adults.
    b. confused autonomy with autonomous morality.
    c. confused moral reasoning with moral behavior.
    d. underestimates the importance of culture.

14. Carol Gilligan has criticized Kohlberg's theory for
    a. overemphasizing people's connectedness and communication with other people.
    b. emphasizing moral behavior and ignoring moral reasoning.
    c. relying on a single method to assess individual's moral reasoning.
    d. understating the importance of interpersonal relationships in moral development.

15. Adolescents' moral performance is influenced by
    a. skills.
    b. awareness of moral rules.
    c. cognitive-sensory processes.
    d. motivation.

16. Which theory distinguishes between moral competence and moral performance?
    a. psychosocial
    b. moral development

    c.   cognitive social learning

    d.   behavioral moral reasoning

17.   Psychoanalytic theorists say that guilt develops when a child
    a.   turns her hostility inward following the withdrawal of parental love.
    b.   harnesses the drives of the superego and maintains the world as a safe place.
    c.   becomes disillusioned with the moral and religious beliefs she acquired during childhood.
    d.   participates in the feelings of an adult with whom she has identified.

18.   The part of the superego that enables us to feel proud when we do the right thing, even if no one else will know, is the
    a.   conscience.
    b.   ego ideal.
    c.   empathic aspect.
    d.   altruistic channel.

19.   Martin Hoffman believes that parents promote the moral development of their children and adolescents through
    a.   love withdrawal.
    b.   power assertion.
    c.   induction.
    d.   altruism.

20.   The failure to develop empathy, if not altruism, is associated with
    a.   excessive achievement orientation.
    b.   vulnerability to cults.
    c.   antisocial behaviors.
    d.   chronic depression.

21.   If a person can experience another's feelings and respond in a similar way, this is called
    a.   pity.
    b.   empathy.
    c.   sympathy.
    d.   understanding.

22.   Which of the following is an example of altruism?
    a.   sharing possessions
    b.   resisting temptation
    c.   saying thank you
    d.   not eating with your fingers

23.   Which term is used when a person "releases the injurer from possible behavioral retaliation"?
    a.   altruism
    b.   empathy
    c.   sympathy
    d.   forgiveness

24. Schools are one of the settings in which moral development occurs. The moral climate of the school is called the
    a. administrative morale.
    b. Damon Comprehensive Approach.
    c. hidden curriculum.
    d. classroom conscience.

25. According to a poll, _____ percent of the adolescents said that they prayed.
    a. 10
    b. 35
    c. 50
    d. 75

26. An adolescent refused to attend church, telling his parents that he would believe what he wants to believe, not what they tell him to believe. This adolescent demonstrates
    a. reflective faith.
    b. individuative-reflective faith.
    c. catastrophic conversion.
    d. moral fundamentalism.

ADOLESCENCE ON THE SCREEN

■ *A Clockwork Orange* An immoral and violent young man becomes the subject of an experiment to eradicate his violent tendencies.

■ *Saving Private Ryan* Examines morality and the need for personal sacrifice in the context of war and military duty.

■ *Stand by Me* Four 12-year-old boys trek into the wilderness to find the body of a missing boy.

■ *Lost and Delirious* Tracks the moral development of a young girl at an all-girls boarding school, before and after young love goes sour.

ADOLESCENCE IN BOOKS

■ *Meeting at the Crossroads*, by Lyn Mikel Brown and Carol Gilligan (Harvard University Press: MA, 1992), provides a vivid portrayal of how adolescent girls are often ignored and misunderstood.

■ *The Lost Boys*, by James Garbarino (the Free Press: NY, 1999). Outstanding compilation of theories and facts related to why children "go bad" and what can be done to stop this.

■ *She Said Yes: The Unlikely Martyrdom of Cassie Bernall,* by Misty Bernall (the Plough Publishing House: UK, 1999). A wrenching and honest portrayal of a troubled teenage girl who, just after turning her life around, ends up being a victim in the Columbine massacre.

■ *Postconventional Thinking*, by James Rest, Darcia Naraez, Muriel Bebeau, and Stephen Thoma (Erlbaum: NJ, 1999), presents a neo-Kolhbergian analysis of moral development.

Answer Key

KEY TERMS

1. **moral development** Thoughts, feelings, and behaviors regarding standards of right and wrong.

2. **heteronomous morality** The first stage of moral development in Piaget's theory, occurring at 4 to 7 years of age. Justice and rules are conceived of as unchangeable properties of the world, removed from the control of people.

3. **autonomous morality** The second stage of moral development in Piaget's theory, displayed by older children (about 10 years of age and older). The child becomes aware that rules and laws are created by people and that, in judging an action, one should consider the actor's intentions as well as the consequences.

4. **immanent justice** Piaget's concept that if a rule is broken, punishment will be meted out immediately.

5. **cognitive disequilibrium theory** Hoffman's theory that adolescence is an important period in moral development, in which, because of broader experiences associated with the move to high school or college, individuals recognize that their set of beliefs is but one of many and that there is considerable debate about what is right and wrong.

6. **internalization** The developmental change from behavior that is externally controlled to behavior that is controlled by internal standards and principles.

7. **preconventional reasoning** The lowest level in Kohlberg's theory of moral development. The individual shows no internalization of moral values—moral reasoning is controlled by external rewards and punishment.

8. **conventional reasoning** The second, or intermediate, level in Kohlberg's theory of moral development. Internalization is intermediate. Individuals abide by certain standards (internal), but they are the standards of others (external), such as parents or the laws of society.

9. **postconventional reasoning** The highest level in Kohlberg's theory of moral development. Morality is completely internalized.

10. **justice perspective** A moral perspective that focuses on the rights of the individual; individuals independently make moral decisions.

11. **care perspective** The moral perspective of Carol Gilligan, that views people in terms of their connectedness with others and emphasizes interpersonal communication, relationships with others, and concern for others.

12. **social cognitive theory of moral development** The theory that distinguishes between moral competence—the ability to produce moral behaviors—and moral performance—those behaviors in specific situations.

13. **altruism** Unselfish interest in helping another person.

14. **forgiveness** This is an aspect of altruism that occurs when an injured person releases the injured from possible behavioral retaliation.

15. **ego ideal** The component of the superego that involves ideal standards approved by parents.

16. **conscience** The component of the superego that involves behaviors disapproved of by parents.

17. **love withdrawal** Is a discipline technique in which a parent removes attention or love from the child.

18. **power assertion** A discipline technique in which a parent attempts to gain control over a child or a child's resources.

19. **induction** A discipline technique in which a parent uses reason and explanation of the consequences for others of a child's actions.

20. **empathy** Reacting to another's feelings with an emotional response that is similar to the other's response.

21. **hidden curriculum** The pervasive moral atmosphere that characterizes schools.

22. **character education** A direct moral education approach that involves teaching students a basic moral literacy to prevent them from engaging in immoral behavior or doing harm to themselves or others.

23. **values clarification** Helping people to clarify what their lives are for and what is worth working for. Students are encouraged to define their own values and understand others' values.

24. **cognitive moral education** Is based on the belief that students should learn to value things like democracy and justice as their moral reasoning develops; Kohlberg's theory has been the basis for many of the cognitive moral education approaches.

25. **service learning** A form of education that promotes social responsibility and service to the community.

26. **values** Beliefs and attitudes about the way people think things should be.

KEY PEOPLE IN THE STUDY OF ADOLESCENCE

1.	D	5.	J	9.	H	13.	M
2.	G	6.	K	10.	F		
3.	C	7.	L	11.	B		
4.	I	8.	A	12.	E		

"DR. DETAIL'S" STAGE MASTERY EXERCISE

Stage	Characteristic
Preconventional Reasoning	Individual shows no internalization of moral values; moral reasoning is controlled by external rewards and punishment.
Heteronomous morality	Moral thinking is tied to punishment.
Individualism, instrumental purpose, and exchange	Individuals pursue their own interests but let others do the same.
Conventional Reasoning	Internalization is intermediate. Individuals abide by certain internal standards, but they are the standards of others, such as parents or the laws of society.
Mutual interpersonal expectations, relationships, and interpersonal conformity	Individuals value trust, caring, and loyalty to others as a basis of moral judgment.
Social systems morality	Moral judgments are based on understanding the social order, law, justice, and duty.
Postconventional Reasoning	Morality is completely internalized and is not based on others' standards. The individual recognizes alternative moral courses, explores the options, and then decides on a personal moral code.
Social contract or utility and individual rights	Individuals reason that values, rights, and principles underscore or transcend the law.
Universal ethical principles	The person has developed a moral standard based on universal human rights.

DOMAINS OF MORAL DEVELOPMENT
SECTION REVIEW

1.   It involves thoughts, feelings, and behaviors regarding standards of right and wrong.

2.   (a) How do adolescents think about rules for ethical conduct? (b) How do adolescents actually behave in moral circumstances? (c) How do adolescents feel about moral matters?

3.   Heteronomous morality is the first stage of moral development. Justice and rules are conceived of as unchangeable properties of the world, removed from the control of people. Autonomous morality is the second stage. Here the child becomes aware that rules and laws are created by people and that in judging an action one should consider the actor's intentions as well as the consequences.

4.   Piaget's concept that if a rule is broken, punishment will be meted out immediately.

5.   This states that adolescence is an important period in moral development, especially as individuals move from the relatively homogeneous grade school to the more heterogeneous high school and college environments, where they are faced with contradictions between the moral concepts they have accepted and experiences outside their family and neighborhood.

6.   The developmental change from behavior that is externally controlled to behavior that is controlled by internal standards and principles.

7. According to Kohlberg, there are three levels of moral development: Preconventional—moral reasoning is controlled by external rewards and punishments. Conventional reasoning—individuals abide by others standards, such as the laws of society. Postconventional reasoning—morality is completely internalized and is not based on other's standards. The individual recognizes alternative moral courses, explores options, and then decides on a personal moral code.

8. Justice perspective is a moral perspective that focuses on the rights of the individual; individuals who stand alone and independently make moral decisions. The care perspective is a moral perspective that views people in terms of their connectedness with others and emphasizes interpersonal communication, relationships with others, and concern for others.

9. Some of the major criticisms of Kohlberg's theories are that they are culturally and gender biased.

10. The DIT attempts to determine which moral issues individuals feel are more critical in a given situation by presenting them with a series of dilemmas.

11. (a) an ethic of autonomy, (b) an ethic of community, and (c) an ethic of diversity.

12. Adolescents were more likely to cheat when their friends pressured them to do so and when the chances of being caught were slim.

13. The theory distinguishes between moral competence and moral performance.

14. Moral competence—the ability to produce moral behaviors. Moral performance—those behaviors in specific situations.

15. Altruism is an unselfish interest in helping another person.

16. Forgiveness is an aspect of altruism that occurs when the injured person releases the injurer from possible behavioral retaliation.

17. "Extra-moral" factors are things such as the desire to avoid embarrassment, which may cause children to fail to do what they believe to be morally right.

18. Trying to probe and elicit their child's opinions, instead of giving too much information that may come across as preaching or lecturing.

19. It is often difficult for the victim of harm to try to take steps toward forgiveness. His friends can encourage him to consider why that might be the better response.

20. Ego ideal is the component of the superego that involves ideal standards approved by parents, whereas conscience is the component of the superego that involves behaviors not approved of by parents.

21. Specific moral learning in childhood, ideological concerns in adolescence, and ethical consolidation in adulthood.

MORAL DEVELOPMENT
SECTION REVIEW

1.   Love withdrawal is a discipline technique in which a parent withholds attention or love from the adolescent. This leads to insecurity in the adolescent. Power assertion is a discipline technique in which a parent attempts to gain control over the adolescent or his/her resources. Spanking is an example. Induction is where parents explain consequences of actions and likely outcomes. These adolescents are the most well-rounded emotionally.

2.   They are warm and supportive. They provide opportunities for their children to learn about others' feelings. They use inductive discipline. They involve children in decision making. They stimulate adolescents to question and expand their moral reasoning. They model moral behaviors and thinking for their children.

3.   William Bennett's *Book of Virtues* (1993) and William Damon's *Greater Expectations* (1995).

4.   Hidden curriculum is conveyed by the moral atmosphere that is a part of every school.

5.   Character education is a direct approach that involves teaching students a basic moral literacy to prevent them from engaging in immoral behavior and doing harm to themselves or others.

6.   It is an educational approach that is intended to help people clarify what their lives are for and what is worth working for.

7.   It is an educational approach based on the belief that students should learn to value things like democracy and justice.

8.   Service learning is a form of education that promotes social responsibility and service to the community.

VALUES, RELIGION, AND CULTS
SECTION REVIEW

1.   Values are beliefs and attitudes about the way things should be.

2.   Over the past two decades, adolescents have shown increased concern for personal well-being and less concern for the well-being of others.

3.

	Name of Stage	Developmental Period	Characteristics
1.	Intuitive-Projective Faith	Early Childhood	Intuitive images of good and evil; fantasy and reality are the same.
2.	Mythical-Literal Faith	Middle/Late Childhood	More logical, concrete thought; literal interpretation of religious stories.
3.	Synthetic-Conventional Faith	Early Adolescence	More abstract thought; conformity to religious beliefs of others.
4.	Individuative-Reflective Faith	Late Adolescence, Early Adulthood	Capable of taking full responsibility for religious beliefs; In-depth exploration of one's own values and beliefs.

5. Conjunctive Faith	Middle Adulthood	More open to opposing viewpoints; awareness of one's finiteness and limitations.
6. Universalizing Faith	Middle and Late Adulthood	Transcending belief systems to achieve a sense of oneness with all.

4. Piaget felt that they progressed through three stages: preoperational intuitive religious thought; concrete operational religious thought; and formal operational religious thought.

5. They are usually controlled by a charismatic leader and their energies and focus are turned inward, as opposed to outward. The more isolated the cult is, the greater likelihood of abuse or dangerous practices.

6. They are usually normal, regular people who are in a transitional phase of life. Only about 5 percent are disturbed.

COGNITIVE CHALLENGE

1. Individual activity. No answers provided.

2. Individual activity. No answers provided.

3. Individual activity. No answers provided.

ADOLESCENCE IN RESEARCH

The hypothesis was that moral behavior is situationally dependent. The researchers observed the moral responses of 11,000 children and adolescents who were given the opportunity to lie, cheat, and steal in a variety of circumstances—at home, school, social events, and in athletics. Situation-specific moral behavior was the rule. Adolescents were more likely to cheat when their friends pressured them to do so and when the chances of getting caught were slim.

☒ COMPREHENSIVE REVIEW

1.	b	8.	d	15.	d	22.	a
2.	c	9.	a	16.	c	23.	d
3.	b	10.	a	17.	a	24.	c
4.	d	11.	c	18.	b	25.	d
5.	c	12.	c	19.	c	26.	b
6.	d	13.	d	20.	c		
7.	b	14.	d	21.	b		

⌘

Chapter 9   Families

Learning Goals with Key Terms and Key People in Boldface

1.0   DISCUSS THE NATURE OF FAMILY PROCESSES IN ADOLESCENCE
    A.   Reciprocal Socialization and the Family As A System
        1.1   What is **reciprocal socialization,** and how does it affect adolescent development?
        1.2   What is meant by parent-adolescent **synchrony?**
        1.3   What defines a family's social system?
        1.4   Why is marriage satisfaction often related to good parenting?
    B.   The Developmental Construction of Relationships
        1.5   What is the **developmental construction** of relationships?
        1.6   Why are close relationships with parents important for adolescent's development?
        1.7   What are the two main variations of the **developmental construction** views?
        1.8   What is the difference between the **continuity view** and the **discontinuity view?**
        1.9   What research evidence exists in support of each view?
    C.   Maturation
        1.10   What parental and adolescent maturation processes affect parent-adolescent interaction?
        1.11   What are the major changes in adolescence that influence parent-adolescent relationships?
        1.12   What dimensions of the adolescent's cognitive world contribute to parent-adolescent relationships?
        1.13   What parental changes contribute to parent-adolescent relationships?
        1.14   How does the timing of parenthood affect parent-adolescent interaction?
    D.   Sociocultural and Historical Changes
        1.15   What sociocultural and historical changes affect family processes?
        1.16   What impact did the Great Depression have on families?
        1.17   What sociocultural changes have made families different than they were 50 years ago?
        1.18   What roles have television and computers played in the changing family.

2.0   DESCRIBE PARENT-ADOLESCENT RELATIONSHIPS
    A.   Parents as Managers
        2.1   What do we mean when we say that parents should manage their adolescent's lives?
        2.2   How can parents effectively monitor their adolescent?
    B.   Parenting Styles
        2.3   What are the four main parenting categories according to **Baumrind,** and which one is most closely associated with socially competent behavior?

2.4   What is the nature of **authoritarian, authoritative, neglectful,** and **indulgent** parenting styles?

2.5   Which is the most effective parenting style?

2.6   Do the benefits of authoritative parenting transcend the boundaries of ethnicity, socioeconomic status, and household composition?

C.   Gender, Parenting, and Coparenting

2.7   What is the mother's role in raising adolescents?

2.8   What major changes have the roles of fathers in families undergone over time?

2.9   How involved are today's fathers in the lives of their adolescents?

2.10   What does the recent research on coparenting suggest?

D.   Parent-adolescent Conflict

2.11   What is the nature and extent of parent-adolescent conflict?

2.12   How are adolescent-parent conflicts usually resolved?

2.13   What is the subject of most parental-adolescent conflict?

2.14   Who do adolescents most often have disagreements with?

2.15   What is the generation gap?

2.16   How much empirical support is there for the existence of a generation gap?

2.17   What percentage of families is parent-adolescent conflict high?

2.18   What problems are associated with intense, prolonged conflict?

2.19   Do patterns of adolescent conflict differ across cultures?

E.   Autonomy and Attachment

2.20   How important are autonomy and attachment in an adolescent's successful adaptation to adulthood?

2.21   What is the difference between autonomy and **emotional autonomy?**

2.22   What are the four distinct patterns of adolescent autonomy that typically emerge from an analysis of high school students?

2.23   What problems do parents have with their adolescent's achieving autonomy?

2.24   Are there gender differences seen with regards to adolescent autonomy?

2.25   What developmental transition signals autonomy?

2.26   Why do some adolescents run away from home, and what problems might they be susceptible to as a result?

2.27   What recommendation might one give a parent regarding their adolescent's need for autonomy?

2.28   Why is it important that adolescents be both autonomous and attached to their parents?

2.29   What is the difference between **secure attachment** and **insecure attachment?**

2.30   Why is secure attachment related social competence and successful adaptation to the world?

2.31   What is the Adult Attachment Interview (AAI)?

2.32   What is the difference between **dismissing/avoidant attachment, preoccupied/ambivalent attachment,** and **unresolved/disorganized attachment?**

3.0   CHARACTERIZE SIBLING RELATIONSHIPS IN ADOLESCENCE

A.   Sibling Roles

3.1   What is the nature and extent of conflict in many sibling relationships?

3.2   How much does conflict characterize adolescent relationships?

B.   Developmental Changes

3.3   How do sibling relationships change over time?

    C.   **Birth Order**

3.4   How does birth order affect sibling and parent relationships?

3.5   Is an only child likely to be a "spoiled brat"?

3.6   What is the most reasonable conclusion to be gained from research about the effects of birth order on adolescent behavior and achievement?

4.0   **DESCRIBE THE CHANGING FAMILY IN A CHANGING SOCIETY**

    A.   **Divorce**

4.1   How do adolescents adjust to divorce in their families?

4.2   Should parents stay together for the sake of their children and adolescents?

4.3   How much do parenting skills matter in divorced families?

4.4   How much do post-divorce family processes affect adolescent adjustment to divorce?

4.5   What factors contribute to adolescent risk and vulnerability to divorce?

4.6   What role does socioeconomic status play in the lives of adolescents in divorced families?

    B.   **Stepfamilies**

4.7   How is the make-up of step families different than other families?

4.8   What are the three common types of stepfamily structures?

4.9   Over time stepfamilies fall into three types based on their relationships. What are these?

4.8   What adjustment problems are associated with adolescents who live in stepfamilies?

4.9   What is the most difficult time for adolescents to experience their parents' remarriage?

4.10   What is **boundary ambiguity?**

4.11   How do you compare adolescent's relationships with their biological and stepparents?

    C.   **Working Parents**

4.13   What is the effect of parental work on the development of children and adolescents?

4.14   What effect do working mothers have on adolescent development?

4.15   What are the special adjustment problems of latchkey adolescents?

4.16   What is the effect of relocation on adolescent development?

4.17   How does parental unemployment affect adolescents?

    D.   **Gay and Lesbian Parents**

4.18   How common are gay or lesbian parents?

4.19   Are children raised by gay or lesbian parents different than other children?

    E.   **Culture and Ethnicity**

4.20   What roles do culture and ethnicity play in families?

4.21   What is the effect of culture on parental roles and discipline styles and family support systems?

4.22   In what ways do ethnic minority families differ from White American families?

4.23   What are the main differences between White-American families and African-American and Latino families?

5.0   **EXPLAIN WHAT IS NEEDED FOR IMPROVED SOCIAL POLICY INVOLVING ADOLESCENTS AND THEIR FAMILIES**

5.1   What are the recommendations of the Carnegie Council on Adolescent Development regarding social policies for families with adolescents?

Exercises

KEY TERMS COMPLETION EXERCISE

Each key term is presented in the form of an incomplete sentence. Complete each sentence by either defining the term or giving an example. Compare your definitions with those given at the end of the study guide chapter.

1. By using **reciprocal socialization,** SuLin has changed her parents

    _____

    _____

2. **Synchrony** can best be explained as

    _____

    _____

3. According to the **developmental construction view**

    _____

    _____

4. The **continuity view** holds that

    _____

    _____

5. The **discontinuity view** holds that

    _____

    _____

6. Bailey's mom uses **authoritarian parenting** in that

    _____

    _____

7. **Authoritative parenting** allows a child to

    _____

    _____

8.   **Neglectful parenting** can result in

_____

_____

9.   **Indulgent parenting** over time can lead to

_____

_____

10.   **Emotional autonomy** is the capacity to

_____

_____

11.   **Insecure attachment** is a maladaptive pattern that is seen in

_____

_____

12.   **Secure attachment** is very important because

_____

_____

13.   **Dismissing/avoidant attachment** can result in

_____

_____

14.   **Preoccupied/ambivalent attachment** can result in

_____

_____

15.   **Unresolved/disorganized attachment** can lead to

_____

_____

16.   **Boundary ambiguity** can be a problem in stepfamilies because

_____

_____

KEY PEOPLE IN THE STUDY OF ADOLESCENCE

Match the person with the event or concept in adolescent development with which they are associated.

_____	1. Andrew Collins	A.	Parenting styles
_____	2. Diana Baumrind	B.	Infant attachment research
_____	3. John Bowlby and Mary Ainsworth	C.	Adolescent adjustment to parental divorce
_____	4. Joseph Allen	D.	Adolescent-parental attachment
_____	5. E. Mavis Hetherington	E.	Adolescent cognitive changes
_____	6. Lois Hoffman	F.	Studied effects of maternal employment

"DR. DETAIL'S" LIBRARY EXERCISE

Go to the library at your institution and look up archival materials that go into some detail as to what family life was in the year 1900. Then, using that information, compare families then with families now. How are they similar, and how are they different?

_____

_____

_____

_____

_____

_____

_____

_____

FAMILY PROCESSES
SECTION REVIEW

1. Describe how a child might use the process of reciprocal socialization to his/her advantage.

_____

_____

2. Differentiate between reciprocal socialization and synchrony.

_____

_____

3. Compare and contrast the continuity and discontinuity views.

_____

_____

4.   In Mark Twain's view, what transforms as adolescents move from childhood to adulthood?

_____

_____

5.   What dimensions of the adolescent's social world contribute to parent-adolescent relationships?

_____

_____

6.   Is parent-child interaction different for families in which parents delay having children until their thirties or forties?

_____

_____

7.   What kinds of effects did the Great Depression have on families?

_____

_____

8.   What role do cognitive processes play in socialization within families?

_____

_____

KEY PEOPLE IN SECTION (Describe the contributions of this individual to the study and understanding of adolescence.)

Alan Sroufe—

_____

_____

Andrew Collins—

_____

_____

Mark Twain—

_____

_____

Margaret Mead—

_____

_____

PARENT-ADOLESCENT RELATIONSHIPS
SECTION REVIEW

1. Match the terms with the correct definitions or descriptions.

    _____ 1. autonomy   A. Parents are uninvolved
    _____ 2. emotional autonomy   B. Highly restrictive, punitive parenting style
    _____ 3. authoritarian parenting style   C. Adolescents de-emphasize the importance of
                                                    attachment
    _____ 4. authoritative parenting style   D. Adolescents are hypertuned to attachment issues
    _____ 5. indulgent parenting style   E. Parenting style associated with social competence
    _____ 6. neglectful parenting style   F. Parenting style associated with social incompetence
    _____ 7. dismissing/avoidant   G. Relinquishing childlike dependence on parents
              attachment
    _____ 8. preoccupied/ambivalent   H. Adolescent has an unusually high fear
              attachment
    _____ 9. unresolved/disorganized   I. Caregiver (usually mom) is used as a secure base from
              attachment   which to explore the environment
    _____ 10. secure attachment   J. Related with independence and self-direction
    _____ 11. insecure attachment   K. Infants avoid the caregiver or show ambivalence
                                                    toward them

2. What are the four main parenting categories according to Baumrind?

    _____

    _____

3. What major changes have the roles of fathers in families undergone over time?

    _____

    _____

4. What are the four distinct patterns of adolescent autonomy that typically emerge form an analysis
    of high school students?

    _____

    _____

5. Why do adolescents run away from their homes?

    _____

    _____

KEY PEOPLE IN SECTION (Describe the contributions of this individual to the study and understanding of adolescence.)

Diana Baumrind—

_____

_____

Judith Smetana—

_____

_____

Reed Larson—

_____

_____

John Bowlby—

_____

_____

Mary Ainsworth—

_____

_____

SIBLING RELATIONSHIPS
SECTION REVIEW

1.　How much of a problem is sibling conflict in adolescence?

_____

_____

2.　What are later-born children like as compared to first-born?

_____

_____

3.　Is the "only child" typically a "spoiled brat?"

_____

_____

THE CHANGING FAMILY IN A CHANGING SOCIETY
SECTION REVIEW

1.   What factors affect the adolescent's individual risk and vulnerability in a divorced family?

   _____

   _____

2.   What role does socioeconomic status play in the lives of adolescents in divorced families?

   _____

   _____

3.   How much do family processes matter in a divorce?

   _____

   _____

4.   What are the three common types of stepfamily structures?

   _____

   _____

5.   Do children in stepfamilies have more adjustment problems than other children?

   _____

   _____

6.   What are some negative experiences faced by "latchkey" adolescents?

   _____

   _____

7.   What effect does unemployment have on families and on adolescents' development?

   _____

   _____

8.   Are children raised by gay or lesbian parents different from other children?

   _____

   _____

9.   In what ways do minority families differ from White American families?

_____

_____

10.   What is the mother's role in the family?

_____

_____

11.   What is the father's role in the family?

_____

_____

12.   How actively are today's fathers involved with their children and adolescents?

_____

_____

KEY PEOPLE IN SECTION (Describe the contributions of this individual to the study and understanding of adolescence.)

James Bray—

_____

_____

E. Mavis Hetherington—

_____

_____

Lois Hoffman—

_____

_____

Nancy Galambos—

_____

_____

Thomas and Lynette Long—

_____

_____

Joan Lipsitz—

_____

_____

Frank Furstenburg and Kathleen Harris—

_____

_____

SOCIAL POLICY, ADOLESCENTS, AND FAMILIES
SECTION REVIEW

1.   What must parents do if they wish to see their adolescents develop in a competent manner?

_____

_____

EXPLORATIONS IN ADOLESCENCE

1.   Compare and contrast the extended family structures in African-American and Mexican-American families. What positive effects do these systems have on adolescent development?

_____

_____

COGNITIVE CHALLENGE

1.   Write down your ideas for how an adolescent boy or girl (you choose which one you would like to discuss) and his or her parents could engage in collaborative problem solving to set ground rules for dating.

_____

_____

2.   Talk to one of your friends or acquaintances whose parents separated when they were teenagers (or use yourself if your parents did so). When, how, and what did their parents tell them about the separation? Could they have done it in a better way? What suggestions would they give to parents of teenagers who are about to separate?

_____

_____

ADOLESCENCE IN RESEARCH

Concerning Diana Baumrind's 1991 research analyzing parenting styles and social competence in adolescence, state the hypothesis, the research methods (if known), the research conclusions, and the implications and applications for adolescent development.

_____

_____

 COMPREHENSIVE REVIEW

1.   The carefully coordinated interaction between the parent and the child or adolescent.
      a.   reciprocal socialization
      b.   maturation
      c.   discontinuity
      d.   synchrony

2.   Relationships more likely to consist of participants who relate to each other on equal terms.
      a.   sibling-child
      b.   parent-child
      c.   peer-child
      d.   teacher-child

3.   _____ once remarked that when he was 14 his father was so ignorant he could hardly stand him, but by age 21 he was surprised at how much his father had learned in those 7 years.
      a.   Jean Piaget
      b.   Charles Darwin
      c.   Mark Twain
      d.   Sigmund Freud

4.   This is the time when marital dissatisfaction is greater.
      a.   when offspring is a newborn
      b.   when offspring is an adolescent
      c.   when offspring is a child
      d.   when offspring is an adult

5.   What frequently happens between adolescents and parents?
      a.   They compete for family resources.
      b.   They violate one another's expectations.

    c.   They reject one another's personal space.
    d.   They get along well because they share similar levels of cognitive development.

6.   Marital dissatisfaction is greatest when the couple's offspring are
    a.   adolescents.
    b.   young children.
    c.   older children.
    d.   adults.

7.   Which of the following is NOT one of Baumrind's four types of parenting?
    a.   indulgent
    b.   power assertion
    c.   authoritarian
    d.   neglectful

8.   A restrictive, punitive style of parenting is
    a.   indulgent.
    b.   authoritative.
    c.   authoritarian.
    d.   neglectful.

9.   Parents who encourage their adolescents to be independent, but still place limits on what they can do are
    a.   indulgent.
    b.   authoritative.
    c.   authoritarian.
    d.   neglectful.

10.   A style in which the parent is very uninvolved in the life of the adolescent is
    a.   indulgent.
    b.   authoritative.
    c.   authoritarian.
    d.   neglectful.

11.   Diana Baumrind describes authoritative parents as
    a.   restrictive, punitive, and allowing little verbal guide.
    b.   encouraging independence and placing limits on adolescents' actions.
    c.   power assertive, rejecting, unresponsive, and parent centered.
    d.   undemanding, rejecting, uninvolved, and controlling.

12.   Jeremy's parents have few rules for household conduct or academic expectations. They do not punish Jeremy when he violates rules, but merely accept his behavior. Jeremy is likely to develop
    a.   social competence because his parents unconditionally accept him.
    b.   anxiety about social comparisons and social inferiority feelings.
    c.   self-reliance, social responsibility, and autonomy.
    d.   little impulse control and disregard for rules.

13.   The increased independence that typifies adolescence is known as
    a.   synchrony.
    b.   autonomy.

c.   indulgence.
d.   reciprocal socialization.

14.   Conflict between adolescents and parents is typically strongest in early adolescence, and may be a healthy aspect of the development of
a.   autonomy.
b.   attachment.
c.   parenting skills.
d.   dating skills.

15.   You are depressed because you argue with your 10-year-old daughter almost daily, and these arguments last for several minutes. Experts on adolescents would tell you that
a.   this high level of conflict will lead to later disturbances.
b.   this type of conflict is normal, and you should not worry about it.
c.   if you are arguing this much now, your arguments will increase in later adolescence.
d.   these arguments will prevent your daughter from developing an autonomous identity.

16.   The most crucial transition for the development of adolescent autonomy is from
a.   school to work.
b.   high school to college.
c.   middle school to high school.
d.   virginity to sexual activity.

17.   What percent of American adolescents currently have one or more siblings?
a.   50%
b.   25%
c.   60%
d.   80%

18.   Adolescents who are securely attached to their parents
a.   cannot adequately develop autonomy.
b.   show less secure attachment to peers.
c.   have more difficulty engaging with peers and separating from parents.
d.   have higher self-esteem than insecurely attached peers.

19.   Sibling conflict is often lower in adolescence than in childhood due to changes in
a.   social development.
b.   physical development.
c.   the power relationship.
d.   the way parents deal with conflict.

20.   Firstborn children are
a.   more achievement-oriented than those born later.
b.   less achievement-oriented than those born later.
c.   more psychologically well adjusted than those born later.
d.   on the average, less socially responsible than those born later.

21.   Which of the following is NOT one of the three common types of stepfamily structures?
a.   stepfather
b.   compound

c.   complex
d.   stepmother

22. _____ refers to the confusion in stepfamilies regarding the membership of the family and each individual's responsibility.
    a.   family blending
    b.   boundary ambiguity
    c.   stepfamily dynamism
    d.   stepfamily individuation

23. According to James Bray, given time stepfamilies fall into three types based on their relationships. Which of the following is NOT one of those types?
    a.   neo-traditional
    b.   matriarchal
    c.   romantic
    d.   new breed

24. After coming home from school, Juan washes the breakfast dishes, does a load of laundry, and starts dinner before his parents get home at 6 P.M. Juan is a
    a.   hurried child.
    b.   latchkey child.
    c.   neglected child.
    d.   stepchild.

25. Ethnic families tend to differ from White American families in that the former
    a.   are smaller.
    b.   show more extended networks.
    c.   encourage more autonomy among girls than boys.
    d.   have more employed mothers.

26. It is a mistake to attribute the problems of adolescents to their mothers because
    a.   fathers spend more time with children and adolescents than ever before.
    b.   mothers and fathers are partners in parenting.
    c.   behavior is determined by multiple factors.
    d.   peers and siblings have more influence on adolescents than parents.

27. Fathers of adolescents who are older than most other fathers of children that age are
    a.   more likely to enforce rules than younger fathers.
    b.   warmer and communicate better than younger fathers.
    c.   more aloof than younger fathers.
    d.   more demanding than younger fathers.

28. African American and Latino adolescents are most likely to differ from White adolescents in that the former are more likely to
    a.   live in extended families.
    b.   live in rural areas.
    c.   attend church.
    d.   use drugs.

29. In studies of social relationships, adolescents report more disagreements with this person than any other.
    a. best friend
    b. father
    c. mother
    d. younger sibling

30. This observation came out of the most recent studies on divorce.
    a. Japanese families are now the most likely to divorce.
    b. African-American families are now the least likely to divorce.
    c. Divorce rates in America are now the highest ever.
    d. Divorce rates in America, after decades of increase, are now starting to decline.

ADOLESCENCE ON THE SCREEN

- *Ordinary People* concerns parents and their teenage son's struggle to deal with the death of a younger sibling. The surviving son feels guilt and blame, leading him to suicidal depression.

- *Tumbleweeds* is the story of a displaced single mother and her teenage daughter who move from place to place and live on a shoestring, while the mother looks for a man who will give them a better life.

- *Liberty House* depicts the changing sociopolitical climate of the 1950s, including integration, interracial dating, and changing family structure and influence.

ADOLESCENCE IN BOOKS

- *Between Parent & Teenager*, by Haim Ginott (Avon: NY, 1999), continues to be one of the most widely read and recommended books for parents who want to communicate more effectively with their teenagers.

- *Surviving the Breakup: How Children and Parents Cope with Divorce*, by Judith Wallerstein & Joan B. Kelly (Basic Books: NY, 1996), adds more empirical data to back up theories regarding what happens after divorce.

- *Growing Up with Divorce*, by Neil Kalter (Free Press: NY, 1990), provides divorced parents with information to help their children and youth avoid emotional problems.

- *I'm Not Mad, I Just Hate You!* by R. Cohen-Sandler & M. Silver (Viking: NY, 1999), deals with adolescent mother/daughter conflict.

- *The Shelter of Each Other: Rebuilding Our Families*, by Mary Pipher (Ballantine: NY, 1996), calls for strengthening the family for the benefit of children, parents, and grandparents.

Answer Key

KEY TERMS

1. **reciprocal socialization** The process by which children and adolescents socialize parents, just as parents socialize them.

2. **synchrony** The carefully coordinated interaction between the parent and the child or adolescent in which, often unknowingly, they are attuned to each other's behavior.

3. **developmental construction views** Views sharing the belief that as individuals grow up, they acquire modes of relating to others. There are two main variations of this view. One emphasizes continuity and stability in relationships throughout the life span, the other emphasizes discontinuity and changes in relationships throughout the life span.

4. **continuity view** A developmental view that emphasizes the role of early parent-child relationships in constructing a basic way of relating to people throughout the life span.

5. **discontinuity view** A developmental view that emphasizes change and growth in relationships over time.

6. **authoritarian parenting** This is a restrictive, punitive style in which the parent exhorts the adolescent to follow the parent's directions and to respect work and effort. Firm limits and controls are placed on adolescents, and little verbal exchange is allowed. This style is associated with adolescents' socially incompetent behavior.

7. **authoritative parenting** This style encourages adolescents to be independent but still places limits and controls on their actions. Extensive verbal give-and-take is allowed, and parents are warm and nurturing toward the adolescent. This style is associated with adolescents' socially competent behavior.

8. **neglectful parenting** A style in which the parent is very uninvolved in the adolescent's life. It is associated with adolescents' social incompetence, especially a lack of self-control.

9. **indulgent parenting** A style in which parents are highly involved with their adolescents but place few demands or controls on them. This is associated with adolescents' social incompetence, especially a lack of self-control.

10. **emotional autonomy** The capacity to relinquish childlike dependencies on parents.

11. **insecure attachment** In this attachment pattern, infants either avoid the caregiver or show considerable resistance or ambivalence toward the caregiver. This pattern is theorized to be related to difficulties in relationships and problems in later development.

12. **secure attachment** In this attachment pattern infants use their primary caregiver, usually the mother, as a secure base from which to explore the environment. Secure attachment is theorized to be an important foundation for psychological development later in childhood, adolescence, and adulthood.

13. **dismissing/avoidant attachment** An insecure attachment category in which individuals de-emphasize the importance of attachment. This category is associated with consistent experiences of rejection of attachment needs by caregivers.

14. **preoccupied/ambivalent attachment** An insecure attachment category in which adolescents are hypertuned to attachment experiences. This is thought to occur mainly because parents are inconsistently available to the adolescents.

15. **unresolved/disorganized attachment** An insecure category in which the adolescent has an unusually high level of fear and is disoriented. This may result from such traumatic experiences as a parent's death or abuse by parents.

16. **boundary ambiguity** The uncertainty in stepfamilies about who is on or out of the family and who is performing or responsible for certain tasks in the family system.

KEY PEOPLE IN THE STUDY OF ADOLESCENCE

1.	E	4.	D
2.	A	5.	C
3.	B	6.	F

"DR. DETAIL'S" LIBRARY EXERCISE

Individual answers will vary, but most should report changes in the size of the family and mobility of the family. Other issues could be income, divorce rates, etc.

FAMILY PROCESSES
SECTION REVIEW

1. Reciprocal socialization is the process by which children and adolescents socialize parents just as parents socialize them.

2. Synchrony refers to the carefully coordinated interaction between the parent and the child or adolescent, in which, often unknowingly, they are attuned to each other's behavior.

3. The continuity view emphasizes the role that early parent-child relationships play in constructing a basic way of relating to people throughout the life span. The discontinuity view emphasizes change and growth in relationships over time.

4. Twain felt that as adolescents grow older, they come to understand their parents better.

5. Adolescents today are required to function in a more anonymous, larger environment with multiple and varying teachers.

6. The primary difference found is that the fathers are warmer and communicate better with their children.

7. During its height, the depression produced economic deprivation, adult depression and discontent, marital conflict, inconsistent child-rearing, and unhealthy behaviors (e.g., drinking).

8. Cognitive processes are increasingly believed to be central to understanding socialization in the family.

KEY PEOPLE IN SECTION

Alan Sroufe—Found in his research support for continuity.

Andrew Collins—In his longitudinal study, he found evidence for the discontinuity view of relationships.

Mark Twain—Once remarked that when he was 14 his father was so ignorant he could hardly stand to have the man around, but when Twain turned 21, he was astonished at how much his father had learned in those seven years.

Margaret Mead—Described subtle changes in a culture that have significant influences on the family.

PARENT-ADOLESCENT RELATIONSHIPS
SECTION REVIEW

1. Matching Answers:

1.	J		**7.**	C
2.	G		**8.**	D
3.	B		**9.**	H
4.	E		**10.**	I
5.	F		**11.**	K
6.	A			

2. Authoritarian parenting, which emphasizes a restrictive punitive style. Authoritative parenting, which encourages adolescents to be independent and active in decision making. Neglectful parenting, where parents are not actively involved in their child's lives. Indulgent parenting, where parents allow too many freedoms to their children.

3. The current role of father in the family presents a shift from breadwinner and moral guardian to a role that incorporates far more nurturing and involvement in day-to-day living.

4. Permissiveness in outside activities; permissiveness in age-related activities; parent regard for judgement; activities with status implications.

5. The reasons are numerous. Some escape poverty, abuse, overcontrolling parents and still others are just simply adventure-seeking.

KEY PEOPLE IN SECTION

Diana Baumrind—believes that parents should be neither punitive nor aloof from their adolescents, but rather should develop rules and be affectionate with them.

Judith Smetana—believes that parent-adolescent conflict can be better understood by considering the adolescent's changing social cognitive abilities.

Reed Larson—spent six months in India studying middle-SES adolescents and their families; he observed that in India there is little parent-adolescent conflict and many would fit Baumrind's model of "authoritarian."

John Bowlby—argued that secure attachment in infancy is central to the development of social competence.

Mary Ainsworth—argued that secure attachment in infancy is central to the development of social competence.

SIBLING RELATIONSHIPS
SECTION REVIEW

1. Sibling relationships show a higher degree of conflict than with relationships with other social agents (parents, peers, teachers, and romantic partners).

2. Later-borns usually enjoy better relations with peers than first-born children.

3. Contrary to public opinion of "spoiled brat," most research suggests goal orientation and many positive personality traits.

THE CHANGING FAMILY IN A CHANGING SOCIETY
SECTION REVIEW

1. Most research suggests that adolescents from divorced families show poorer adjustment, such as externalizing disorders.

2. One of the biggest adjustments following divorce is lower SES. There is a greater decline if the child lives with the mother.

3. They matter a lot. When divorced parents have a harmonious relationship, the children do much better.

4. a. stepfather, b. stepmother, and c. blended or complex families

5. Yes. Their adjustment problems are very similar to those of kids in divorced families.

6. Abusing siblings, stealing, vandalizing, using substances, etc.

7. Deprived adolescents show less positive peer interaction.

8. Researchers have found no discernable differences between adolescents raised by gay and/or lesbian parents as opposed to heterosexual parents.

9. Ethnic minority families differ from White American families in their size, structure, reliance on kinship networks, level of income, and education.

10. Mothers tend to get little of the credit for their children's successes and much of the blame for their failures.

11.   During the Industrial Revolution, fathers gained the role of breadwinner, although moral role model has also been a historic part of the father's role as well.

12.   Today's fathers spend only a small portion of their time with their children. As little as 1/3 what mothers do. They have adapted a more nurturing role as opposed to primarily bread winner.

KEY PEOPLE IN SECTION

James Bray—found that over time stepfamilies often fall into three types based on their relationships: neo-traditional, matriarchal, and romantic.

E. Mavis Hetherington—prominent researcher regarding the effects of divorce on children.

Lois Hoffman—a leading authority on maternal employment; she says it's a fact of life.

Nancy Galambos—studied the effects of parents' work overload on their relationships with their adolescent on the adolescent's development.

Thomas and Lynette Long—concluded that a slight majority of latchkey children had negative experiences.

Joan Lipsitz—called the lack of adult supervision of children and adolescents in the after-school hours one of the nation's major problems.

Frank Furstenburg and Kathleen Harris—documented how nurturant fathering can overcome children's difficult life circumstances.

SOCIAL POLICY, ADOLESCENTS, AND FAMILIES
SECTION REVIEW

1.   Show them warmth and respect; demonstrate sustained interest in their lives; recognize and adapt to their changing cognitive and socioemotional development; communicate expectations for high standards of conduct and achievement; display authoritative, constructive ways of dealing with problems and conflict.

EXPLORATIONS IN ADOLESCENCE

Both ethnic groups tend to "stick together." African-American grandmothers are a great resource for mothers and infants. Mothers of adolescents who have good relationships with their mothers pass that on to their children. Family support has been directly related to adolescent school success and self-reliance. In Mexican-American families the father is the undisputed authority but the mother is the main source of affection and care. These families exist more for each other, rather than for themselves. Self-reliance is not valued as highly as it is in African-American (and White) families.

COGNITIVE CHALLENGE

1.   Example: Parents and adolescent should set aside a time when the teen first indicates an interest in dating to discuss only this issue. Each come to the "meeting" with a list of what they feel they

"must" have and what they would "like" to have. Beginning with the "must" have list, they should discuss and negotiate, then move on to the "like" to have list. They should come up with a written agreement that both are comfortable with signing. The agreement could have a method for resolving disputes that arise about dating, such as submitting the issue to a respected and neutral party (such as an aunt or uncle).

2.   Example: Parents should tell their child as soon as the separation is decided upon. Both parents should be present and should make it clear that they respect each other and love their child, and that the separation is no fault of the child's. The teenager should be consulted about which parent he or she wishes to live with and the arrangements for visiting the other parent. The teen should be given the opportunity to ask questions and express his or her feelings.

ADOLESCENCE IN RESEARCH

The researcher assessed 139 boys and girls 14 years of age and their parents. The hypothesis was that parents with problems would be more likely to have adolescents with problems. The results supported the hypothesis. The adolescents were very directly impacted by the adjustment levels of the parents.

⊠ COMPREHENSIVE REVIEW

1.	d	9.	b	17.	d	25.	b
2.	c	10.	d	18.	d	26.	c
3.	c	11.	b	19.	c	27.	b
4.	b	12.	d	20.	a	28.	a
5.	b	13.	b	21.	b	29.	c
6.	a	14.	a	22.	b	30.	d
7.	b	15.	c	23.	d		
8.	c	16.	b	24.	b		

⌘

Chapter 10   Peers

Learning Goals with Key Terms and Key People in Boldface

1.0   **DISCUSS THE ROLE OF PEER RELATIONS IN ADOLESCENT DEVELOPMENT**

    A.   **Peer Group Functions**

        1.1   What are **peers,** and how are they important to adolescent social development?

        1.2   How do **peers** provide a basis for social comparison and a source of information about the world outside the family?

        1.3   Why are good peer relations necessary for normal social development?

        1.4   What do adolescents do when they are with their peers?

        1.5   How can peer relations be either positive or negative?

        1.6   What did Jean Piaget and Harry Stack Sullivan stress about peer relations?

        1.7   According to Hartup, in what ways do peer relations vary?

    B.   **Family-Peer Linkages**

        1.8   How do healthy family relations promote healthy peer relations?

        1.9   What are some of the ways in which the worlds of parents and peers are connected?

        1.10   What is the main difference between the quality of adolescent's relations with their peers and parents?

    C.   **Peer Conformity**

        1.11   What is **conformity?**

        1.12   How can **conformity** to peer pressure in adolescence be positive or negative?

        1.13   At what point does conformity to antisocial standards of peers peak?

        1.14   How can the effects of peer pressure be observed?

    D.   **Peer Statuses**

        1.15   How would you describe **popular children?**

        1.16   What is the peer status of **neglected children?**

        1.17   How well do **rejected children** fare among their peers?

        1.18   Where do **controversial children** fit in with their peer group?

    E.   **Social Cognition and Emotion**

        1.19   How is social knowledge associated with improved peer relations?

        1.20   How do good information processing skills improve peer relations?

        1.21   What are the five steps children go through in processing information about their social world?

        1.22   What part does the ability to regulate emotion play in successful peer relations?

    F.   **Strategies for Improving Social Skills**

        1.23   How do **conglomerate strategies** improve social skills?

        1.24   How can neglected children and adolescents be trained to interact more effectively with their peers?

2.0 FRIENDSHIP
    A.   It's Important
        2.1   What is a **friend?**
        2.2   What are the six functions that friendship plays in adolescence?
    B.   Sullivan's Idea
        2.3   How does research support or refute **Sullivan's** ideas?
    C.   Intimacy and Similarity
        2.4   What are the key characteristics of friendship?
        2.5   What similarities do friends share?
    D.   Mixed-Age Friendships
        2.6   What happens to adolescents who become close friends with older individuals?

3.0 SUMMARIZE WHAT TAKES PLACE IN ADOLESCENT GROUPS
    A.   Group Function and Formation
        3.1   How do groups satisfy adolescents' personal needs, reward them, provide information, raise their self-esteem, and give them an identity?
        3.2   How do **norms** and **roles** play a part in any group?
        3.3   What are group **norms?**
        3.4   What are group **roles?**
    B.   Children Groups and Adolescent Groups
        3.5   In what ways do children's groups differ from those of adolescents?
        3.6   What did Dexter Dunphy learn about adolescent groups?
    C.   Cliques and Crowds
        3.7   What is the difference between a **clique** and a **crowd?**
        3.8   What different cliques are found in most secondary schools?
        3.9   With what type of cliques is membership associated with high self-esteem?
        3.10   What is the main feature distinguishing a **crowd?**
        3.11   What are Brown's conclusions about adolescent crowds?
    D.   Youth Organizations
        3.12   In what way do youth organizations influence adolescent development?
        3.13   What is the mission of boys' clubs and girls' clubs?

4.0 DESCRIBE THE ROLES OF GENDER AND CULTURE IN ADOLESCENT PEER GROUPS AND FRIENDSHIPS
    A.   Gender
        4.1   How do boys and girls differ when interacting with various groups?
        4.2   What are some features of lower-socioeconomic status groups?
        4.3   Why do ethnic minority adolescents often have two sets of peers?
        4.4   Why do ethnic minority adolescents turn to peer groups more than White adolescents?
    B.   Culture
        4.5   Why is access to peers restricted in some countries?
        4.6   Explain the role of the dormitory in the Murian culture.

5.0 CHARACTERIZE ADOLESCENT DATING AND ROMANTIC RELATIONSHIPS
    A.   Functions of Dating
        5.1   What is dating and what are its functions?
        5.2   What eight functions can be served by dating?
    B.   Types of Dating and Developmental Changes
        5.3   At what age do adolescents start to hang out together in heterosexual groups?
        5.4   What is cyberdating?

5.5   How much time do young adolescents spend thinking about the opposite sex as opposed to actually being with them?

5.6   What are common myths associated with dating among sexual minority youth?

5.7   What special problems do immigrant adolescents face with their families in relationship to dating?

C.   **Emotion and Romantic Relationships**

5.8   How do romantic relationships affect an adolescent's life?

5.9   What emotions are associated with adolescent romantic relationships?

D.   **Romantic Love and Its Construction**

5.10   What is the difference between **romantic love** and **affectionate love?**

5.11   How does the relationship of the adolescents parents impact their own dating relationships?

5.12   What role does secure attachment play in adolescent relationships?

5.13   What is the developmental construction view of romantic love?

5.14   According to Mavis Hetherington, how are the relationships of girls and boys impacted by the divorce of their parents?

5.15   What is Sullivan's conceptualization of collaboration in dating?

5.16   How important are peers and friends in adolescent romantic relationships?

5.17   What is the relationship between group leadership and dating?

E.   **Gender and Culture**

5.18   Do male and female adolescents bring different motivations to the dating experience?

5.19   What are the differences between male and female **dating scripts?**

5.20   How is adolescent dating different for Latinos than traditional American dating styles?

Exercises

KEY TERMS COMPLETION EXERCISE

Each key term is presented in the form of an incomplete sentence. Compare each sentence by either defining the term or giving an example. Compare your definitions with those given at the end of the study guide chapter.

1.   To adolescents, **peers** are

 children or adolescents who are about the same age or maturity level.

2.   **Conformity** means to

 occurs when individuals adopt the attitudes or behaviour of others bc of real or imagined pressure from them.

3. **Popular children** are those who

   are frequently nominated as a best friend and rarely are disliked by peers.

4. **Neglected children** are very likely to

   are infrequently nominated as a best friend but are not disliked by their peers.

5. **Rejected children** often

   are infrequently nominated as someone's best friend and are actively disliked by peers.

6. **Controversial children** are those who

   are frequently nominated both as someone's best friend and as being disliked.

7. **Conglomerate strategies** are meant to

   involve the use of a combo of techniques, rather than single approach, to improve adols' social skills.

8. **Friends** are those who

   are a subset of peers who engage in mutual companionship, support, and intimacy. (relationships are more involved and closer)

9. **Intimacy in friendship** is exemplified by

   self disclosure or sharing of private thoughts.

10. Examples of **norms** are

    rules that apply to all members of a group. ie/ GPA level in honour society, weights in off-season for football

11. The importance of **roles** is

    certain positions in a group that are governed by rules and expectations. Roles define how adols should behave in those positions

12. **Cliques** are meant to

sm. groups that range from 2-12 individuals (ave 5-6). members usually same sex, similar age.
— share ideas, hangout, develop an in-group identity.

13. **Crowds** are seen when

larger group structure than cliques. membership usually based on reputation. Less personal than cliques.

14. **Dating scripts** are used by

_____

_____

15. An example of **romantic love** is

_____

_____

16. An example of **affectionate love** is

_____

_____

KEY PEOPLE IN THE STUDY OF ADOLESCENCE

_____	1. Reed Larson	A. Studied conformity
_____	2. Thomas Berndt	B. Studied nature and function of adolescent and children's groups, emphasizing change in sexual make-up
_____	3. John Coie and Kenneth Dodge	C. Studied role of attachment patterns in adolescent romantic relationships
_H_	4. William Hartup	D. Studied role of peers in romantic involvement
_G_	5. Harry Stack Sullivan	E. Encouraged structured volunteer activities as a way to develop initiative
_____	6. Candice Feiring	F. Studied the impact of insecure attachment on dating relationships
_B_	7. Dexter Dunphy	G. Psychoanalytical theorist who emphasized importance of friendship for adolescents
_____	8. Wyndol Furman	H. Studied nature of child and adolescent friendships
_____	9. Bradford Brown	I. Studied role of peer influences in child and adolescent aggression and antisocial behavior
_____	10. Jennifer Connolly	J. Found that males and females bring different motivations to the dating experience

EXPLORING PEER RELATIONS
SECTION REVIEW

1. How they are seen by peers is the most important aspect of many adolescents' lives. Why?

    _____

    _____

2. What do adolescents do when they are with their peers?

    _____

    _____

3. How important are good peer relationships for normal social development in adolescence?

    _____

    _____

4. What are some of the ways the worlds of parents and peers are connected?

    _____

    _____

5. What is conformity?

    _____

    _____

6. According to developmentalists, what are three types of children who have a different status than popular children?

    _____

    _____

7. How can the effects of peer pressure be observed?

    _____

    _____

8. In peer relations, what role is played by appropriate cognitive skills?

    _____

    _____

9. How can conglomerate strategies be used to improve adolescents' social skills?

_____

_____

10. How can neglected children and adolescents be trained to interact more effectively with their peers?

_____

_____

KEY PEOPLE IN SECTION (Describe the contributions of this individual to the study and understanding of adolescence.)

Anna Freud—

_____

_____

Jean Piaget and Harry Stack Sullivan—

_____

_____

Thomas Berndt—

_____

_____

James Coleman—

_____

_____

Kenneth Dodge—

_____

_____

FRIENDSHIP
SECTION REVIEW

1. What is a friend?

_____

_____

2. What six functions do adolescent friendships serve?

_____

_____

3. List and give an example of five appropriate strategies for making friends.

_____

_____

4. List and give examples for three inappropriate strategies for making friends.

_____

_____

5. How important is similarity in forming friendships?

_____

_____

6. What happens to adolescents who become close friends with older individuals?

_____

_____

KEY PEOPLE IN SECTION (Describe the contributions of this individual to the study and understanding of adolescence.)

Harry Stack Sullivan—

_____

_____

Willard Hartup—

_____

_____

ADOLESCENT GROUPS
SECTION REVIEW

1. Why does an adolescent join a group?

_____

_____

2.   What two things do all groups have in common?

_____

_____

3.   Describe what Dunphy found to be the five stages of progression of peer group relations in adolescence.

_____

_____

4.   Summarize the conclusions of Bradford Brown and colleagues' most recent research on cliques.

_____

_____

5.   Compare and contrast cliques and crowds.

_____

_____

6.   What impact can youth organizations have on adolescents?

_____

_____

KEY PEOPLE IN SECTION (Describe the contributions of this individual to the study and understanding of adolescence.)

Dexter Dunphy—

_____

_____

Bradford Brown—

_____

_____

Jane Lohr—

_____

_____

Reed Larson—

_____

_____

GENDER AND CULTURE
SECTION REVIEW

1.   How do boys and girls differ when interacting with various groups?

_____

_____

2.   Why is access to peers restricted in some countries?

_____

_____

3.   Explain the role of the dormitory in the Murian culture?

_____

_____

DATING AND ROMANTIC RELATIONSHIPS
SECTION REVIEW

1.   What eight functions are served by dating?

_____

_____

2.   a.   Describe the three main activities involved in the male dating script and give an example of each.

_____

_____

b.   Describe the three main activities involved in the female dating script and give an example of each.

_____

_____

3.   What is romantic love?

_____

_____

4.   What is affectionate love?

_____

_____

5.   According to Mavis Hetherington, how are the relationships of girls and boys impacted by the divorce of their parents?

_____

_____

6.   How is adolescent dating different for Latinos than traditional American dating styles?

_____

_____

KEY PEOPLE IN SECTION (Describe the contributions of this individual to the study and understanding of adolescence.

Candice Feiring—

_____

_____

Wyndol Furman and Elizabeth Wehner—

_____

_____

Peter Blos—

_____

_____

Mavis Hetherington—

_____

_____

Harry Stack Sullivan—

_____

_____

Jennifer Connolly—

_____

_____

EXPLORATIONS IN ADOLESCENCE

1.   What did the 1995 Search Institute study find regarding barriers to participation in youth programs?

_____

_____

COGNITIVE CHALLENGE

1.   How did your relationship with your parents affect your peer relationships and friendships in adolescence? How did your parents influence your choice of peers and friends? How did your parents' marital relationship affect your dating and romantic relationships?

_____

_____

2.   Think back over your adolescent dating experiences. How were your experiences different when you were 13, 15, and 17? What would you do differently if you could begin anew today? What advice would you offer today's teenagers of those ages?

_____

_____

ADOLESCENCE IN RESEARCH

Concerning Brown and Lohr's 1987 research dealing with the self-esteem of students in grades 7 through 12, state the hypothesis, the research methods (if known), the research conclusions, and the implications and applications for adolescent development.

_____

_____

⊠ COMPREHENSIVE REVIEW

1.   Jason is a sixth-grader who spends a lot of time with his peers. Statistically speaking, in which activity is he most likely engaging?
   a.   going to stores
   b.   watching television
   c.   team sports
   d.   girl-watching

2. Most cooperative group programs have been conducted in these settings.
   a. children's homes
   b. video arcades
   c. academic settings
   d. hospitals

3. Participating in a newspaper drive with one's club because the club wants everyone to be involved in this activity is an example of _____ conformity.
   a. negative
   b. positive
   c. independent
   d. responsible

4. Thomas Berndt found that adolescent conformity to antisocial, peer-endorsed behavior _____ in late high school years, and _____ agreement between parents and peers begins to occur in some areas.
   a. decreases; greater
   b. decreases; lesser
   c. increases; greater
   d. increases; lesser

5. The adolescent who does not have significant interactions with peers is likely to be
   a. handicapped.
   b. antisocial.
   c. neglected.
   d. mature and independent.

6. Kenneth Dodge indicates that adolescents go through five steps when processing information about their social world. Which of the following is NOT one of these steps?
   a. response search
   b. selecting an optimal response
   c. decoding of social cues
   d. elaboration of possibilities

7. Which of the following is NOT a characteristic of a popular child?
   a. enthusiasm
   b. self-confidence
   c. conceit
   d. list well

8. Children who are frequently nominated as a best friend and are rarely disliked by their peers are
   a. popular children.
   b. neglected children.
   c. rejected children.
   d. controversial children.

9. Children who are infrequently nominated as a best friend but are not disliked by their peers are
   a. popular children.
   b. neglected children.

    c.   rejected children.
    d.   controversial children.

10.   Children who are infrequently nominated as a best friend and are actively disliked by their peers are
    a.   popular children.
    b.   neglected children.
    c.   rejected children.
    d.   controversial children.

11.   Children who are frequently nominated both as a best friend and as being disliked are
    a.   popular children.
    b.   neglected children.
    c.   rejected children.
    d.   controversial children.

12.   Which of the following is NOT one of the six functions served by friendship?
    a.   intimacy/affection
    b.   personal gain
    c.   ego support
    d.   stimulation

13.   Rules that apply to all members of a group are
    a.   mandates.
    b.   roles.
    c.   values.
    d.   norms.

14.   _____ are small groups that range from two to about twelve individuals and average about five to six individuals.
    a.   Cliques
    b.   Chumships
    c.   Crowds
    d.   Youth organizations

15.   Which of the following is not one of the myths regarding the romantic relationships of sexual minority youth?
    a.   There is a great deal of complexity in the romantic possibilities of sexual minority youth.
    b.   Adolescents who sexually desire the same sex always fall in love with the same sex.
    c.   All gay and lesbian youth only have same-sex attractions.
    d.   All sexual minority youth quietly struggle with same-sex attractions in childhood, shun heterosexual dating, and gradually sense that they are gay in mid- to late-adolescence.

16.   Which theorist stressed the importance of friendship to adolescent development?
    a.   Kenneth Dodge
    b.   Erik Erikson
    c.   Muzafer Sherif
    d.   Harry Stack Sullivan

17.   As the parent of an adolescent male, you are concerned about his friends who are 3–5 years older than he is. Your concern is
        a.   not justified.
        b.   not justified, because he will probably not drop out of school.
        c.   justified because his friend is probably a drug user.
        d.   justified because your son will likely engage in deviant behavior.

18.   A subset of peers who engage in mutual companionship, support, and intimacy is called
        a.   friends.
        b.   cohorts.
        c.   cliques.
        d.   a gang.

19.   Compared to adolescent groups, children's groups
        a.   are not as formalized.
        b.   include a broader array of members.
        c.   have well-defined rules and regulations.
        d.   are composed of large cliques.

20.   An adolescent who has older friends is LEAST likely to become
        a.   pregnant.
        b.   involved in drug use.
        c.   involved in underage drinking of alcohol.
        d.   class valedictorian.

21.   Sarah is 16 years old and does not want to belong to any clique. She "does her own thing" and is good at what she does. Her level of self-esteem is likely
        a.   the same as that of the "jocks."
        b.   lower than that of the "populars."
        c.   lower than that of the" normals."
        d.   the same as that of the "nobodies."

22.   Which of the following is NOT a main function of adolescent dating?
        a.   recreation
        b.   status
        c.   socialization
        d.   procreation

23.   Small groups that range from two to about twelve individuals and average about five to six individuals are called
        a.   cohorts.
        b.   cliques.
        c.   crowds.
        d.   chumships.

24.   Affectionate love is also referred to as
        a.   *eros.*
        b.   *agape.*
        c.   passionate love.
        d.   companionate love.

25. Cindy is a teenage girl who has been interacting with a teenage boy, Simon, she has only met on the Internet. Simon might be referred to as
    a. a pedophile.
    b. Michael Jackson.
    c. a cyber boyfriend.
    d. a Web date.

26. Boys are more likely than girls to be involved in all of the following EXCEPT
    a. collaborative discourse.
    b. risk taking.
    c. ego displays.
    d. conflict.

ADOLESCENCE ON THE SCREEN

- *Diner* follows a group of friends during high school and graduation.

- *Breakfast Club* depicts how students who must spend Saturday morning in detention develop into a cohesive group.

- *Trainspotting* involves a group of friends whose lives revolve around using drugs.

- *Romeo and Juliet*, a Shakespearean classic about romantic love, appeals to today's adolescents.

ADOLESCENCE IN BOOKS

- *Just Friends*, by Lillian Rubin (HarperCollins: NY, 1985), explores the nature of friends and intimacy.

Answer Key

KEY TERMS

1. **peers** Children or adolescents who are of about the same age or maturity level.

2. **conformity** This occurs when individuals adopt the attitudes or behaviors of others because of real or imagined pressure from them.

3. **popular children** Children who are frequently nominated as a best friend and are rarely disliked by their peers.

4. **neglected children** Children who are infrequently nominated as a best friend but are not disliked by their peers.

5. **rejected children** Children who are infrequently nominated as a best friend and are actively disliked by their peers.

6. **controversial children** Children who are frequently nominated both as being a best friend and as being disliked.

7. **conglomerate strategies** Involves the use of a combination of techniques, rather than a single approach, to improve adolescents' social skills.

8. **friends** A subset of peers who engage in mutual companionship, support, and intimacy.

9. **intimacy in friendship** In most research, this is defined narrowly as self-disclosure or sharing of private thoughts.

10. **norms** Rules that apply to all members of a group.

11. **roles** Certain positions in a group that are governed by rules and expectations. Roles define how adolescents should behave in those positions.

12. **cliques** These units are smaller, involve more intimacy, and are more cohesive than crowds. They are, however, larger and involve less intimacy than friendships.

13. **crowd** The largest, most loosely defined, and least personal unit of adolescent peer society. Crowds often meet because of their mutual interest in an activity.

14. **dating scripts** The cognitive models that adolescents and adults use to guide and evaluate dating interactions.

15. **romantic love** Also called passionate love or Eros, this love has strong sexual and infatuation components, and it often predominates in the early part of a love relationship.

16. **affectionate love** Also called companionate love, this love occurs when an individual wants to have another person near and has a deep, caring affection for that person.

KEY PEOPLE IN THE STUDY OF ADOLESCENCE

1.	E	4.	H	7.	B	10.	D
2.	A	5.	G	8.	F		
3.	I	6.	J	9.	C		

EXPLORING PEER RELATIONS
SECTION REVIEW

1. To be excluded means stress, frustration, and sadness. So many will do most anything to be included.

2. For boys (more so than girls) a lot of time was spent doing sports activities. General play and going places was common for both sexes.

3. Good peer relationships might be necessary for normal social development.

4. Parents choose where they will work, live, churches, school districts, etc. All impact the children.

5.   When individuals adopt the attitudes or behavior of others because of real or imagined pressure from them.

6.   Neglected children, rejected children, and controversial children.

7.   Peer pressure is a pervasive theme of adolescents' lives. Its power can be observed in almost every dimension of adolescents' behavior—their choice of dress, music, language, values, leisure activities, and so on.

8.   They help generate correct interpretations of situations, which lessens the likelihood of conflict.

9.   Refers to coaching to improve an adolescent's social skills.

10.   Training programs help them attract attention from their peers in positive ways and to hold their attention by asking questions, by listening in a warm and friendly way, and by saying things about themselves that relate to the peers' interests.

KEY PEOPLE IN SECTION

Anna Freud—studied peer attachment with six children from different families whose parents were killed in WWII.

Jean Piaget and Harry Stack Sullivan—were influential theorists who stressed that it is through peer interaction that children and adolescents learn the symmetrical reciprocity mode of relationships.

Thomas Berndt—focused on the negative, neutral, and positive aspects of peer conformity.

James Coleman—pointed out that for adolescents in the average range, there is little or no relation between physical attractiveness and popularity.

Kenneth Dodge—found that aggressive boys are more likely to perceive another child's actions as hostile when the peer's intentions are ambiguous.

FRIENDSHIP
SECTION REVIEW

1.   A subset of peers who engage in mutual companionship, support, and intimacy.

2.   Companionship; stimulation; physical support; ego support; social comparison; intimacy/affection.

3.   Initiate interaction; be nice; engage in prosocial behavior; show respect for self and others; provide social support.

4.   Using psychological aggression, having a negative self-presentation; engaging in antisocial behavior.

5.   Friends are generally similar in terms of age, sex, ethnicity, and other factors.

6.   These relationships often lead to delinquency and sexual activities.

KEY PEOPLE IN SECTION

Harry Stack Sullivan—was the most influential theorist to discuss the importance of friendship.

Willard Hartup—studied peer relations across four decades, recently concluding that children and adolescents often use friends as cognitive and social resources.

ADOLESCENT GROUPS
SECTION REVIEW

1.   Groups satisfy adolescents' personal needs, reward them, provide information, raise self-esteem, and give them an identity.

2.   Norms and roles.

3.   a.   Precrowd stage of isolated, unisex groups
        b.   Beginning of the crowd; unisex groups start group-group interaction
        c.   Crowd in structural transition; unisex groups are forming mixed-sex groups
        d.   Fully developed crowd; mixed-sex groups are closely associated
        e.   Crowd begins to disintegrate as loosely associated groups of couples pair off

4.   a.   The influence of cliques is not entirely negative
        b.   The influence of cliques is not uniform for all adolescents
        c.   Development changes occur in cliques

5.   Cliques are small groups that range from two to about 12 individuals and average about five. Crowds are a larger group structure than cliques. Adolescents are usually members of a crowd based on reputation.

6.   Youth organizations can have an important influence on the adolescent's development, depending on which they are.

KEY PEOPLE IN SECTION

Dexter Dunphy—indicated that opposite-sex participation in groups increases during adolescence.

Bradford Brown—researched the role of crowds in adolescence.

Jane Lohr—examined self-esteem of adolescents.

Reed Larson—proposed that structured activities, such as selling Girl Scout cookies, are especially well-suited for the development of initiative.

GENDER AND CULTURE
SECTION REVIEW

1.   There is increasing evidence that gender plays an important role in the peer group and friendships. The evidence related to the peer group focuses on group size and interaction. Boys are more likely than girls to associate in clusters. Boys are more likely than girls to engage in competition.

2.   In some countries, adults restrict adolescents' access to peers. Examples are India and Arab countries.

3.   In the Murian culture of India, male and female children live in a dormitory from the age of 6 until they get married. The dormitory is a religious community.

DATING AND ROMANTIC RELATIONSHIPS
SECTION REVIEW

1.   Dating can be a form of recreation. Dating is a source of status and achievement. Dating is part of the socialization process in adolescence. Dating involves learning about intimacy and serves as an opportunity to establish a unique, meaningful relationship with a person of the opposite sex. Dating can be a context for sexual experimentation. Dating can provide companionship through interaction and shared activities. Dating experiences contribute to identity formation and development. Dating can be a means of mate sorting and selection.

2.   a. (1) Initiating the date; (2) controlling the public domain; and (3) initiating physical contact. b. (1) Concern for the private domain; (2) participating in structure of the date; and (3)responding to sexual gestures.

3.   Also called passionate love or Eros; it has strong sexual and infatuation components and often predominates in the early parts of a relationship.

4.   Also called companionate love; occurs when individuals desire to have another person near and have a deep, caring affection for that person.

5.   According to Hetherington, divorce is associated with a stronger heterosexual orientation in daughters. Girls also had a more negative opinion of males when they came out of a divorced family.

6.   Most Latino youths' parents view U.S. style dating as a violation of traditional courtship styles. As a result, dating for Latinos is often described as full of tension and conflict.

KEY PEOPLE IN SECTION

Candice Feiring—found that male and female adolescents bring different motivations to the dating experience.
Wyndol Furman and Elizabeth Wehner—discussed how specific insecure attachment styles might be related to adolescents' romantic relationships.

Peter Blos—noted that at the beginning of adolescence, boys and girls try to separate themselves from opposite-sex parents as a love object.

Mavis Hetherington—found that divorce was associated with a stronger heterosexual orientation of adolescent daughters.

Harry Stack Sullivan—believed that it is through intimate friendships that adolescents learn a mature form of love he referred to as "collaborative."

Jennifer Connolly—documented the role of peers in the emergence of romantic involvement in adolescence.

EXPLORATIONS IN ADOLESCENCE

This study, based in Minneapolis, found that more than 50 percent of the youth said they don't participate in any type of youth program in a typical week. More than 40 percent reported no participation in youth programs during the summer months.

COGNITIVE CHALLENGE

No answers. Individual activity.

ADOLESCENCE IN RESEARCH

Two hundred twenty-one adolescents were either associated with major cliques (jocks, populars, normals, druggies/toughs, and nobodies) or not associated with any clique. The self-esteem of the jocks and populars was the highest, whereas that of the nobodies was the lowest. Those involved with no clique—the independents—had self-esteem equivalent to the jocks and the populars.

⊠ COMPREHENSIVE REVIEW

1.	c	8.	a	15.	a	22.	d
2.	c	9.	b	16.	d	23.	b
3.	b	10.	c	17.	d	24.	d
4.	a	11.	d	18.	a	25.	c
5.	c	12.	b	19.	a	26.	a
6.	d	13.	d	20.	d		
7.	c	14.	a	21.	a		

⌘

Chapter 11   Schools

Learning Goals with Key Terms and Key People in Boldface

1.0   DESCRIBE APPROACHES TO EDUCATING STUDENTS
A.   **Historical Aspects**
   1.1   How have secondary schools changed since the nineteenth century?
   1.2   What is the make up of a comprehensive high school?
   1.3   What functions of secondary schools are being debated today?
   1.4   How did the open education movement of the 1970s fail in the United States?
   1.5   What is the **back-to-basics movement?**
   1.6   What arguments are being made for schools to fulfill more comprehensive functions?
   1.7   What is **direct instruction approach** to student learning?
   1.8   What are **cognitive constructivist approaches** to student learning?
   1.9   What are **social constructivist approaches** to student learning?
   1.10   What is the American Psychological Association's learner centered psychological principles?
   1.11   What are the Carnegie Council on Adolescent Development's eight principles for transforming adolescent's educational experiences?
   1.12   How do the social contexts of schools differ at the preschool, elementary school, and secondary school levels?

2.0   DISCUSS TRANSITIONS IN SCHOOLING FROM EARLY ADOLESCENCE TO EMERGING ADULTHOOD
A.   **Transition to Middle or Junior High School**
   2.1   What is the origin of junior high schools?
   2.2   What were the justifications for junior high schools?
   2.3   How has the role of ninth grade been resolved over time?
   2.4   Why have middle schools become more popular than the junior high model?
   2.5   How are middle schools related to pubertal development?
   2.6   Is the transition to sixth- through eighth-grade middle schools easier for students than the transition to traditional junior highs (7–9)?
   2.7   Why is the transition to middle- or junior-high school stressful?
   2.8   What is the **top-dog phenomenon?**
B.   **What Makes A Successful Middle School?**
   2.9   According to **Lipsitz**, what makes a middle school successful?
   2.10   What did the Carnegie Foundation recommend about the redesign of middle schools?
C.   **The American High School**
   2.11   According to the National Commission on the High School Senior, what problems do America's high schools need to address for the 21st century?

D.   **High School Dropouts and Non-college Youth**

2.12   Over the past half century, what has been the reason for the drop in the numbers of dropouts?

2.13   What educational deficiencies do students who drop out experience in adulthood?

2.14   What are the extent and characteristics of ethnic minority students who drop out?

2.15   What factors are associated with dropping out?

2.16   What is the optimal size of a high school, with regard to avoiding high numbers of dropouts?

2.17   What approaches can be used to reduce the rate of dropping out and improve student experiences?

E.   **Transition from High School to College**

2.18   What happens to parental interaction during the transition?

2.19   What are the effects of discontinuity between high school and college?

2.20   Why are today's college freshmen suffering from more depression and stress than in the past?

F.   **Transition from College to Work**

2.21   Why is the transition from college to work a difficult one?

3.0   **EXPLAIN HOW THE SOCIAL CONTEXTS OF SCHOOL INFLUENCE ADOLESCENT DEVELOPMENT**

A.   **Changing Social Developmental Contexts**

3.1   How does the social context change at the different educational levels?

B.   **Size and Climate**

3.2   What are the most desirable classroom and school sizes?

3.3   What are some benefits of a small school?

3.4   What are some of the drawbacks of large schools?

3.5   What are some benefits of a large school?

3.6   Which class size best benefits student learning?

3.7   What are the components of a positive classroom climate?

3.8   What is the **authoritative strategy of classroom management?**

3.9   What is the **authoritarian strategy of classroom management?**

3.10   What is the **permissive strategy of classroom management?**

3.11   To what variables are classroom climate generally linked?

3.12   What is the effect of school climate on student achievement?

C.   **Person-Environment Fit and Aptitude-Treatment Interaction**

3.13   What happens when the schools do not meet the adolescent's needs?

D.   **Teachers and Parents**

3.14   Can a profile of a competent teacher be compiled?

3.15   How does parental involvement with schools change as students move into adolescence?

3.16   Why do student-teacher relationships often deteriorate after the transition to junior high?

3.17   Why is greater collaboration between schools, families, and communities needed?

3.18   What is Epstein's framework for improving parent involvement in adolescents' schooling?

E.   **Peers**

3.19   How does the structure of the middle school lead to more peer interaction?

3.20   Is popularity related to academic outcomes?

3.21   How significant is the problem of bullying in American schools?

3.22   What are common characteristics of victims of bullies?

F.   Culture

3.23   What is the effect of poverty on student learning?

3.24   What are the characteristics of schools in low-income neighborhoods?

3.25   How does ethnicity impact school experiences?

3.26   What is the role of teachers' positive expectations of ethnic students?

3.27   What are some effective teaching strategies for improving relations with ethnically diverse students?

3.28   What is a **jigsaw classroom?**

3.29   How can the concept of the **jigsaw classroom** be used to improve American schools?

3.30   What has been the evaluation of the effectiveness of the Comer schools?

3.31   What are some similarities and dissimilarities between American high schools and those in other countries?

4.0   CHARACTERIZE ADOLESCENTS WHO ARE EXCEPTIONAL AND THEIR EDUCATION

A.   Who Are Adolescents with Disabilities?

4.1   How many U.S. students receive special education services?

4.2   What percentage of students receiving special education has **learning disabilities?**

B.   Learning Disabilities

4.3   What are the characteristics of a **learning disability?**

4.4   Are gender differences observed among those with learning disabilities?

4.5   How are **learning disabilities** defined?

4.6   What is the most common problem for students with a learning disability?

C.   Attention Deficit/Hyperactivity Disorder (ADHD)

4.7   How is **ADHD** defined?

4.8   What is the controversy related to the diagnosis and treatment of **ADHD?**

4.9   What interventions are recommended for children and adolescents with **ADHD?**

D.   Educational Issues Involving Adolescents with Disabilities

4.10   What is **Public Law 92–142?**

4.11   What is **The Individuals with Disabilities Act (IDEA)?**

4.12   What does **least restrictive environment (LRE)** mean?

4.13   What is meant by **inclusion?**

E.   Adolescents Who Are Gifted

4.14   What are the criteria for giftedness?

4.15   According to **Winner,** what are the three characteristics of adolescents who are gifted?

4.16   What are some characteristics that characterize **gifted adolescents?**

4.17   What program options exist for students who are gifted?

EXERCISES

KEY TERMS COMPLETION EXERCISE

Each key term is presented in the form of an incomplete sentence. Complete each sentence by either defining the term or giving an example. Compare your definitions with those given at the end of the study guide chapter.

1.   According to the **back-to-basics movement,**

_____

_____

2.   A benefit of the **direct instruction approach** is

_____

_____

3.   The **cognitive constructivist approaches** emphasize

_____

_____

4.   **Social constructivist approaches** focus on

_____

_____

5.   You typically see evidence of the **top-dog phenomenon** in

_____

_____

6.   The benefits of an **authoritative strategy of classroom management** are

_____

_____

7.   The benefits of an **authoritarian strategy of classroom management** are

_____

_____

8.   A **permissive strategy of classroom management** can lead to

_____

_____

9.   The **aptitude-treatment interaction (ATI)** stresses the importance of

_____

_____

10.   I can tell that Jovan is in a **jigsaw classroom** because

_____

_____

11.   Having a **learning disability** means

_____

_____

12.   Having an **attention deficit/hyperactivity disorder (ADHD)** suggests

_____

_____

13.   With the institution of **Public Law 94–142** came

_____

_____

14.   The **Individuals with Disabilities Education Act (IDEA)** is

_____

_____

15.   Placement in the **least restrictive environment** means

_____

_____

16.   **Inclusion** means

_____

_____

17.   **Adolescents who are gifted** are

_____

_____

KEY PEOPLE IN THE STUDY OF ADOLESCENCE

Match the person with the concept of adolescent development with which they are associated.

_____ 1. Joan Lipsitz   A. Believed teachers should help students achieve industry
_____ 2. Jacqueline Eccles   B. Pioneered research on the jigsaw classroom
_____ 3. Erik Erikson   C. Studied how developmentally appropriate school environments could meet students' needs
_____ 4. Joyce Epstein   D. Conducted research into what makes a good middle school
_____ 5. Jonathan Kozol   E. Believes that parents needs to be more involved in schools
_____ 6. John Ogbu   F. Anthropologist who says American schools exploit minority students
_____ 7. Elliot Aronson   G. Author of *Savage Inequities*
_____ 8. Ellen Winner   H. Believes that a community team approach is the best way to educate students
_____ 9. James Comer   I. Conducted research about gifted children

"DR. DETAIL'S" MATCHING EXERCISE

Match the person with his/her contribution to the understanding of adolescents.

_____ 1. Arthur Powell,   A. Searched the nation finding and describing the best middle schools
             Eleanor Farrar, and
             David Cohen
_____ 2. Roberta Simmons   B. Philanthropist who donated money to start the I Have A Dream Program.
             and Dale Blyth
_____ 3. Joan Lipsitz   C. Studied self-esteem in students participating in varied numbers of extracurricular activities
_____ 4. Margaret Beale   D. Developed the metaphor of the "shopping mall" high school
             Spencer
_____ 5. Eugene Lang   E. Suggested that "well-meaning" teachers, acting out of misguided liberalism, fail to challenge students of color to achieve
_____ 6. Diana Baumrind   F. Described the effective teacher as one secure in his/her own identity and sexuality
_____ 7. Jacob Kounin   G. Provided the original idea of an authoritative classroom management strategy
_____ 8. Stephanie Feeney   H. Studied classroom management styles to identify effective teachers

APPROACHES TO EDUCATING STUDENTS
SECTION REVIEW

1.   How have secondary schools changed since the nineteenth century?

_____

_____

2.　　What is the comprehensive high school?

_____

_____

3.　　What functions of secondary schools are being debated today?

_____

_____

4.　　What is the back-to-basics movement?

_____

_____

5.　　What is the direct instruction approach to student learning?

_____

_____

6.　　What are cognitive constructivist approaches to student learning?

_____

_____

7.　　What are social constructivist approaches to student learning?

_____

_____

8.　　Match the APA Learner-Centered Psychological Principle with its description.

Cognitive and Metacognitive Factors

_____ 1. nature of the learning process

A. Successful learners can create a repertoire of thinking and reasoning strategies to achieve complex goals.

_____ 2. goals of the learning process

B. Successful learners can create meaningful, coherent representations of knowledge.

_____ 3. construction of knowledge

C. Higher order strategies for selecting and monitoring mental operations facilitate creative and critical thinking.

_____ 4. strategic thinking

D. The learning of complex subject matter is more effective when it is an intentional process of constructing meaning and experience.

_____ 5. thinking about thinking

E. Successful learners can link new information with existing knowledge in meaningful ways.

_____ 6. context of learning

F. Learning is influenced by environmental factors, including culture, technology, and instructional practices.

Motivational, Instructional, Developmental, Social, and Individual Difference Factors

_____ 1. motivational and emotional influences on learning

    A. The learner's creativity, higher order thinking, and natural curiosity all contribute to motivation to learn.

_____ 2. intrinsic motivation to learn

    B. Acquiring complex knowledge and skills requires extended learner effort and guided practice. Without learners' motivation to learn, the willingness to exert this effort is unlikely without coercion.

_____ 3. effects of motivation on effort

    C. What and how much is learned is influenced by the learner's motivation, which, in turn, is influenced by the learner's emotional states, beliefs, interests, goals, and habits of thinking.

_____ 4. developmental influences on learning

    D. Setting appropriately high and challenging standards and assessing the learner and learning progress are integral aspects of the learning experience.

_____ 5. social influences on learning

    E. Learning is influenced by social interactions, interpersonal relations, and communication with others.

_____ 6. individual differences in learning

    F. Learners have different strategies, approaches, and capabilities for learning that are a function of prior experience and heredity.

_____ 7. learning and diversity

    G. Learning is most effective when differential development within and across physical, cognitive, and socioemotional domains is taken into account.

_____ 8. standards and assessment

    H. Learning is most effective when differences in learner's linguistic, cultural, and social backgrounds are considered.

9. What are the Carnegie Council on Adolescent Development's eight principles for transforming adolescent's educational experiences?

_____

_____

_____

_____

10. How does the social context of schools differ at the preschool, elementary school, and secondary school levels?

_____

_____

TRANSITIONS IN SCHOOLING
SECTION REVIEW

1. What is the origin of junior high schools?

_____

_____

2.   How has the role of ninth grade been resolved over time?

_____

_____

3.   Why have middle schools become more popular than the junior highs?

_____

_____

4.   Is the sixth- through eighth-grade middle school transition easier than the transition to junior high?

_____

_____

5.   Why is the transition to middle- or junior-high school stressful?

_____

_____

6.   What is the top-dog phenomenon?

_____

_____

7.   According to Lipsitz, what makes a middle school successful?

_____

_____

8.   What did the Carnegie Foundation recommend about the redesign of middle schools?

_____

_____

9.   Why are today's college freshmen suffering from more depression and stress than in the past?

_____

_____

10.   Over the past 40 years, what has accounted for the drop in the numbers of dropouts?

_____

_____

11.   What educational deficiencies do students who drop out experience in adulthood?

_____

_____

12.   What factors are associated with dropping out of school?

_____

_____

13.   What approaches can be used to reduce the rate of dropping out and improve students' experiences?

_____

_____

THE SOCIAL CONTEXTS OF SCHOOLS
SECTION REVIEW

1.   What is the most desirable classroom/school size?

_____

_____

2.   What are some benefits of a small school?

_____

_____

3.   What are some benefits of a large school?

_____

_____

4.   What are the components of a positive classroom climate?

_____

_____

5.   What is the authoritative strategy of classroom management?

_____

_____

6. What is the authoritarian strategy of classroom management?

    _____

    _____

7. What is the permissive strategy of classroom management?

    _____

    _____

8. How does parental involvement with schools change as students get older?

    _____

    _____

9. Why do student-teacher relationships often deteriorate after the transition to junior high?

    _____

    _____

10. What is Epstein's framework for improving parent involvement in schooling?

    _____

    _____

11. List three things teachers can do to improve the likelihood that students will cooperate with them in the classroom.

    _____

    _____

12. Is popularity related to academic outcomes?

    _____

    _____

13. How significant is the problem of bullying in American schools?

    _____

    _____

14. What is the effect of poverty on student learning?

    _____

    _____

15.   How does ethnicity impact school experiences?

_____

_____

16.   What is a jigsaw classroom?

_____

_____

17.   What are some social policy recommendations for improving schools for adolescents?

_____

_____

ADOLESCENTS WHO ARE EXCEPTIONAL
SECTION REVIEW

1.   What are the characteristics of a learning disability?

_____

_____

2.   How are learning disabilities defined?

_____

_____

3.   How is ADHD defined?

_____

_____

4.   What is the controversy related to the diagnosis and treatment of ADHD?

_____

_____

5.   What interventions are recommended for adolescents with ADHD?

_____

_____

6.   What is Public Law 92–142?

_____

_____

7.   What is the Individuals with Disabilities Education Act (IDEA)?

_____

_____

8.   What does least restrictive environment mean?

_____

_____

9.   What is inclusion?

_____

_____

10.   According to Winner, what are the three characteristics of adolescents who are gifted?

_____

_____

11.   What are some characteristics that characterize gifted adolescents?

_____

_____

12.   What program options exist for students who are gifted?

_____

_____

EXPLORATIONS IN ADOLESCENT DEVELOPMENT

Compare and contrast the following aspects of secondary schools in Australia, Brazil, Germany, Japan, Russia, and the United States: (a) mandatory age: (b) number of levels; (c) role of sports; (d) entrance and exit exams;
(e) content and philosophy; and (f) foreign language education.

_____

_____

COGNITIVE CHALLENGE

1.   In three sections, list the things you liked most about high school, liked least about high school, and would change about schools in general to make them more effective.

liked most

_____

_____

liked least

_____

_____

would change

_____

_____

2.   Think back on your high school classmates that were of diverse ethnic, religious, and socioeconomic background. How well did your school meet the social and educational needs of these students? Knowing what you know now, how would you have responded to the needs of these students if you had been a teacher at the school?

_____

_____

ADOLESCENCE IN RESEARCH

Describe two attributes that were found in adolescents of the 8–4 arrangement and researchers' conclusions.

 COMPREHENSIVE REVIEW

1.   In the 1970s, three independent panels that examined the benefits of secondary school for adolescents concluded that high schools
    a.   increase adolescents' exposure to adults.
    b.   restrict the transition to adulthood.
    c.   decrease adolescents' sense of alienation.
    d.   increase employment opportunities for adolescents.

2.   Which kind of school has been referred to as "teenage warehouses?"
    a.   middle school
    b.   elementary school

    c.   high school
    d.   military school

3.   In which country are martial arts classes a standard?
    a.   United States
    b.   Russian
    c.   Brazil
    d.   Japan

4.   A major current concern among educators regarding middle schools or junior highs is that
    a.   there are not enough of them to accommodate the growing population.
    b.   they are becoming "watered down" versions of high school.
    c.   the curriculum is too basic for the growing needs of children of that age.
    d.   there is a shortage of teachers for these schools.

5.   According to the back-to-basics movement, the main function of schools should be to
    a.   provide extracurricular activities.
    b.   enhance the social and emotional development of adolescents.
    c.   be comprehensive and provide a multifaceted curriculum.
    d.   develop an intellectually mature person by emphasizing training in basic subjects.

6.   The major rationale for the establishment of junior high schools in the 1920s–1930s was that
    a.   early adolescents experience many changes at this time and need to be segregated.
    b.   the poor economic conditions put pressure upon the schools to provide more "babysitting" space.
    c.   too many older adolescents were fighting with the young adolescents.
    d.   high schools were "upgraded" and reorganized to encourage students to go on to college.

7.   The top-dog phenomenon refers to
    a.   the superior formal operational reasoning of high school students compared to junior high students.
    b.   the dating advantage that junior high school girls have over junior high school boys.
    c.   the self-perceptions of junior high school students who attend supportive and stable schools.
    d.   the lowered status experienced by students when they move from elementary to junior high school.

8.   Darren has been complaining about not being able to make good grades. He says he used to feel good in school, but now feels like a little fish in a big pond. Darren
    a.   probably has the same school crises as girls of his age.
    b.   is struggling with the transition to junior high school.
    c.   is becoming self-conscious because of the emergence of formal operational thought.
    d.   probably has developed the underdog adjustment disorder associated with junior high entry.

9.   Effective schools for young adolescents have all of the following characteristics EXCEPT
    a.   similar methods of grouping students.
    b.   emphasis on the school context as a community.
    c.   curricula emphasizing self-exploration and definition.
    d.   responsiveness to their community political milieus.

10. In which country would you find a *juku* or *cramming school?*
    a. United States
    b. Australia
    c. Germany
    d. Japan

11. Freddy is the oldest boy in his middle school and the best athlete. Which of the following is likely true about Freddy?
    a. He is probably very unpopular.
    b. He is probably a poor student.
    c. He is probably a *top dog.*
    d. He is probably truant.

12. Which of the following is NOT a recommendation by the 1989 Carnegie Council on Adolescent Development?
    a. involving parents and community leaders in the schools
    b. boosting students' health and fitness with more in-school programs and helping students who need public health care get it
    c. merging multiple small school districts into larger districts so as to offer more programs and better utilize resources
    d. lowering student-to-counselor ratios from several hundred-to-1 to 10 to 1

13. The report from the Carnegie Commission encourages
    a. disbanding middle schools in favor of a longer stay in elementary school.
    b. eliminating high schools and moving from junior high directly to college prep schools.
    c. arranging middle school students in smaller groups.
    d. eliminating middle schools in favor of junior high schools.

14. The students least likely to complete high school are
    a. African Americans.
    b. from single-parent homes.
    c. Native Americans.
    d. Urban Hispanics.

15. About 50 percent of the dropouts do so for school-related reasons, whereas another 20 percent drop out of high school
    a. for economic reasons.
    b. because they are unable to read and write well.
    c. because they are in trouble with law-enforcement authorities.
    d. for cultural reasons.

16. Small schools are more likely to
    a. be associated with prosocial behavior than large schools.
    b. provide fewer opportunities for school participation than large schools.
    c. promote better academic achievement than large schools.
    d. promote more antisocial behavior than large schools.

17. The _____ classroom is characterized by teachers who serve as facilitators of student learning rather than teaching in the traditional manner.
    a. open
    b. new wave
    c. multi-dimensional
    d. California

18. Young adolescents appear to respond well to teachers who
    a. let the students set the limits in the classroom.
    b. are pals.
    c. are insensitive to student criticism.
    d. use natural authority.

19. A teacher says to a student, "Thank you for being quiet in class today for a change." With which type of student is this more likely to occur?
    a. a "trouble-maker"
    b. a White-American student
    c. an African-American student
    d. the "best" student in the class

20. Among minority youth who stay in school, poor academic performance is linked to
    a. the refusal of other students to study with them.
    b. the unwillingness to engage in cooperative learning.
    c. the language barriers.
    d. coming from a poor, single-parent family.

21. The Education for All Handicapped Children Act mandated that all states do which of the following for all handicapped children?
    a. provide free health care
    b. provide educational programs for their parents
    c. provide free testing programs
    d. provide individualized educational programs

22. Inclusion refers to
    a. teaching handicapped children in public schools.
    b. assigning handicapped children to regular classrooms.
    c. giving handicapped children a high educational priority.
    d. assuring handicapped children interact with nonhandicapped children whenever possible.

23. Shawna, a second grader, has no trouble with math, science, or art; but she cannot spell, read, or write. It is likely that Shawna has a(n)
    a. visual impairment.
    b. speech handicap.
    c. learning disability.
    d. attention deficit.

24. Timothy is suffering from attention-deficit hyperactivity disorder (ADHD). He is most likely to be experiencing all but one of the following symptoms?
    a. short attention span.
    b. easily distracted.

    c.   below-normal intelligence.

    d.   high levels of physical activity.

25.   What type of drug is used to control attention-deficit hyperactivity disorder?

    a.   stimulant

    b.   depressant

    c.   tranquilizer

    d.   relaxant

26.   The I Have a Dream program (IHAD) was created by Eugene Lang to help in

    a.   alleviating the school violence problem in America.

    b.   to boost student literacy rates.

    c.   to decrease the likelihood of a child dropping out of school.

    d.   to get troubled kids off of the streets.

27.   What is the best school size?

    a.   500 to 600 or fewer

    b.   800 to 1,000

    c.   1,000 to 1,500

    d.   2,000 or more

28.   _____ is the only country in the world that has high school athletics and sports as an integral part of the educational system.

    a.   South Africa

    b.   Japan

    c.   Italy

    d.   The United States

29.   During a lifetime, a college graduate will earn approximately _____ more than a high school graduate will.

    a. $40,000

    b. $400,000

    c. $60,000

    d. $600,000

30.   Boys are identified as learning disabled _____ as often as girls.

    a.   three times

    b.   twice

    c.   equally

    d.   four times

ADOLESCENCE ON THE SCREEN

- *To Sir, With Love* is the story of a black engineer who takes a job in a rough London school.

- *The Breakfast Club* portrays how students in a Saturday detention class coalesce as a group.

- *Dangerous Minds* depicts a female teacher struggling to deal with tough inner city teenagers.

- *Dead Poet's Society* stars Robin Williams playing an English teacher, who tries to change the way students learn literature.

- *Middle School Confessions* (HBO) is a documentary that portrays in shocking detail the crisis in today's middle schools in America.

ADOLESCENCE IN BOOKS

- *Adolescence in the 1990s,* edited by Ruby Takanishi (Teachers College Press, 1993), features a number of experts on adolescence addressing the risks and opportunities for adolescents in today's world. Many chapters focus on improving the quality of schooling for adolescents.

- *Successful Schools for Young Adolescents*, by Joan Lipsitz (Transaction Books: NJ, 1984), is a classic resource for people involved in middle school education.

- *Endangered Minds*, by Jane M. Healy (Simon and Schuster: NY, 1999), depicts clearly the problems existing in our schools and makes specific suggestions on how to change things.

- *Failure to Connect: How Computers Affect Our Children's Minds, and What We Can Do About It*, by Jane M. Healy (Simon and Schuster: NY, 1999) presents a very strong case "against" the use of computers in modern classrooms.

ADOLESCENCE IN RESEARCH

Concerning the 1987 study by Simmons and Blyth comparing school systems with a 6–3–3 arrangement and those with an 8–4 arrangement, state the hypothesis, the research methods (if known), the research conclusions, and the implications and applications for adolescent development.

_____

_____

Answer Key

KEY TERMS

1. **back-to-basics movement** This philosophy stresses that the function of schools should be the rigorous training of intellectual skills through such subjects as English, mathematics, and science.

2. **direct instruction approach** A teacher-centered approach that is characterized by teacher direction and control, mastery of academic skills, high expectations for students' progress, and maximum time spent on learning tasks.

3. **cognitive constructivist approaches** Emphasizes the adolescent's active, cognitive construction of knowledge and understanding; an example of this approach is Piaget's theory.

4. **social constructivist approach** Focus on collaboration with others to produce knowledge and understanding; an example of this approach is Vygotsky's theory.

5. **top-dog phenomenon** The circumstance of moving from the top position (in elementary school, the oldest, biggest, and most powerful students) to the lowest position (in middle or junior high school, the youngest, smallest, and least powerful).

6. **authoritative strategy of classroom management** Encourages students to be independent thinkers and doers but still involves effective monitoring. Authoritative teachers engage students in considerable verbal give-and-take and show a caring attitude toward them. However, they still declare limits when necessary.

7. **authoritarian strategy of classroom management** Is restrictive and punitive. The focus is mainly on keeping order in the classroom rather than on instruction and learning.

8. **permissive strategy of classroom management** Offers students considerable autonomy but provides them with little support for developing learning skills or managing their behavior.

9. **aptitude-treatment interaction (ATI)** This interaction stresses the importance of both the attitudes and the characteristics of the adolescent, such as academic potential or personality traits, and the treatments or experiences, such as the educational techniques that the adolescent receives. *Aptitude* refers to such characteristics as the academic potential and personality characteristics on which students differ; *treatment* refers to educational techniques, such as structured versus flexible classrooms.

10. **jigsaw classroom** Students from different cultural backgrounds are placed in a cooperative group in which they have to construct different parts of a project to reach a common goal.

11. **learning disability** Describes individuals who 1) are of normal intelligence or above, 2) have difficulties in a least one academic area and usually several, and 3) their difficulties cannot be attributed to any other diagnosed problem or disorder, such as mental retardation.

12. **attention deficit/hyperactivity disorder (ADHD)** Is a disability in which children and adolescents show one or more of the following characteristics over a period of time: 1) inattention, 2) hyperactivity, and 3) impulsivity.

13. **Public Law 94–142** The Education for All Handicapped Children Act, which requires all students with disabilities to be given a free, appropriate education and provides the funding to help implement this education.

14. **Individuals with Disabilities Education Act (IDEA)** This spells out broad mandates for services to all children and adolescents with disabilities. These include evaluation and eligibility determination, appropriate education and the Individualized Education Program (IEP), and least restrictive environment.

15. **least restrictive environment** A setting that is as similar as possible to the one in which the children, or adolescents without a disability are educated; under the Individuals with Disabilities Education Act, the child or adolescent must be educated in this setting.

16. **inclusion** Educating a child or adolescent with special education needs full-time in a general school program.

17. **adolescents who are gifted** They are characterized by having above average intelligence (usually defined as an IQ of 120 or higher) and/or superior talent in some domain such as art, music, or mathematics.

KEY PEOPLE IN THE STUDY OF ADOLESCENCE

1.	D	4.	E	7.	B
2.	C	5.	G	8.	I
3.	A	6.	F	9.	H

"DR. DETAIL'S" MATCHING EXERCISE

1.	D	3.	A	5.	B	7.	H
2.	C	4.	E	6.	G	8.	F

APPROACHES TO EDUCATING STUDENTS SECTION REVIEW

1. In the late 1800s, most states passed laws prohibiting child labor. These coincided a move toward compulsory secondary education.

2. This is the popular notion of the 1970s to build high schools that offered some of everything, like shopping malls.

3. The basis of the debate is between frills or back to the basics.

4. This is the movement to focus more on basic curriculum, e.g., math, reading, and science.

5. A teacher-centered approach that is characterized by teacher direction and control, mastery of skills, high expectations for students' progress, and maximum time spent on learning tasks.

6. These emphasize the adolescent's active, cognitive construction of knowledge, and understanding.

7. These focus on collaboration with others to produce knowledge and understanding.

8. ***Cognitive and Metacognitive Factors***

1.	D	3.	E	5.	C
2.	B	4.	A	6.	F

Motivational, Instructional, Developmental, Social, and Individual Difference Factors

1.	C	4.	G	7.	H
2.	A	5.	E	8.	D
3.	B	6.	F		

9. Create communities for learning; teach a core of common knowledge; provide an opportunity for all students to succeed; strengthen teachers and principals; prepare teachers for the middle

grades; improve academic performance through better health and fitness; engage families in the education of adolescents; connect schools with communities.

10. They start out as protected environments and become increasingly more complex, especially socially.

TRANSITIONS IN SCHOOLING
SECTION REVIEW

1. Junior highs were justified on the basis of physical, cognitive, and social changes that characterize early adolescence.

2. Middle schools appear to better suit the maturation rates of children, so ninth grade has slowly become part of high school again.

3. Again, sixth to eighth grade seems to cover a phase of maturation and the transition to high school is easier in the ninth grade. In junior high, one problem is that ninth graders are far more mature than the other children.

4. The sixth through eighth transition generally goes well, but can be complicated by the fact that this period encompasses much of puberty for the average child.

5. Because of the onset of puberty.

6. The circumstance of moving from the top, power position to the lowest position, due to changing schools.

7. These schools emphasize the importance of creating an environment that was positive for the adolescent's social and emotional development.

8. Develop smaller communities; lower student-to-counselor ratios; involve parents and community leaders; develop curriculum that produces competent students; have teachers team-teach in more flexible curriculum blocks; boosting students' health and fitness.

9. Many report that they feel overwhelmed.

10. Laws requiring more time in school have been passed and there is a general consensus that a high school diploma is the basis for finding a good job.

11. They have lower grades, especially in reading.

12. Reasons can be school-related, economic, family-related, peer-related, and personal.

13. Approaches that bridge the gap between school and work, such as the "I Have a Dream" foundation.

THE SOCIAL CONTEXTS OF SCHOOLS
SECTION REVIEW

1. Classrooms about 20, schools 500–600.

2. Safe, personalized climate.

3. More course offerings.

4.   Teachers who more carefully monitor activities have the better classroom climates.

5.   Encourages students to be independent thinkers and doers but still involves effective monitoring. Authoritative teachers involve students in considerable verbal give and take.

6.   This is restrictive and punitive to maintain order.

7.   This offers students considerable autonomy but provides them with little support for developing learning skills or managing their behavior.

8.   Parents are often active in early education, but become less involved when children grow into adolescents.

9.   Part of the problem appears to be higher self-confidence and self-efficacy found in teachers of children in lower grades, as opposed to those teaching seventh grade or above.

10.   a.   Parents need to be knowledgeable about adolescent health and safety issues.
       b.   Schools need to communicate with families about school programs and the individual progress of the adolescents.
       c.   Parents need to be more involved in schools assisting teachers.
       d.   Parents need to be involved in their children's homework.
       e.   Parents need to be involved in decision making at school.
       f.   Schools need to collaborate with community organizations.

11.   a.   Develop a positive relationship with students.
       b.   Get students to share and assume responsibility.
       c.   Reward appropriate behavior.

12.   Being popular is associated with academic success, whereas being rejected by peers is related to more negative academic outcomes.

13.   Thirty percent of sixth- through tenth-graders say they have been involved in moderate or frequent bullying,

14.   Adolescents from backgrounds of poverty have more difficulties on average.

15.   Ethnicity and poverty tend to go hand-in-hand with fewer educational opportunities and poorer schools for those children from impoverished backgrounds.

16.   Where students from different cultural backgrounds are placed in cooperative groups in which they have to construct different parts of a project to reach a common goal.

17.   Comer recommends (1) a governance and management team that develops a comprehensive school plan, (2) a mental health or school support team, and (3) a parents program.

ADOLESCENTS WHO ARE EXCEPTIONAL
SECTION REVIEW

1.   Normal intelligence versus sub-normal performance.

2. Adolescents with a learning disability are of normal intelligence and have difficulties in a least one academic area and usually several, and their difficulty cannot be attributed to any other diagnosed problem.

3. ADHD is a disability in which children and adolescents show one or more of the following characteristics over a period of time: inattention, hyperactivity, and impulsivity.

4. The controversy is that in many parts of the country it is over-diagnosed and over-medicated.

5. Many recommend a combination of academic, behavioral, and medical interventions to help students.

6. The Education for All Handicapped Children Act.

7. IDEA spells out broad mandates for services to all children and adolescents with disabilities.

8. A setting that is similar as possible to the one in which the children without a disability are educated.

9. Inclusion used to be called mainstreaming. It means educating a child or adolescent with special education needs full-time in a general school program

10. (a) precocity, (b) marching to their own drummer, and (c) a passion for mastery

11. Above average intelligence and/or superior talent in some domain, such as art, music or math.

12. (a) Special classes, (b) acceleration and enrichment in the regular classroom setting, (c) mentor and apprenticeship programs, (d) work/study and community service programs.

EXPLORATIONS IN ADOLESCENT DEVELOPMENT

1. Brazil—14; Russia—17; Germany, Japan, Australia, and U.S.—15 to 16.

2. Most schools have two or more levels (elementary, junior/middle, and high school), but Germany has three ability tracks.

3. U.S. is the only country in the world that has integrated sports into the public school system. Private schools in other countries may have organized sports.

4. Japanese secondary schools have entrance exam, but other five countries do not; only Australia and Germany have exit exams.

5. Russia emphasizes preparation for work, but gifted students attend special schools; Brazil requires that students take four foreign languages, due to the country's international characters; Australian students take courses in sheep husbandry and weaving, activities important to the country's economics and culture; Japanese students take courses in Western languages, literature, physical education, and art.

COGNITIVE CHALLENGE

1. No answer provided. Individual activity.

2. No answer provided. Individual activity.

ADOLESCENCE IN RESEARCH

The adolescents in the 8–4 arrangement had higher self-esteem and participated more in extracurricular activities than the adolescents in the 6–3–3 arrangement, who had to change schools twice. The researchers concluded that the earlier the school transitions occur in adolescence, the more difficult it likely is for students.

☒ COMPREHENSIVE REVIEW

1.	b	**9.**	a	**17.**	a	**25.**	a
2.	c	**10.**	d	**18.**	d	**26.**	c
3.	d	**11.**	c	**19.**	c	**27.**	a
4.	b	**12.**	c	**20.**	d	**28.**	d
5.	d	**13.**	c	**21.**	d	**29.**	d
6.	a	**14.**	c	**22.**	d	**30.**	a
7.	d	**15.**	a	**23.**	b		
8.	b	**16.**	a	**24.**	c		

⌘

Chapter 12   Achievement, Careers, and Work

Learning Goals with Key Terms and Key People in Boldface

1.0   **DISCUSS ACHIEVEMENT IN THE LIVES OF ADOLESCENTS**

    A.   **The Importance of Adolescence in Achievement**

        1.1   What is the importance of achievement in adolescence?

        1.2   What determines how well adolescents adapt to social and academic pressures?

    B.   **Achievement Processes**

        1.3   What is **intrinsic motivation?**

        1.4   What is **extrinsic motivation?**

        1.5   What are the self-determining characteristics of **intrinsic motivation?**

        1.6   What can be done to increase students' internal motivation?

        1.7   What is **Csikszentmihalyi's** concept of **flow?**

        1.8   When is **flow** most likely to occur?

        1.9   What is **attribution theory?**

        1.10   What, according to **Weiner**, are the three dimensions of causal attributions?

        1.11   What are locus, stability, and controllability?

        1.12   How do these dimensions produce different explanations of failures?

        1.13   What is **mastery orientation?**

        1.14   What is meant by **helpless orientation?**

        1.15   What is **performance orientation?**

        1.16   What is **self-efficacy?**

        1.17   What is **Bandura's** view of **self-efficacy?**

        1.18   What is **Schunk's** view of **self-efficacy?**

        1.19   What are some educational applications for **self-efficacy?**

        1.20   How does goal-setting benefit students' self-efficacy and achievement?

        1.21   How do **Dweck** and **Nicholls** define goals?

        1.22   What are the characteristics of a good planner?

        1.23   What is the nature of **anxiety?**

        1.24   Where does high anxiety come from?

        1.25   What can be done to help students cope with anxiety?

    C.   **Ethnicity and Culture**

        1.26   What are the respective roles of ethnicity and culture in achievement?

        1.27   Why is it important to consider diversity of achievement within an ethnic group?

        1.28   How do American adolescents size up against their Asian counterparts in terms of achievement?

    D.   **Motivating Low-Achieving Adolescents**

        1.29   What are the characteristics of students in need of help?

        1.30   According to **Brophy,** what constitutes a hard-to-reach student?

1.31   What is **failure syndrome,** and where does it come from?

1.32   What strategies benefit adolescents who are motivated to protect self-worth and avoid failure?

1.33   What are **self-handicapping strategies?**

1.34   According to **Covington,** what strategies can teachers use to protect student self-worth and avoid failure?

2.0   WORK

A.   Sociohistorical Context of Adolescent Work

2.1   How likely are adolescents to hold full-time jobs today as opposed to in the 1800s?

2.2   How many adolescents work part-time?

2.3   What kind of jobs are adolescents working today?

2.4   Do male and female adolescents take the same types of jobs, and are they paid equally?

B.   Advantages and Disadvantages of Part-Time Work in Adolescence

2.5   Does the increase in work have benefits for adolescents?

2.6   What are the advantages of part-time work for adolescents?

2.7   What are the disadvantages of part-time work for adolescents?

C.   Work Profiles of Adolescents Around the World

2.8   How does work in adolescence vary in different countries around the world?

D.   Working While Going to College

2.9   What percentage of U.S. undergraduate students work?

2.10   Does work during college increase the likelihood of dropping out?

E.   The Transition from School to Work

2.11   What are the rates of adolescent unemployment?

2.12   What can be done to bridge the gap between school and work?

F.   Work/Career-Based Learning

2.13   What is work/career-based learning?

2.14   What three types of high schools exemplify a college-and-career approach?

2.15   What are single-theme schools?

2.16   What are schools-within-schools?

2.17   What are majors, clusters, or pathways in the school curriculum?

2.18   What is the value of cooperative education programs?

3.0   CAREER DEVELOPMENT

A.   Theories of Career Development

3.1   What are the three theories of career development?

3.2   What are the characteristics of **Ginzberg's developmental career choice theory?**

3.3   What are the characteristics of **Super's** vocational **career self-concept theory?**

3.4   What is the nature of **Holland's personality type theory** of career development?

B.   Cognitive Factors

3.5   Why do adolescents have difficulties making career choices?

3.6   How is career development related to identity development in adolescence?

3.7   According to **Csikszentmihalyi** and **Schneider** (2000), how do U.S. adolescents develop attitudes and acquire skills to achieve their career goals?

C.   Social Contexts

3.8   What are the most important social contexts that influence career development?

3.9　　What roles do socioeconomic status, parents and peers, schools, gender, and ethnicity play in career development?

Exercises

KEY TERMS COMPLETION EXERCISE

Each key term is presented in the form of an incomplete sentence. Complete each sentence by either defining the term or giving an example. Compare your definition with those given at the end of the study guide chapter.

1.　　**Extrinsic motivation** causes

_____

_____

2.　　**Intrinsic motivation** is noted when

_____

_____

3.　　**Flow** describes

_____

_____

4.　　**Attribution theory** suggests that individuals are

_____

_____

5.　　**Mastery orientation** is a very good approach to

_____

_____

6.　　A **helpless orientation** can lead to

_____

_____

7.　　When people have a **performance orientation** they

_____

_____

8.   **Self-efficacy** is a belief

_____

_____

9.   Symptoms of **anxiety** are

_____

_____

10.   Simon suffers from the **failure syndrome** because

_____

_____

11.   **Self-handicapping strategies** are used when

_____

_____

12.   **Developmental career choice theory** is Ginzberg's theory that

_____

_____

13.   **Career self-concept theory** is Super's theory that

_____

_____

14.   **Personality type theory** is Holland's belief that

_____

_____

KEY PEOPLE IN THE STUDY OF ADOLESCENCE

Match the person with the concept of adolescent development with which they are associated.

_____ 1. Mihalyi Csikszentmihalyi

_____ 2. Bernard Weiner

_____ 3. Carol Dweck

_____ 4. Albert Bandura

_____ 5. Dale Schunk

_____ 6. Sandra Graham

_____ 7. Harold Stevenson

A. Believe that today's parents are pressuring adolescents to achieve too much

B. Proponent of the career self-concept theory

C. Examined the work experience of California students

D. Credited with the development of the personality type theory of career development

E. Conceptualized the developmental career choice theory

F. Studies cross-cultural comparisons of school performance

G. Believes that self-efficacy influences a student's choice of tasks

_____	8. Martin Covington	H. Believes that self-efficacy is a critical factor in student development
_____	9. Eli Ginzberg	I. Studies ethnic differences in achievement
_____	10. Donald Super	J. Proposed strategies that teachers can use to help adolescents protect self-worth and avoid failure
_____	11. John Holland	K. Believes that parent-child relationships play an important role in occupation selection
_____	12. David Elkind	L. Developed strategies for improving motivation of hard-to-teach and low-achieving adolescents
_____	13. Anna Roe	M. Theorized about the three dimensions of causal attribution
_____	14. Ellen Greenberger and Laurence Steinberg	N. Uses the term "flow" to refer to optimal experiences in life

"DR. DETAIL'S" THEORY MASTERY EXERCISE

Complete the table by listing the career areas that match each of Holland's personality types.

Personality Type	Career
Realistic	
Intellectual	
Social	
Conventional	
Enterprising	
Artistic	

Complete the table by listing the career areas that match each of Ginzberg's career choice stages.

Career Choice Stage	Careers
Fantasy	
Tentative	
Realistic	

Complete the table by listing the developmental information that match each of Super's career choice phases.

Phase	Developmental Information
crystallization	
specification	
implementation	
stabilization	
consolidation	

ACHIEVEMENT
SECTION REVIEW

1.   What determines how well adolescents adapt to social and academic pressures?

_____

_____

2. Complete the table by filling in the outcomes for each of the combinations of students' perceived level of skill and challenge.

Students' Perceived Level of Skill

Perceived Level of Challenge	Low	High
Low		
High		

3. Complete the table by listing students' reasons for failure that correspond with the given combination of Weiner's three main categories of attributions: locus (internal-external), stability (stable-unstable), and controllability (controllable-uncontrollable).

Combination of Causal Attributes	Reason Students Give for Failure
Internal-Stable-Uncontrollable	
Internal-Stable-Controllable	
Internal-Unstable-Uncontrollable	
Internal-Unstable-Controllable	
External-Stable-Uncontrollable	
External-Stable-Controllable	
External-Unstable-Uncontrollable	
External-Unstable-Controllable	

4. What are the self-determining characteristics of intrinsic motivation?

_____

_____

5. What is flow?

_____

_____

6. When is flow most likely to occur?

_____

_____

7. What is attribution theory?

_____

_____

8. What, according to Weiner, are the three dimensions of causal attributions?

_____

_____

9.   What are locus, stability, and controllability?

        _____

        _____

10.   What is mastery orientation?

        _____

        _____

11.   What is helpless orientation?

        _____

        _____

12.   What is performance orientation?

        _____

        _____

13.   What is self-efficacy?

        _____

        _____

14.   Contrast Bandura's and Schunk's views of self-efficacy.

        _____

        _____

15.   How do Dweck and Nicholls define goals?

        _____

        _____

16.   What are the respective roles of ethnicity and culture in achievement?

        _____

        _____

17.   How do American adolescents size up against their Asian counterparts in terms of achievement?

        _____

        _____

18. According to Brophy, what does it take to reach a discouraged student?

_____

_____

19. What is failure syndrome and where does it come from?

_____

_____

20. What are self-handicapping strategies?

_____

_____

21. According to Covington, what strategies can teachers use to protect student self-worth and avoid failure?

_____

_____

WORK
SECTION REVIEW

1. How many adolescents work full-time today, as opposed to in the 1800s?

_____

_____

2. Do male and female adolescents take the same types of jobs, and are they paid equally?

_____

_____

3. What are the advantages of part-time work for adolescents?

_____

_____

4. How does work in adolescence vary in different countries around the world?

_____

_____

5.   Does work during college increase the likelihood of dropping out?

_____

_____

6.   What can be done to bridge the gap between school and work?

_____

_____

7.   What are single-theme schools?

_____

_____

CAREER DEVELOPMENT
SECTION REVIEW

1.   What are the three theories of career development?

_____

_____

2.   How is career development related to identity development in adolescence?

_____

_____

3.   What are the most important social contexts that influence career development?

_____

_____

4.   Why do adolescents have difficulties making career choices?

_____

_____

COGNITIVE CHALLENGE

1.   What are your career dreams? With your dreams in mind, write down your specific work, job, and career goals for the next 20 years, 10 years, and 5 years. Begin with the long-term goals first so that you can envision how to plan now to reach that "dream" career goal.

_____

_____

2. What achievement-related challenges did you encounter in middle school and high school? How did you resolve them? Looking back, how might you have coped with these challenges in a more effective way?

_____

_____

3. How long have you had your current career goals? Since kindergarten? Since elementary school? Since secondary school? Or has it only been recently that you have started to focus on your career?

_____

_____

ADOLESCENCE IN RESEARCH

Concerning the research of Mihalyi Csikszentmihalyi and Barbara Schneider (2000), state the hypothesis, the research methods (if known), the research conclusions, and the implications and applications for adolescent development.

_____

_____

_____

_____

_____

_____

☒ COMPREHENSIVE REVIEW

1. The motive with the greatest impact on the quality of adult life is
   a. sexuality.
   b. fear.
   c. affiliation.
   d. achievement.

2. Aaron studies very hard. He concentrates on the sciences because he wants to become an environmental biologist. Aaron could be described as
   a. motivated.
   b. intelligent.
   c. unrealistic.
   d. a hurried adolescent.

3.   Attribution theory indicates that individuals attribute people's behavior to two causes:
        a.   direct and indirect.
        b.   inferred and observed.
        c.   internal and external.
        d.   scientific and psychological.

4.   A parent of an adolescent decides to join the community band. His daughter asks why he joined, since he won't make any money and few people attend the concerts. He responds, "I just like playing with the band." He is _____ motivated.
        a.   achievement
        b.   intrinsically
        c.   extrinsically
        d.   mastery

5.   One key feature of the helpless orientation is
        a.   attributing failure to internal causes.
        b.   overestimating the role of effort.
        c.   underestimating the importance of external incentives.
        d.   fear of failure.

6.   It is very difficult and dangerous to make sweeping generalizations about achievement motivation in ethnic minority adolescents because
        a.   it has never been studied systematically.
        b.   there is more variability within groups than among groups.
        c.   all American groups score lower than Asian groups.
        d.   social class is a more powerful predictor.

7.   Japanese children often outperform American children in math and science areas, perhaps because all of the following are true except that
        a.   Japanese parents have higher expectations.
        b.   Japanese children spend more time in school each week.
        c.   Japanese teachers are better trained in math and science.
        d.   the Japanese school year is longer.

8.   According to your text, the major reason for the "super achiever" image of Asian American adolescents (whose parents immigrated to the United States in the late 1960s to mid-1970s) is that
        a.   their families have had more time to adjust to the culture.
        b.   they are more intelligent.
        c.   the males are encouraged to excel more than the females.
        d.   they come from better-educated families.

9.   According to Eli Ginzberg, youngsters between the ages of 11 and 17 years progressively evaluate three aspects of career choice. The order of occurrence is:
        a.   values, capacities, and interests.
        b.   interests, capacities, and values.
        c.   interests, values, and capacities.
        d.   capacities, values, and interests.

10. When individuals complete their education or training and enter the workforce, Donald Super refers to this as the _____ stage.
    a. crystallization
    b. implementation
    c. stabilization
    d. specification

11. Your son always had a way with words and got along well with peers and adults. According to John Holland, he would prefer the job of
    a. social worker.
    b. bank teller.
    c. construction worker.
    d. sales manager.

12. The most important contribution made by John Holland's personality type theory to the career field was its
    a. consideration of the role of motivation on job performance.
    b. introduction of the conventional personality type.
    c. focus on psychological testing as a way of insuring job suitability.
    d. emphasis on linking individuals' personalities to the characteristics of given jobs.

13. In order to benefit from career guidance courses and to show more systematic career planning, students need
    a. accurate knowledge concerning the educational requirements of careers.
    b. self-directed opportunities to engage in career exploration.
    c. courses that are taught by trained guidance counselors.
    d. to be in the implementation stage of vocational choice.

14. When both parents work and seem to enjoy it,
    a. the parents try to live vicariously through their children's occupational choices.
    b. boys and girls learn work values from both parents.
    c. boys and girls aspire to higher status occupations.
    d. schools don't need to motivate students to get a good education.

15. Which kind of job employs the most adolescents in part-time work?
    a. unskilled laborers
    b. clerical assistants
    c. restaurant work
    d. retail

16. An adolescent female (16 years of age) who takes a part-time job can expect to
    a. make more money than males.
    b. work shorter hours than males.
    c. easily find a job as a newspaper carrier.
    d. easily find a job as a gardener.

17. Which of the following represents an advantage of working during adolescence?
    a. extensive on-the-job training
    b. improved ability to manage money

    c.   improved school grades
    d.   greater enjoyment of school

18.   A number of adolescent problem behaviors are associated with part-time work, such as insufficient sleep and exercise. At what level of work does this begin to be apparent?
    a.   1 to 5 hours per week
    b.   6 to 10 hours per week
    c.   15 to 20 hours per week
    d.   more than 20 hours per week

19.   Which foundation in the United States has been very active in developing programs for unemployed youth?
    a.   John S. Sage
    b.   William T. Grant
    c.   Richard B. Williams
    d.   John F. Kennedy Education

20.   When a recent study compared the top 25 percent of students in different countries, the U.S. students
    a.   were found to be much stronger than students from other countries.
    b.   compared favorably to the "select" group from other countries.
    c.   did not do well in comparison.
    d.   were stronger in physical education, but weaker in math.

21.   Sherry consistently blames her poor performance on tests on high levels of anxiety. This is an example of
    a.   setting unreachable goals.
    b.   procrastination.
    c.   sham effort.
    d.   the academic wooden leg.

22.   Out of every ten students attending school in the U.S. today, _____ will receive a high school diploma.
    a.   9
    b.   8
    c.   7
    d.   5

ADOLESCENCE ON THE SCREEN

- *Cider House Rules* depicts an orphan who rejects the medical profession his foster father planned for him—until he chooses it for himself.

- *October Sky* is the true story of Homer Hickman, a West Virginia coal miner's son, who went from setting off rockets in his back yard to joining the NASA space program.

- *Stand and Deliver* is the story of Jaime Escalante's math classrooms in a predominantly Chicano Southern California high school.

ADOLESCENCE IN BOOKS

- *All Grown Up & No Place to Go: Teenagers in Crisis*, by David Elkind (Addison-Wesley: MA, 1984), argues that teenagers are expected to confront adult challenges too early in their development.

- *Mentors*, by Thomas Evans (Peterson's Guides: NJ, 1992), describes the experiences of motivated individuals, from corporate executives to parents.

- *What Color Is Your Parachute?* by Richard Bolles (Ten Speed Press: CA, 2000), is a popular book on career choice that is updated annually.

Answer Key

KEY TERMS

1. **extrinsic motivation** Response to external incentives such as rewards and punishments.

2. **intrinsic motivation** Internal motivational factors such as self-determination, curiosity, challenge, and effort.

3. **flow** Csikszentmihalyi's concept that describes optimal life experiences, which he believes occur most often when people develop a sense of mastery and are absorbed in a state of concentration when they are engaged in a activity.

4. **attribution theory** The concept that individuals are motivated to discover the underlying causes of their own behavior or performance in their effort to make sense of it.

5. **mastery orientation** An outlook in which individuals focus on the task rather than on their ability, have positive affect, and generate solution-oriented strategies that improve performance.

6. **helpless orientation** An outlook in which individuals focus on their personal inadequacies often attribute their difficulty to a lack of ability, and display negative affect (including boredom and anxiety). This orientation undermines performance.

7. **performance orientation** An outlook in which individuals are concerned with performance outcome rather than performance process. For performance-oriented students, winning is what matters.

8. **self-efficacy** The belief that one can master a situation and produce positive outcomes.

9. **anxiety** A vague, highly unpleasant feeling of fear and apprehension.

10. **failure syndrome** Having low expectations for success and giving up at the first sign of difficulty.

11. **self-handicapping strategies** Some adolescents deliberately do not try in school, put off studying until the last minute, and use other self-handicapping strategies so that if their subsequent performance is at a low level, these circumstances, rather than lack of ability, will be seen as the cause.

12. **developmental career choice theory** Ginzberg's theory that children and adolescents go through three career-choice stages: fantasy, tentative, and realistic.

13. **career self-concept theory** Super's theory that individuals' self-concepts play a central role in their career choices and that in adolescence individuals first construct their career self-concept.

14. **personality type theory** Holland's belief that an effort should be made to match an individual's career choice with his or her personality.

KEY PEOPLE IN THE STUDY OF ADOLESCENCE

1.	N	5.	G	9.	E	13.	K
2.	M	6.	I	10.	B	14.	C
3.	L	7.	F	11.	D		
4.	H	8.	J	12.	A		

"DR. DETAIL'S" THEORY MASTERY EXERCISE

Holland's personality type:

Personality Type	Career
Realistic	labor, farming, truck driving, construction
Intellectual	math and science careers
Social	teaching, social work, counseling
Conventional	bank tellers, secretaries, file clerks
Enterprising	sales, politics, management

Ginzberg's career choice stages:

Career Choice Stage	Careers
Fantasy	Doctor, superhero, teacher, movie star, etc.
Tentative	Big plans of youth are changed to fit skills and abilities.
Realistic	Explore careers and settle upon one within reach that fits their goals and personality

Super's career choice phases:

Phase	Developmental Information
Crystallization	Age 14 to 18, develop ideas that mesh with existing self-concept
Specification	Age 18 to 22, narrow career choices and take steps toward career
Implementation	Age 21 to 24, compete education and training
Stabilization	Age 25 to 35, enter their career of choice
Consolidation	After 35, seek to reach higher status positions

ACHIEVEMENT
SECTION REVIEW

1. Psychological, motivational, and contextual factors.

2. **Students' Perceived Level of Skill**

Perceived Level of Challenge	Low	High
Low	Apathy	Boredom
High	Anxiety	Flow

3.

Combination of Causal Attributes	Reason Students Give for Failure
Internal-Stable-Uncontrollable	Low aptitude
Internal-Stable-Controllable	Never study
Internal-Unstable-Uncontrollable	Sick the day of the test
Internal-Unstable-Controllable	Did not study for this particular test
External-Stable-Uncontrollable	School has tough requirements
External-Stable-Controllable	The instructor is biased
External-Unstable-Uncontrollable	Bad luck
External-Unstable-Controllable	Friends failed to help

4. Adolescents want to believe that they are doing something because of their own will.

5. The concept of optimal life experiences, which occur most often when people develop a sense of mastery.

6. More likely to occur when materials are mastered.

7. This states that in their effort to make sense out of their own behavior or performance, individuals are motivated to discover its underlying causes.

8. Locus, stability, and controllability.

9. Locus—whether the cause is internal or external; stability—the extent to which the cause remains the same or changes; controllability—the extent to which the individual can control the cause.

10. Focusing on the task rather than on ability and generating solution-oriented strategies to completion.

11. Focusing too much on personal inadequacies and displaying negative affect.

12. Involves being concerned with outcome rather than process.

13. The belief that one can master a situation and produce favorable outcomes.

14.   Bandura—believes that self-efficacy is a crucial factor in whether or not adolescents achieve. Schunk—believes that self-efficacy influences a student's choice of activities; therefore it has an important indirect role.

15.   They define goals in terms of immediate achievement-related focus and definition of success.

16.   Ethnicity and culture play and important role in achievement. The orientation of the parents in particular is important. SES is more associated with poor achievement than is ethnicity or culture.

17.   There are differences in school, parent attitudes and the likelihood of students doing homework. Taken together, Asian students often out-perform American students.

18.   Convince them that effort and work pay off.

19.   Having low expectations for success. It comes from falling behind and struggling with academics with mostly failure as a result.

20.   Some adolescents deliberately do not try in school; this way they have an excuse if they fail.

21.   (a) Give these adolescents assignments that are interesting and stimulate curiosity. (b) Establish a reward system. (c) Help adolescents set challenging but realistic goals. (d) Strengthen the association between effort and self-worth. (e) Encourage students to have positive beliefs about their abilities. (f) Improve teacher-student relations.

WORK
SECTION REVIEW

1.   In the 1800's fewer than 1 in 20 graduated from high school, so most worked. The number working full time has decreased today with 9 of 10 receiving diplomas before entering the workforce full time.

2.   Males work more labor-intensive jobs, work longer hours, and get paid more than females.

3.   Better time management skills, and spending money.

4.   In many developing countries where it is common for adolescents to not attend school on a regular basis, and boys are more likely to earn an income. High school aged kids in the U.S. are more likely to hold a job. Kids in Europe and Asia also often have jobs, more so than most other countries.

5.   As the number of hours worked increases, the likelihood of dropping out of college also increases.

6.   (a) monitored work experiences, (b) community youth-guided services, (c) vocational education should be redirected, (d) incentives need to be introduced, (e) career information and counseling need to be improved, and (f) more school volunteers should be used.

7.   The curriculum is organized around a single theme, such as agriculture.

CAREER DEVELOPMENT
SECTION REVIEW

1. Ginzberg's development theory, Super's self-concept theory, and Holland's personality type theory.

2. Career decidedness and planning are positively related to identity achievement, whereas career planning and decidedness are negatively related to identity moratorium and identity diffusion statuses.

3. SES, parents and peers, schools, gender, culture, and ethnicity.

4. It is suggested that most do not spend nearly enough time with career counselors in high school (under 3 hours).

COGNITIVE CHALLENGE

1. Individual activity. No answers provided.

2. Individual activity. No answers provided.

3. Individual activity. No answers provided.

ADOLESCENCE IN RESEARCH

Csikszentmihalyi and Schneider studied how U.S. adolescents develop attitudes and acquire skills to achieve their career goals and expectations. They assessed (using questionnaires) the progress of more than 1,000 students from 13 school districts across the United State (cross-sectional). Among the findings: (a) girls anticipated the same lifestyles as boys in terms of education and income; (b) lower-income minority students were more positive about school than more affluent students; (c) students who got the most out of school were those who perceived school as more playlike than worklike; and (d) clear vocational goals and good work experiences did not guarantee a smooth transition to adult work.

⊠ COMPREHENSIVE REVIEW

1.	d	7.	c	13.	a	19.	b
2.	a	8.	d	14.	b	20.	c
3.	c	9.	b	15.	d	21.	d
4.	b	10.	b	16.	b	22.	a
5.	a	11.	a	17.	b		
6.	d	12.	d	18.	a		

⌘

Chapter 13   Culture

Learning Goals with Key Terms and Key People in Boldface

1.0   DISCUSS THE ROLE OF CULTURE IN ADOLESCENCE DEVELOPMENT
    A.   What is Culture?
        1.1   What is **culture?**
        1.2   What is **socioeconomic status?**
        1.3   What is **ethnicity?**
    B.   The Relevance of Culture for the Study of Adolescence
        1.4   What is the relevance of **culture** for the study of adolescence in the twenty-first century?
        1.5   What is an example of **ethnocentrism?**
        1.6   Are ethnic differences often interpreted as deficits?
    C.   Cross-Cultural Comparisons
        1.7   What are **cross-cultural studies?**
        1.8   In what context did the study of adolescence emerge in **cross-cultural** comparisons?
        1.9   How do adolescents around the world spend their time?
    D.   Models of Cultural Change
        1.10   What four models have been used to understand cultural changes within and between cultures?
        1.11   What is **assimilation?**
        1.12   What is **acculturation?**
        1.13   What is **alternation model?**
        1.14   What is the multiculturalism?
        1.15   What is the advantage of using the **multicultural model?**
    E.   Rites of Passage
        1.16   What is meant by **rites of passage?**
        1.17   How are rites of passage different for American and primitive cultures?
2.0   SUMMARIZE HOW ETHNICITY IS INVOLVED IN ADOLESCENT DEVELOPMENT
    A.   Immigration
        2.1   What stressors are experienced by immigrants?
        2.2   Is there a relationship between acculturation and adolescent problems in the United States?
    B.   Adolescence: A Special Juncture for Ethnic Minority Individuals
        2.3   Are ethnic minority youth impacted by a lack of role models?
    C.   Ethnicity Issues
        2.4   How do history, the economy, and social experiences produce legitimate differences between ethnic minority groups and between ethnic minority groups and the White majority?

2.5   How does failure to recognize diversity lead to stereotyping?

2.6   What is **prejudice?**

2.7   In what ways do ethnic minority adolescents experience prejudice, discrimination, and bias?

2.8   Why is adolescence a critical juncture in the development of ethnic minority individuals?

2.9   What are some of the complicating effects of the "browning" of America?

D.   **Ethnic Minority Adolescents**

2.10   What are some defining characteristics of African-American adolescents?

2.11   Why is low SES a problem among black youth?

2.12   What helps to diminish the impact of single parent families amongst African-American youth?

2.13   Where are national origins of Latino adolescents?

2.14   What is a **Chicano?**

2.15   What roles do families play in the lives of Latino youth?

2.16   What countries do Asian American adolescents represent?

2.17   What accounts for the strong achievement orientation of Asian American youth?

2.18   What discriminations have Native American adolescents endured?

2.19   How is America a cultural mosaic?

2.20   What are included in Canadian cultures?

2.21   How do adolescents in Canada compare to adolescents in the United States?

2.22   What are the main ethnic ties of Canadian adolescents?

3.0   DESCRIBE HOW SOCIOECONOMIC STATUS AND POVERTY ARE RELATED TO ADOLESCENT DEVELOPMENT

A.   **What is Socioeconomic Status**

3.1   What is meant by socioeconomic status?

3.2   What is the significance of socioeconomic status for adolescent development?

3.3   How does socioeconomic status affect the families, neighborhoods, and schools of adolescents?

3.4   What effect do socioeconomic variables in families, neighborhoods, and schools have on adolescent development?

3.5   How do low-socioeconomic parents differ from their middle-SES counterparts?

B.   **Poverty**

3.6   What is poverty?

3.7   What percentage of U.S. children lives in poverty?

3.8   Why is poverty among American youth so high?

3.9   What is the nature of the subculture of the poor?

3.10   What is meant by the **feminization of poverty?**

3.11   What effects do persistent and long-lasting poverty have on development?

3.12   What was the impact of the Quantum project?

4.0   CHARACTERIZE THE ROLES OF THE MEDIA AND TECHNOLOGY IN ADOLESCENT DEVELOPMENT

A.   **Functions and Use of Media**

4.1   What are the functions of media?

4.2   How do adolescents use media?

B.   **Television**

4.3   What are the functions of television for adolescents?

4.4   What are the special concerns raised by television today?

4.5   How strongly does televised violence influence a person's behavior?

4.6   What impact is television having on the sexual behaviors of youth?

C.   **The Media and Music**

     4.7   How important is music to adolescents?

     4.8   How do adolescents' music tastes change during the course of adolescence?

     4.9   What adolescent needs does music fulfill?

D.   **Technology, Computers, and the Internet**

     4.10   How is the technological revolution affecting teenagers today?

     4.11   What is the **Internet?**

     4.12   What are some concerns surrounding **Internet** regulation?

     4.13   What is **E-mail?**

     4.14   What is the importance of **E-mail** for adolescents?

     4.15   What are some concerns regarding how adolescents use the **Internet?**

     4.16   What inequities might arise as a result of the technological revolution?

     4.17   How have computers impacted schools?

     4.18   What is the relationship between technology and adolescent learning?

E.   **Social Policy and Media**

     4.19   What social policy recommendations concerning the media would benefit adolescents?

Exercises

KEY TERMS COMPLETION EXERCISE

Each key term is presented in the form of an incomplete sentence. Complete each sentence by either defining the term or giving an example. Compare your definitions with those given at the end of the study guide chapter.

1.   **Culture** is the

     _____

     _____

2.   A person's **socioeconomic status (SES)** is

     _____

     _____

3.   Because of Octavio's **ethnicity,** he often

     _____

     _____

4.   **Ethnocentrism** leads to

     _____

     _____

5.   **Cross-cultural studies** are used in order to

_____

_____

6.   **Assimilation** is seen when

_____

_____

7.   **Acculturation** results from

_____

_____

8.   The **alternation model** assumes that

_____

_____

9.   The **multicultural model** promotes

_____

_____

10.   **Rites of passage** are evidenced in

_____

_____

11.   An example of **prejudice** is

_____

_____

12.   The term **Chicano** means

_____

_____

13.   The **Internet** is the

_____

_____

14.　　**E-mail** is used for

_____

_____

15.　　**Feminization of poverty** refers to

_____

_____

KEY PEOPLE IN THE STUDY OF ADOLESCENCE

Match the person with the concept of adolescent development with which they are associated.

_____　1.　Richard Brislin　　　A.　Asian American researcher who studies prejudice and discrimination

_____　2.　Vonnie McLoyd　　　B.　A cross-cultural psychologist who argues that intimate contact reduces conflict between individuals from different ethnic backgrounds

_____　3.　Stanley Sue　　　　C.　Psychologist who observed that one function of education is to rearrange prejudice

_____　4.　James Jones　　　　D.　Studied the effect on children of ethnic minority mothers' poverty and stress

_____　5.　Sandra Calvert　　　E.　Co-director of the Harvard Immigration Projects

_____　6.　Carola Suárez-Orozco　F.　Studies the role of the technological revolution in adolescent development

"DR. DETAIL'S" PUZZLE EXERCISE

Across

1.　　A dimension of culture based on heritage, nationality, race, religion, and language.
2.　　Cultural change that occurs with first-hand contact between two cultural groups.

3.   An unjustified negative attitude toward a person due to his/her membership in a group.
4.   The name politically conscious Mexican American adolescents give themselves.
5.   The core of computer-mediated communication.

Down

1.   The behavior, patterns, and beliefs of a particular group of people.
2.   Absorption of ethnic minority groups into a dominant group.
3.   Stands for electronic mail.

CULTURE AND ADOLESCENCE
SECTION REVIEW

1.   List the seven features of culture according to Richard Brislin (1993).

a.   _____

b.   _____

c.   _____

d.   _____

e.   _____

f.   _____

g.   _____

2.   What is socioeconomic status?

_____

3.　　What is ethnicity?

_____

_____

4.　　List five common features of ethnocentrism present in all cultures.

　　　a.　_____

_____

　　　b.　_____

_____

　　　c.　_____

_____

　　　d.　_____

_____

　　　e.　_____

_____

5.　　What are cross-cultural studies?

_____

_____

6.　　What four models have been used to understand the process of adaptation within and between cultures?

_____

_____

7.　　What is the alternation model?

_____

_____

8.　　What is multiculturalism?

_____

_____

9.   What is meant by rites of passage?

_____

_____

ETHNICITY
SECTION REVIEW

1.   What is ethnicity?

_____

2.   What are some stressors commonly experienced by immigrants?

_____

_____

3.   Are ethnic minority youth impacted by a lack of role models?

_____

_____

4.   Are ethnic differences often interpreted as deficits?

_____

_____

5.   How does failure to recognize diversity lead to stereotyping?

_____

_____

6.   What is prejudice?

_____

_____

7.   What are some defining characteristics of African-American adolescents?

_____

_____

8.   Why is low SES a problem among black youth?

_____

_____

9.   Where are the national origins of Latino adolescents?

_____

_____

10.   What is a Chicano?

_____

_____

11.   What role do families play in the lives of Latino youth?

_____

_____

12.   What accounts for the strong achievement orientation of Asian American youth?

_____

_____

13.   What discriminations have Native American adolescents endured?

_____

_____

SOCIOECONOMIC STATUS AND POVERTY
SECTION REVIEW

1.   What are four psychological ramifications for adolescents living in poverty.

    a.   _____

    b.   _____

    c.   _____

    d.   _____

2.   What is meant by socioeconomic status (SES)?

_____

_____

3.   What is the most common marker of poverty?

       _____

       _____

4.   Compare the poverty rate of adolescents in the United States to those living in Canada and
       Sweden.

       _____

       _____

5.   Compare the poverty rate of African American and Latino adolescents with the overall
       adolescent poverty rate in the United States.

       _____

       _____

6.   Give three explanations for why poverty is so high among American youth.

       a.   _____

             _____

       b.   _____

             _____

       c.   _____

             _____

7.   What is meant by the feminization of poverty?

       _____

       _____

THE MEDIA AND TECHNOLOGY
SECTION REVIEW

1.   What are the six functions of media for adolescents?

       _____

       _____

2.   How strongly does television influence a child's negative behavior?

       _____

       _____

3. What impact is television having on the sexual behaviors of youth?

_____

_____

4. How important is music to adolescents?

_____

_____

5. What is the Internet?

_____

_____

6. What are some concerns regarding how adolescents use the Internet?

_____

_____

7. What is the relationship between technology and adolescent learning?

_____

_____

8. What social policy recommendations were made by the Carnegie Council on Adolescent Development regarding the effects of the media?

_____

_____

COGNITIVE CHALLENGE

1. Take a moment to imagine how your life might have been different if you were of another race or ethnic background. Would your friends be the same? Would you live in the same neighborhood? How might your family be different? Would your attitude toward education be different?

_____

_____

ADOLESCENCE IN RESEARCH

Concerning the evaluation of the Quantum Opportunities Program, comparing mentored students with a nonmentored control group, state the hypothesis, the research methods (if known), the research conclusions, and the implications and applications for adolescent development.

_____

_____

_____

⊠ COMPREHENSIVE REVIEW

1.　The learning and shared behavioral patterns, beliefs, and values of a group of people that are passed on from one generation to the next are known as
　　a.　culture.
　　b.　minority.
　　c.　ethnicity.
　　d.　socioeconomic status.

2.　Family income is a good measure of
　　a.　ethnicity.
　　b.　social class.
　　c.　culture.
　　d.　ethnocentrism.

3.　_____ is a tendency to favor one's own group over others.
　　a.　Ethnicity
　　b.　Social class
　　c.　Culture
　　d.　Ethnocentrism

4.　In comparison to adolescents from other cultures, American adolescents are often described as more
　　a.　passive.
　　b.　rebellious.
　　c.　achievement-oriented.
　　d.　mentally healthy.

5.　Of the different ethnic groups living in America, which is the most achievement oriented?
　　a.　African-American
　　b.　Asian American
　　c.　Latino
　　d.　Anglo-American

6.　The melting pot belief in the United States assumes which process of cultural change?
　　a.　assimilation
　　b.　acculturation
　　c.　accommodation
　　d.　cultural schema shifting

7.　Which of the following is NOT an adolescent rite of passage?
　　a.　gaining of knowledge or secrets associated with maturity
　　b.　participation in athletics

    c.   experimentation with sexuality

    d.   gaining entry into the adult world

8.   Which of the following is NOT a disadvantage experienced by ethnic minority youth in poverty?

    a.   prejudice

    b.   bias

    c.   affirmative action

    d.   discrimination

9.   Children from low-SES backgrounds are at high risk for all of the following EXCEPT

    a.   depression.

    b.   peer conflict.

    c.   academic success.

    d.   low self-confidence.

10.   Which of the following is LEAST likely to make use of the extended family unit?

    a.   African American

    b.   Anglo-American

    c.   Latino

    d.   Asian American

11.   According to research by Lee, successful African-American students are most likely to have mentioned _____ as having an important influence on their lives.

    a.   their father

    b.   Bill Clinton

    c.   Jesus Christ

    d.   Jessie Jackson

12.   Rituals such as bar mitzvah and confirmation are examples of

    a.   rites of passage.

    b.   cultural transitions of sexuality.

    c.   evidence of ethnocentrism.

    d.   family traditions.

13.   The most common rite of passage for American adolescents is probably

    a.   a religious ceremony.

    b.   going off to college.

    c.   graduating from high school.

    d.   buying the first car.

14.   ___ percent of the adolescents in the United States live in poverty.

    a.   Eleven

    b.   Thirty-three

    c.   Seventeen

    d.   Twenty

15.   The adolescent raised in a single-parent, female-headed household is more likely than not to be

    a.   sexually active.

    b.   promiscuous.

c.   in trouble with the law.

d.   poor.

16.   When an adolescent has a negative attitude about another individual because that individual belongs to a particular group, the adolescent is exhibiting

      a.   values.

      b.   an opinion.

      c.   prejudice.

      d.   cognitive narrowing.

17.   El Puente is a social program for _____ Latinos.

      a.   low-income

      b.   female

      c.   Protestant

      d.   English-speaking

18.   Which ethnic minority adolescent group has the highest suicide rate in the United States?

      a.   African American

      b.   Hispanic

      c.   Native American

      d.   Asian

19.   Compared to the United States, the ethnic subcultures of Canadian adolescents tend to be organized more along the lines of

      a.   economic power.

      b.   political affiliation.

      c.   religious participation.

      d.   gender differences.

20.   Adolescents spend approximately _____ of their waking hours with some form of mass media.

      a.   one-eighth

      b.   one-third

      c.   one-half

      d.   two-thirds

21.   Television has been criticized for all of the following EXCEPT

      a.   teaching adolescents that problems are easily resolved.

      b.   declining national achievement test scores.

      c.   increasing the leisure activities of adolescents.

      d.   creating passive learners.

22.   Which is the most accurate conclusion about the long-term effects of watching television violence?

      a.   Watching television violence causes crime.

      b.   Watching television violence has no relationship to crime.

      c.   Watching television violence may be associated with violence in some young people.

      d.   Watching television violence makes young people less afraid of being a victim.

ADOLESCENCE ON THE SCREEN

- *Of Hopscotch and Little Girls* A powerful documentary film that explores the plight of girls growing up to be women in different cultures.

- *Daughters of the Dust* explores life and development on a barrier island off the coast of South Carolina. The Gullah subculture, an isolated African-American group, is the focus.

- *Saturday Night Fever* highlights the lives of older adolescents during the disco era of the 1970s.

- *Pulp Fiction* is a parody of drug use, violence, and down-and-out diner bandits.

- *Woodstock* captures the drug and rock culture of the 1960s.

- *Fresh* shows the challenges faced by a 12-year-old trying to grow up in one of America's roughest neighborhoods.

- *Whale Rider* deals with the challenges associated with upholding cultural tradition in a changing world.

ADOLESCENCE IN BOOKS

- *The Adolescent & Young Adult Fact Book*, by Janet Simons, Belva Finlay, and Alice Yang (Children's Defense Fund, 1991), describes the role of poverty and ethnicity in adolescent development.

- *Children's Journey Through the Information Age*, by Sandra Calvert (McGraw-Hill: IA, 1999), covers topics related to the information age, including television and computers.

- *Understanding Culture's Influence on Behavior*, by Richard Brislin (Harcourt Brace: FL, 1993), details the role of culture in behavior and development.

- *Failure to Connect: How Computers Affect Our Children's Minds, and What We Can Do About It*, by Jane M. Healy (Simon and Schuster: NJ, 1999) presents a very strong case against the use of computers in modern classrooms.

Answer Key

KEY TERMS

1. **culture** The behavior, patterns, beliefs, and all other products of a particular group of people that are passed on from generation to generation.

2. **socioeconomic status (SES)** A grouping of people with similar occupational, educational, and economic characteristics.

3. **ethnicity** A dimension of culture based on cultural heritage, nationality, race, religion, and language.

4. **ethnocentrism** A tendency to favor one's own group over other groups.

5. **cross-cultural studies** Studies that compare a culture with one or more other cultures. Such studies provide information about the degree to which adolescent development is similar, or universal, across cultures, or about the degree to which it is culture specific.

6. **assimilation** The absorption of ethnic minority groups into the dominant group, which often means the loss of some or virtually all of the behavior and values of the ethnic minority group.

7. **acculturation** Cultural change that results from continuous, first-hand contact between two distinctive cultural groups.

8. **alternation model** This model assumes that it is possible for an individual to know and understand two different cultures. It also assumes that individuals can alter their behavior to fit a particular social context.

9. **multicultural model** This model promotes a pluralistic approach to understanding two or more cultures. It argues that people can maintain their distinctive identities while working with others from different cultures to meet common national or economic needs.

10. **rites of passage** Ceremonies or rituals that mark an individual's transition from one status to another, especially into adulthood.

11. **prejudice** An unjustified negative attitude toward an individual because of her or his membership in a group.

12. **Chicano** The name politically conscious Mexican American adolescents give themselves, reflecting the combination of their Spanish-Mexican-Indian heritage and Anglo influence.

13. **Internet** The core of computer-mediated communication. The Internet is worldwide and connects thousands of computer networks, providing an incredible array of information adolescents can access.

14. **e-mail** Stands for electronic mail and is a valuable way the Internet can be used. Written messages can be sent to and received by individuals as well as large numbers of people.

15. **feminization of poverty** The fact that far more women than men live in poverty. Likely causes are women's low income, divorce, and the resolution of divorce cases by the judicial system, which leaves women with less money than they and their children need to adequately function.

KEY PEOPLE IN THE STUDY OF ADOLESCENCE

1.	B		4.	C
2.	D		5.	F
3.	A		6.	E

"DR. DETAIL'S" PUZZLE EXERCISE

Across		*Down*	
1.	ethnicity	**1.**	culture
2.	acculturation	**2.**	assimilation
3.	prejudice	**3.**	e-mail
4.	Chicano		
5.	Internet		

CULTURE AND ADOLESCENCE
SECTION REVIEW

1. a. Culture is made up of ideals, values, and assumptions about life that guide people's behaviors.
    b. Culture is made by people.
    c. Culture is transmitted from generation to generation.
    d. Culture's influence is noticed most in well-meaning clashes between people from very different cultural backgrounds.
    e. Despite compromises, cultural values still remain.
    f. People react emotionally when their cultural values are violated or when their cultural expectations are ignored.
    g. People accept a cultural value at one point in their life and reject it at another.

2. SES refers to a grouping of people with similar occupational, educational, and economic characteristics.

3. Ethnicity is based on cultural heritage, nationality, race, religion, and language.

4. a. People believe that what happens in their culture is natural and correct and that what happens in other cultures is unnatural and incorrect.
    b. People perceive their cultural customs as universally valid, that is, good for everyone.
    c. People behave in ways that favor their own cultural group.
    d. People feel proud of their cultural group.
    e. People feel hostile toward other cultural groups.

5. These involve the comparison of a culture with one or more other cultures, which provides information about the degree to which adolescent development is similar, or universal, across cultures, or the degree to which it is culture-specific.

6. (1) assimilation, (2) acculturation, (3) alternation, and (4) multiculturalism.

7. This model assumes that it is possible for an individual to know and understand two different cultures.

8. This model promotes a pluralistic approach to understanding two or more cultures.

9. These are ceremonies or rituals that mark an individual's transition from one status to another, especially into adulthood.

ETHNICITY
SECTION REVIEW

1.   Ethnicity is race and cultural background and tradition.

2.   Language barriers, dislocations, separation from support networks, changes in SES, and the pressure to retain culture while at the same time acculturating.

3.   Within communities there is often a lack of role models. So African-American youth in particular either seek White middle class values, or they are drawn to black role models whose success was gained in atypical ways (e.g., sports).

4.   Traditionally, this has been the case, but it depends on the situation.

5.   Stereotyping discounts individuality. By lumping someone inextricably to an ethnic group and discounting individuality, one increases the likelihood of both positive and negative stereotyping.

6.   Prejudice is an unjustified negative attitude toward an individual because of the individual's membership in a group.

7.   The majority stay in school, do not take drugs, do not prematurely get married or become parents, are employed, are not involved in crime, and grow up to be very productive despite disadvantage.

8.   Low SES places people in worse neighborhoods and at poorer schools. This leads to many other problems.

9.   Most are from Mexico.

10.   Chicano is the name politically conscious Mexican American adolescents give themselves to reflect the combination of their Spanish-Mexican-Indian heritage and Anglo influence.

11.   Church and family are very important in the lives of Latino youth.

12.   There is a general expectation for success that places pressure on these kids to perform at a high level.

13.   Native Americans have experienced an inordinate amount of discrimination. Terrible abuse and punishment, among other things.

SOCIOECONOMIC STATUS AND POVERTY
SECTION REVIEW

1.   a.   The poor are often powerless.
       b.   The poor are often vulnerable to disease and disaster.
       c.   Only a limited number of options (e.g., jobs) are open to them.
       d.   Being poor means having less prestige.

2.   The grouping of people with similar occupational, educational, and economic characteristics.

3.   Its most common marker is the federal poverty threshold.

4.   The overall poverty rate for American adolescents is 17 percent. In Canada it is 9 percent, whereas in Sweden it is only 2 percent.

5.   The overall poverty rate is 17 percent. The poverty rate for African American and Latino adolescents is 40 percent.

6.   a.   Economic changes have eliminated many blue-collar jobs that paid reasonably well.
      b.   Increase in the percentage of youth living in single-parent families headed by the mother.
      c.   Reduction of government benefits during the 1970s and 1980s.

7.   This refers to the fact that far more women than men live in poverty.

THE MEDIA AND TECHNOLOGY
SECTION REVIEW

1.   a.   Entertainment
      b.   Information
      c.   Sensation
      d.   Coping
      e.   Gender-role modeling
      f.   Youth culture identification

2.   Adolescents spend a third or more of their waking hours with some form of mass-media, most often TV. Research has suggested that the amount of TV watched at age 8 is directly correlated with problem behaviors in adulthood.

3.   Adolescents like to watch TV with much sexual content. It tends to lead them to make errors in judgment with regard to what typical sexual activity is.

4.   Very important. Two-thirds of all records and tapes are purchased by those 10- to 24-years old.

5.   The core of computer mediated communication.

6.   Of the 1,000 most visited sites, 10 percent are adult sex oriented. Forty-four percent of adolescents have viewed an adult Internet site. Twenty-five percent of adolescents have visited an Internet site that promotes hate groups. Twleve percent of adolescents have visited a site where they can obtain information about how to purchase a gun.

7.   The numbers of computers in schools have increased dramatically, but it has not impacted adolescent learning.

8.   (a) Encourage socially responsible programming, (b) support public efforts to make the media more adolescent friendly, (c) encourage media literacy programs as part of school curricula, youth and community organizations, and family life, (d) increase media presentations of health promotions,
(e) expand opportunities for adolescents' views to appear in the media.

COGNITIVE CHALLENGE

1.   No answer provided. Individual activity

ADOLESCENCE IN RESEARCH

An evaluation of the Quantum project compared the mentored students with a nonmentored control group. The methods were experimental. The hypothesis was that the features of the Quantum project would help overcome the intergenerational transmission of poverty and its negative outcomes. The mentored students were involved in academic-related activities, community service projects, and cultural enrichment and personal development activities. Students also received financial incentives for participating, including bonuses for every 100 hours of education. Sixty-three percent of the mentored students graduated from high school, but only 42 percent of the control group did. Forty-two percent of the mentored group is currently enrolled in college, but only 16 percent of the control group. The control-group students were twice as likely as mentored students to receive food stamps or be on welfare and they had more arrests. The conclusion is that programs like the Quantum project have the potential to help overcome the intergenerational transmission of poverty and its negative outcomes.

⊠ COMPREHENSIVE REVIEW

1.	a	7.	b	13.	c	19.	a
2.	b	8.	c	14.	c	20.	b
3.	d	9.	c	15.	d	21.	c
4.	c	10.	b	16.	c	22.	c
5.	b	11.	c	17.	a		
6.	a	12.	a	18.	c		

⌘

Chapter 14   Adolescent Problems

Learning Goals with Key Terms and Key People in Boldface

1.0   DISCUSS TWO MAIN APPROACHES TO UNDERSTANDING ADOLESCENT PROBLEMS AND THE CHARACTERISTICS OF THESE PROBLEMS

A.   The Bio-psycho-social Approach
- 1.1   What is the **bio-psycho-social approach?**
- 1.2   What roles do the three factors play in the development of problem behavior?

B.   The Developmental Psychopathology Approach
- 1.3   What is the focus of **developmental psychopathology?**
- 1.4   Compare and contrast **internalizing** and **externalizing problems.**
- 1.5   According to **Sroufe,** anxiety problems in adolescence are linked with what?

C.   Characteristics of Adolescent Problems
- 1.6   What correlation did **Achenbach** find between SES and behavior problems?

D.   Resilience
- 1.7   Why might the study of resilience be important in understanding problem behavior?

2.0   DESCRIBE SOME MAIN PROBLEMS THAT CHARACTERIZE ADOLESCENTS

A.   Drug Use
- 2.1   Why do people use drugs?
- 2.2   What is **tolerance?**
- 2.3   What is **physical dependence?**
- 2.4   What are the characteristics of **psychological dependence?**
- 2.5   What was the nature of drug use in the 1960s and 1970s?
- 2.6   What has been the trend of drug use in the 1980s and 1990s?
- 2.7   How does adolescent drug use in the United States compare to that in other industrialized countries?
- 2.8   What type of drug is alcohol?
- 2.9   How much is alcohol used by American adolescents?
- 2.10   What are some potential negative outcomes of alcohol abuse?
- 2.11   What are the risk factors for adolescent alcohol use?
- 2.12   Is there a genetic predisposition to alcoholism?
- 2.13   Is there a personality profile for someone who is likely to develop an alcohol problem?
- 2.14   What are some possible preventative strategies for alcoholism?
- 2.15   What drugs other than alcohol are harmful to adolescents?
- 2.16   What are the nature and characteristics of **hallucinogens,** LSD, and marijuana?
- 2.17   What are the most widely used **stimulants?**
- 2.18   How does cigarette smoking play a role in the drug problems of youth?
- 2.19   Have school health programs had success in deterring youth from smoking?

2.20   What is the history of cocaine use?

2.21   How many adolescents use cocaine?

2.22   How prevalent is the use of amphetamines among adolescents?

2.23   What is Ecstasy, and what are some special concerns associated with it?

2.24   What are **depressants?**

2.25   How has the use of depressants changed over the past 25 years?

2.26   What are the risks of using **anabolic steroids?**

2.27   What role does early drug use play in adolescent development?

2.28   How can parents and peers help prevent adolescent drug abuse?

2.29   What school-based intervention programs can help reduce adolescent drug use?

B.   **Juvenile Delinquency**

2.30   What is **juvenile delinquency?**

2.31   What is the difference between **index offenses** and **status offenses?**

2.32   Is it appropriate to try juveniles as adults in court?

2.33   What is **conduct disorder?**

2.34   What percentage of adolescents engage in delinquent behaviors?

2.35   In the Pittsburgh Youth Study, what were noted as the three developmental pathways to delinquency?

2.36   What are the predictors of delinquency?

2.37   What is Erikson's beliefs regarding youth and delinquency?

2.38   Can siblings influence delinquency?

2.39   Why is the high rate of youth violence an increasing concern?

2.40   What percent of public schools experience one or more serious violent incidents each year?

2.41   What factors are often present in at-risk youths and seem to propel them toward violence?

2.42   What strategies have been proposed for reducing youth violence?

2.43   What is the **cadre approach** to reducing violence?

2.44   What is meant by the **total student body approach** to reducing school-related violence?

2.45   What are the steps students learn in mediation?

C.   **Depression and Suicide**

2.46   What is the rate of depression in females as opposed to males?

2.47   How serious a problem is depression in adolescence?

2.48   What is a **major depressive disorder?**

2.49   Will a depressed adolescent be more likely to suffer from depression as an adult?

2.50   What are the treatments for depression?

2.51   What is the rate of adolescent suicide and how has it changed since the 1950s?

2.52   Why do adolescents attempt suicide?

2.53   What proximal and distal factors are involved in suicide?

2.54   What is the psychological profile of the suicidal adolescents like?

D.   **Eating Disorders**

2.55   What percent of adolescents are obese?

2.56   What hereditary and environmental factors are involved in obesity?

2.57   What are the characteristics of **anorexia nervosa?**

2.58   Are certain adolescents more prone to anorexia than others?

2.59   What societal, psychological, and physiological causes of **anorexia nervosa** have been proposed?

2.60   What is the nature of **bulimia nervosa?**

3.0   SUMMARIZE THE INTERRELATION OF ADOLESCENT PROBLEMS AND WAYS TO PREVENT OR INTERVENE IN PROBLEMS
   A.   **Adolescents with Multiple Problems**
          3.1   Which four problems affect adolescents the most?
          3.2   Are adolescent problem behaviors interrelated?
   B.   **Prevention and Intervention**
          3.3   What are the common components of successful prevention/intervention programs for adolescent problem behaviors?

Exercises

KEY TERMS COMPLETION EXERCISE

Each key term is presented in the form of an incomplete sentence. Complete each sentence by either defining the term or giving an example of it. Compare your definitions with those given at the end of the study guide chapter.

1.   The **bio-psycho-social approach** focuses on

_____

_____

2.   **Developmental psychopathology** focuses on

_____

_____

3.   **Internalizing problems** appear as

_____

_____

4.   Examples of **externalizing problems** are

_____

_____

5.   **Tolerance** of a drug means

_____

_____

6.   **Physical dependence** on a drug means

_____

_____

7.   **Psychological dependence** on a substance suggests

_____

_____

8.   **Hallucinogens** are a grouping of drugs that

_____

_____

9.   Overuse of **stimulants** can lead to

_____

_____

10.   The use of **depressants** in recent years has

_____

_____

11.   **Anabolic steroids** are used to

_____

_____

12.   Involvement in **juvenile delinquency** leads to

_____

_____

13.   **Index offenses** are crimes that

_____

_____

14.   **Status offenses** are crimes that

_____

_____

15.   Example of a **conduct disorder** is

_____

_____

16.   A **major depressive disorder** is

_____

_____

17.   **Anorexia nervosa** is defined as

_____

_____

18.   **Bulimia nervosa** differs from anorexia in that

_____

_____

KEY PEOPLE IN THE STUDY OF ADOLESCENCE

Match the person with the concept of adolescent development with which they are associated.

_____ 1. Thomas Achenbach and Craig Edelbrock

_____ 2. Lloyd Johnston, Patrick O'Malley, and Gerald Bachman

_____ 3. Norman Garmezy

_____ 4. Joy Dryfoos

_____ 5. James Garbarino

_____ 6. David and Roger Johnson

A. Believe(s) that resilient children triumph over life's adversities

B. Found that adolescents from lower-SES background were more likely to have problems than those from a middle-SES background

C. Monitored the drug use of America's high school students through a project at the University of Michigan

D. Interviewed young men who were murderers

E. Interested in the interrelationship between adolescent problem behaviors

F. Believe(s) in teaching conflict resolution skills in schools

"DR. DETAIL'S" MATCHING EXERCISE

Match the following contributors to the study of adolescence to their area of contribution.

_____ 1. Alan Sroufe

_____ 2. Ann Masten

_____ 3. Sigmund Freud

_____ 4. Lloyd Johnson, Patrick O'Malley, and Gerald Bachman

_____ 5. Robert Cloninger

_____ 6. Cheryl Perry

_____ 7. Judith Brooks

_____ 8. Mary Ann Dentz

A. Experimented with therapeutic uses of cocaine

B. Proposed a developmental model of adolescent drug abuse

C. Studied traits associated with alcoholism

D. Believe(s) that adolescents, whose development has restricted them from acceptable social roles, might choose a negative identity

E. Found that anxiety problems in adolescence are linked with anxious/resistant attachment in infancy

F. Found that good intellectual functioning and parenting served protective roles in keeping adolescent from antisocial behaviors

G. Developed the Midwestern Prevention Program

H. Taught conflict resolution training in schools

_____	9.	Erik Erikson	I.	Have/Has monitored the drug use of American Seniors in public and private schools
_____	10.	David and Roger Johnson	J.	Developed an approach to stop smoking by adolescents

EXPLORING ADOLESCENT PROBLEMS
SECTION REVIEW

1. What are the three factors that might be the basis for adolescent problem behavior?

   _____

   _____

2. What are two social factors that influence the development of adolescent problems?

   _____

   _____

3. What is the focus of developmental psychopathology?

   _____

   _____

4. Compare and contrast internalizing and externalizing problems?

   _____

   _____

5. According to Sroufe, anxiety problems in adolescence are linked with what?

   _____

   _____

6. What correlations did Achenbach find between SES and behavior problems?

   _____

   _____

7. Why might the study of resilience be important in understanding problem behavior?

   _____

   _____

PROBLEMS AND DISORDERS
SECTION REVIEW

1. Identify the class of drugs by placing a "D" for depressants, "S" for stimulants, and "H" for hallucinogens.

_____	1.	Marijuana	_____	5.	Tranquilizers
_____	2.	Alcohol	_____	6.	Cocaine
_____	3.	Barbiturates	_____	7.	Narcotics
_____	4.	Amphetamines	_____	8.	LSD

2.   What is tolerance?

_____

_____

3.   What is physical dependence?

_____

_____

4.   What type of drug is alcohol?

_____

_____

5.   What are the risk factors for adolescent alcohol use?

_____

_____

6.   What are some possible preventative strategies for alcoholism?

_____

_____

7.   Have school health programs had success in deterring youth from smoking?

_____

_____

8.   How many adolescents use cocaine?

_____

_____

9.   What are depressants?

_____

_____

10.   How has the use of depressants changed over the past 25 years?

_____

_____

11.   What seven criteria have been generally accepted as necessary for effective school-based drug abuse prevention programs?

a.   _____

_____

b.   _____

_____

c.   _____

_____

d.   _____

_____

e.   _____

_____

f.   _____

_____

g.   _____

_____

12.   Complete the table for listing the association with delinquency that matches each antecedent of delinquency.

Antecedent	Association with Delinquency
Identity	
Self-control	
Age	
Sex	
Expectations for education and school grades	
Parental influences	

Peer influences	
Socioeconomic status	
Neighborhood quality	

13.   What is the nature of juvenile delinquency?

_____

_____

14.   In the Pittsburgh Youth Study, what were noted as the three developmental pathways to delinquency?

_____

_____

15.   What is Erikson's beliefs regarding youth and delinquency?

_____

_____

16.   What are the four factors often present in at-risk youth that seem to propel them toward acts of violence?

a.   _____

b.   _____

c.   _____

d.   _____

17.   What four recommendations for reducing youth violence were suggested by The Oregon Social Learning Center?

a.   _____

b.   _____

c.   _____

d.   _____

18.   What is the cadre approach to reducing violence?

_____

_____

19.   What is a major depressive disorder?

_____

_____

20.   What proximal and distal factors are involved in suicide?

_____

_____

21.   What hereditary and environmental factors are involved in obesity?

_____

_____

22.   What are the characteristics of anorexia nervosa?

_____

_____

23.   What is the nature of bulimia nervosa?

_____

_____

INTERRELATION OF ADOLESCENT PROBLEMS AND REVENTION/INTERVENTION SECTION REVIEW

1.   What four problems affect the most adolescents?

_____

_____

2.   Are adolescent problem behaviors interrelated?

_____

_____

3.   What are the common components of successful prevention/intervention programs for adolescent problem behaviors?

_____

_____

COGNITIVE CHALLENGE

1. Imagine that you have just been appointed the head of the President's Commission on Adolescent Drug Abuse. What would be the first program you would try to put into place? What would be its main components? Would it be school-focused? What role, if any, would the media play in promoting the program?

    _____

    _____

2. Why are the consequences of risky behavior more serious today than they have ever been?

    _____

    _____

3. What role might David Elkind's conceptualizations of the Personal Fable and Imaginary Audience have played in the atrocities at Columbine and Thurston High Schools?

    _____

    _____

ADOLESCENCE IN RESEARCH

The Search Institute in Minneapolis conducted research that led to the prescription of 40 developmental assets that adolescents need to achieve positive outcomes. State the hypothesis, methods used, and conclusions of the Search Institute research project.

_____

_____

⊠ COMPREHENSIVE REVIEW

1. Scientists who adopt a biological approach usually focus on all of the following EXCEPT
    a.   the brain as a cause of problems.
    b.   drug therapy treatments.
    c.   distorted thoughts as causes of problems.
    d.   genetic factors as causes of problems.

2. The condition where a greater amount of a drug is needed to produce the same effect is referred to as
    a.   tolerance.
    b.   physical dependence.
    c.   psychological dependence.
    d.   emotional dependence.

3.   Physical need for a drug that is accompanied by unpleasant withdrawal symptoms when the drug is withdrawn is referred to as
      a.   tolerance.
      b.   physical dependence.
      c.   psychological dependence.
      d.   emotional dependence.

4.   Strong desire and craving to repeat the use of a drug for various emotional reasons is referred to as
      a.   tolerance.
      b.   physical dependence.
      c.   psychological dependence.
      d.   emotional dependence.

5.   Robin has been told he has an internalizing disorder. Which of the following is NOT something that Robin might have?
      a.   shyness
      b.   attention deficit/hyperactivity disorder
      c.   anxiety
      d.   depression

6.   Which of the following is NOT one of the behavioral problems most likely to cause adolescents to be referred to a clinic for mental health problems?
      a.   sadness
      b.   poor school performance
      c.   anger
      d.   unhappiness

7.   Which therapist experimented with therapeutic uses of cocaine?
      a.   Jean Piaget
      b.   Erik Erikson
      c.   Sigmund Freud
      d.   Lawrence Kohlberg

8.   In which year did cigarette smoking by eighth graders in the U.S. reach its peak?
      a.   1973
      b.   1996
      c.   2001
      d.   2002

9.   Most developmentalists accept an interactionist approach to the study of abnormal behavior because
      a.   the evidence shows that all disorders have both psychological and sociocultural causes.
      b.   neither the biological nor psychological and sociocultural viewpoints can account for the complexity of problems.
      c.   it's the only way to keep peace in the profession.
      d.   adolescents tell us that the interactionist approach is best.

10. Which nation has the highest rate of adolescent drug use?
    a.   Thailand
    b.   Germany
    c.   United States
    d.   France

11. Which of the following is NOT a risk factor for abuse of alcohol?
    a.   heredity
    b.   peer relations
    c.   alcohol tolerance
    d.   family influences

12. Which two behavioral problems are the most common causes for adolescent mental health referrals?
    a.   conflict with parents and substance abuse
    b.   poor school work and depression
    c.   suicide attempt and depression
    d.   substance abuse and poor schoolwork

13. Your textbook indicates that adolescents use drugs
    a.   because Sigmund Freud used cocaine.
    b.   as adaptations to changing environments.
    c.   as aids to sexual gratification.
    d.   because their parents use drugs at home.

14. Drugs that modify an individual's perceptual experiences and produce hallucinations are known as
    a.   stimulants.
    b.   depressants.
    c.   hallucinogens.
    d.   anabolic steroids.

15. Andrew is a 17-year-old adolescent who has been drinking white wine for about three years. Andrew has noticed that over this period, it takes more and more wine to get "looped." This indicates
    a.   the wine producers have decreased the alcoholic content.
    b.   tolerance.
    c.   the disorganized thinking associated with ingesting alcohol at a young age.
    d.   his psychological dependence.

16. The most widely used illicit drug is
    a.   marijuana.
    b.   cocaine.
    c.   barbiturates.
    d.   alcohol.

17. Which of the following is NOT a risk factor for alcohol abuse?
    a.   secure attachment to parents
    b.   having friends who abuse alcohol

c. coming from an unhappy home
d. susceptibility to peer pressure

18. The parents of an 11-year-old boy have been advised by a psychologist to provide more structure in the home, more caring support, and a more stimulating environment. According to Robert Cloninger, what are they trying to prevent in their son?
a. eventually acquiring a sexually transmitted disease
b. attempting suicide
c. alcoholism as an adult
d. the youngster from eventually abusing his parents

19. Nembutal and Seconal are
a. stimulants.
b. hallucinogens.
c. opiates.
d. depressants.

20. Which of the new school-based drug prevention programs appears to be the most promising?
a. counselor-led programs
b. the use of testimonials from ex-drug users
c. social skills training
d. attendance at juvenile court when drug cases are heard

21. In the United States, theft, rape, and assault are _____ offenses.
a. status
b. index
c. matrix
d. conduct

22. Between February and September, Harry, a 14-year-old, ran away from home twice and got involved in a series of break-and-enter offenses. The parents say he is "out of control." According to your text, the court psychiatrist will likely diagnose him as
a. being a delinquent.
b. having a conduct disorder.
c. a problem child.
d. having poor parents.

23. Which of the following individuals would say that delinquency is a manifestation of the search for "Who am I?"
a. Gilbert Botvin
b. Peter Blos
c. John Bowlby
d. Erik Erikson

24. Which of the following is NOT associated with juvenile delinquency?
a. negative identity
b. learned helplessness
c. failed self-control
d. lower-class culture

25.   A recent review of all the approaches to prevention of delinquency by Dryfoos has revealed that
       _____ seems to be effective.
       a.   a multiple components approach
       b.   work experience
       c.   preventative casework
       d.   security guards in school

26.   How common is suicide in adolescence?
       a.   It is the most common cause of death in adolescents.
       b.   It is the second most common cause of death in adolescents.
       c.   It is the third most common cause of death in adolescents.
       d.   It is the fourth most common cause of death in adolescents.

27.   All but one of the following is a characteristic of successful programs for reducing adolescent
       problems.
       a.   Remove adolescents from the situation that seems to be causing their problems.
       b.   Make sure that each adolescent gets personal attention from a responsible adult.
       c.   Coordinate the activities of different agencies and institutions.
       d.   Begin intervention programs early in adolescent's lives.

28.   Which of the following is NOT one of the four problems that affects the most adolescents?
       a.   drug abuse
       b.   juvenile delinquency
       c.   shyness
       d.   school-related problems

ADOLESCENCE ON THE SCREEN

■   *Ordinary People* A young man struggles with depression and thoughts of suicide as a result of
     surviving an accident that took his younger brother's life.

■   *Trainspotting* portrays the grim reality of lives ruined by heroin addiction.

■   *The Killer at Thurston High* (Frontline) portrays the events that led up to Kip Kinkel's assault on
     his parents and the school at Thurston. The content is shocking, but gives much insight.

■   *The River's Edge* A group of high school friends must come to terms with the fact that one of
     them killed another.

ADOLESCENCE IN BOOKS

■   *Developmental Psychopathology*, edited by Suniya Luthar, Jacob Burack, Dante Cicchetti, and
     John Weisz (Cambridge University Press: MA, 1999), explores the many aspects of
     developmental psychopathology.

■   *Lost Boys*, by James Garbarino (The Free Press: NY, 1999), examines why young men grow up
     to be murderers.

Answer Key

KEY TERMS

1. **bio-psycho-social approach** Emphasizes that problems develop through an interaction of biological, psychological, and social factors.

2. **developmental psychopathology** Focuses on describing and exploring the developmental pathways of problems and disorders.

3. **internalizing problems** Occur when individuals turn problems inward. Anxiety and depression.

4. **externalizing problems** Occur when individuals turn problems outward. Such as juvenile delinquency.

5. **tolerance** A greater amount of a drug is needed to produce the same effect.

6. **physical dependence** The physical need for a drug that is accompanied by unpleasant withdrawal symptoms when the drug is discontinued.

7. **psychological dependence** The strong desire and craving to repeat the use of a drug for various emotional reasons, such as a feeling of well-being and reduction of distress.

8. **hallucinogens** Drugs that alter an individual's perceptual experiences and produce hallucinations—also called psychedelic or mind-altering drugs.

9. **stimulants** Drugs that increase the activity of the central nervous system.

10. **depressants** Drugs that slow the central nervous system, bodily functions, and behavior.

11. **anabolic steroids** Drugs derived from the male sex hormone, testosterone. They promote muscle growth and lean body mass.

12. **juvenile delinquency** A broad range of child and adolescent behaviors, including socially unacceptable behavior, status offenses, and criminal acts.

13. **index offenses** Whether they are committed by juveniles or adults, these are criminal acts, such as robbery, rape, and homicide.

14. **status offenses** Performed by youths under a specified age, these are juvenile offenses that are not as serious as index offenses. These offenses may include such acts as drinking under age, truancy, and sexual promiscuity.

15. **conduct disorder** The psychiatric diagnostic category for the occurrence of multiple delinquent activities over a 6-month period. These behaviors include truancy, running away, fire setting, and cruelty to animals, breaking and entering, and excessive fighting.

16. **major depressive disorder** The diagnosis when an individual experiences a major depressive episode and depressed characteristics, such as lethargy and depression, for two weeks or longer and daily functioning becomes impaired.

17. **anorexia nervosa** An eating disorder that involves the relentless pursuit of thinness through starvation.

18. **bulimia nervosa** In this eating disorder, the individual consistently follows a binge-and-purge eating pattern.

KEY PEOPLE IN THE STUDY OF ADOLESCENCE

1. B
2. C
3. A
4. E
5. D
6. F

"DR. DETAIL'S" MATCHING EXERCISE

1. E
2. F
3. A
4. I
5. C
6. J
7. B
8. G
9. D
10. H

EXPLORING ADOLESCENT PROBLEMS
SECTION REVIEW

1. Psychological, Sociocultural, and Biopsychosocial.

2. Socioeconomic status and neighborhood quality.

3. Focuses on describing and exploring the developmental pathways of problems.

4. Internalizing problems occur when individuals turn their problems inward. Externalizing problems occur when problems are turned outward.

5. They are linked with anxious/resistant attachment in infancy.

6. Adolescents from a lower SES background were more likely to have problems than those from a higher SES background.

7. It may give important insight into why some children, against all odds, succeed.

PROBLEMS AND DISORDERS
SECTION REVIEW

1.

1.	H	**5.**	D
2.	D	**6.**	S
3.	D	**7.**	D
4.	S	**8.**	H

2.   A greater amount of a drug is needed to produce the same effect.

3.   Physical need for a drug that is accompanied by unpleasant withdrawal symptoms when the drug is discontinued.

4.   It is a widely used and powerful drug.

5.   Heredity, family influences, peer relations, personality characteristics, and the college transition.

6.   A strong family support system is a very important preventative strategy.

7.   No. While informative, their impact has been minimal.

8.   In 1999 it had dropped to 2.6 percent.

9.   Drugs that slow down the central nervous system, bodily functions, and behavior.

10.   The use of depressants has dropped dramatically over the past 25 years.

11.   a.   Early intervention in schools is believed to be more effective than later intervention.
      b.   School-based drug-abuse prevention requires a kindergarten through grade 12 approach.
      c.   Teacher training is important.
      d.   Social skills training is a most-promising new approach to prevention.
      e.   Peer-led programs are often more effective than those led by teachers or counselors.
      f.   More programs aimed at high-risk kids are needed.
      g.   The most effective programs are often part of community-wide programs.

12.

Antecedent	Association with Delinquency
Identity	Negative identity
Self-control	Low degree
Age	Early initiation
Sex	Males
Expectations for education and school grades	Low expectations and low grades
Parental influences	Low monitoring, low support, ineffective discipline
Peer influences	Heavy influence, low resistance
Socioeconomic status	Low
Neighborhood quality	Urban, high crime, high mobility

13.   It refers to a broad range of behaviors, from socially unacceptable, to status offenses to criminal acts.

14.   (a) authority conflict, (b) covert conflict, and (c) overt conflict.

15.   He believes that adolescents whose development has restricted them from acceptable social roles might choose a negative identity.

16.   a.   Early involvement with drugs and alcohol.
        b.   Easy access to weapons.
        c.   Association with a deviant peer group.
        d.   Pervasive exposure to violence in the media.

17.   a.   Recommit to raising children safely and effectively.
        b.   Make prevention a reality.
        c.   Give more support to schools.
        d.   Forge effective partnerships among families.

18.   In the cadre approach, a small number of students are trained to serve as peer mediators for the entire school.

19.   An individual experiences a major depressive episode and depressed characteristics, such as lethargy and hopelessness, for at least two weeks or longer and daily functioning becomes impaired.

20.   Drugs may present a proximal risk for suicide. Distal risks tend to be things that grow out of the family history or environment.

21.   Some inherit a tendency to be overweight. Only 10% of those children not having obese parents become obese. Strong evidence supporting the role of the environment is the doubling of the rate of obesity since 1900.

22.   It is an eating disorder that involves the relentless pursuit of thinness through starvation. Weighing less than 85% of the recommended weight is a key indicator.

23.   Bulimia is an eating disorder in which the individual consistently follows a binge-and-purge eating pattern.

INTERELATION OF ADOLESCENT PROBLEMS AND PREVENTION/INTERVENTION SECTION REVIEW

1.   Drug abuse; juvenile delinquency; sexual problems; school-related problems.

2.   Adolescents tend to have more than one problem, and researchers tend to suggest that these are interrelated.

3.   (a) Intensive individualized attention, (b) Community-wide multiagency collaborative approaches, and (c) Early identification and intervention.

COGNITIVE CHALLENGE

1.   Individual activity. No answer provided.

2.   Individual activity. No answer provided.

3.   Individual activity. No answer provided.

ADOLESCENCE IN RESEARCH

The research method was survey with descriptive statistics. The hypothesis was that a set of external and internal assets could be used to predict success in life. External assets included things such as support, empowerment, boundaries and expectations, and effective time use. Internal assets included things like commitment to learning, positive values, social competencies, and positive identity. The fewer the assets reported by the 12,000 ninth- to twelfth-graders, the more likely was alcohol use and other problem behaviors.

⊠ COMPREHENSIVE REVIEW

1.	c	11.	c	21.	b
2.	a	12.	b	22.	b
3.	b	13.	b	23.	d
4.	c	14.	c	24.	b
5.	b	15.	b	25.	a
6.	c	16.	d	26.	c
7.	c	17.	a	27.	a
8.	b	18.	c	28.	c
9.	b	19.	d		
10.	c	20.	b		